Panama Lost?

UNIVERSITY PRESS OF FLORIDA

Florida A&M University, Tallahassee
Florida Atlantic University, Boca Raton
Florida Gulf Coast University, Ft. Myers
Florida International University, Miami
Florida State University, Tallahassee
University of Central Florida, Orlando
University of Florida, Gainesville
University of North Florida, Jacksonville
University of South Florida, Tampa
University of West Florida, Pensacola

Panama Lost?

U.S. Hegemony, Democracy, and the Canal

Peter M. Sánchez

University Press of Florida
Gainesville/Tallahassee/Tampa/Boca Raton
Pensacola/Orlando/Miami/Jacksonville/Ft. Myers

12 11 10 09 08 07   6 5 4 3 2 1

Library of Congress Cataloging-in-Publication Data
Sánchez, Peter Michael, 1954-
Panama lost? : U.S. hegemony, democracy, and the Canal /
Peter M. Sánchez.
p. cm.
Includes bibliographical references and index.
ISBN-13: 978-0-8130-3046-3 (alk. paper)
1. Panama—History—20th century. 2. Democratization—Panama—
History—20th century. 3. Hegemony—United States—History—
20th century. 4. Panama—Relations—United States. 5. United
States—Relations—Panama. I. Title.
F1438.S36 2007
972.8705—dc22
2006023148

The University Press of Florida is the scholarly publishing agency
for the State University System of Florida, comprising Florida A&M
University, Florida Atlantic University, Florida Gulf Coast University,
Florida International University, Florida State University, University
of Central Florida, University of Florida, University of North Florida,
University of South Florida, and University of West Florida.

University Press of Florida
15 Northwest 15th Street
Gainesville, FL 32611-2079
http://www.upf.com

Contents

Preface and Acknowledgments

My interest in Panama started over twenty years ago, although at that time I never imagined I would end up writing a book. In the summer of 1983, while teaching at the U.S. Air Force Academy, I arrived in Panama on a one-month assignment at U.S. Southern Command (SOUTHCOM) to assist with the creation of an interagency group that would begin to discuss with the Panamanian government, namely the Panamanian Defense Forces (PDF), the status of U.S. defense facilities in Panama after 1999. While the 1977 Canal Treaties, signed by President Jimmy Carter and General Omar Torrijos, called for the U.S. military presence to be gone by noon, December 31, 1999, some agencies in the U.S. government, particularly the Department of Defense, and some members of Congress were eager to renegotiate that aspect of the treaty so that the U.S. government could maintain a military presence on the isthmus well into the twenty-first century. On my first day at SOUTHCOM, however, I was given a different, much less interesting task because, according to the colonel in charge of J-5 (politico-military affairs), "Noriega was not yet interested in discussing the issue of base rights." The colonel, as well as most officers I met at SOUTHCOM, spoke very negatively about Noriega with regard to his "ultranationalism." This hesitance on the part of Noriega and the PDF generated a great deal of concern and even anger among U.S. military officers, who often exhibited disdain toward the isthmians in general. On several occasions, military officers with whom I spoke would say that SOUTHCOM should send a clear signal to Noriega and the Panamanians by pulling out a few bases "to see how they like it!" The assumption was that Noriega and the Panamanians did not really want the U.S. presence to end and were using the bases simply as negotiating leverage. If the U.S. government began to close down bases, the Panamanians would panic and quickly beg the U.S. government to stop the evacuation. This U.S. gambit was never tried, Washington being the partner that was most enamored with a U.S. military presence on the isthmus.

One year later, I returned to Panama as a politico-military affairs officer at the U.S. Air Force Southern Air Division, the Air Force's SOUTHCOM component, in Howard Air Force Base. I had requested this assignment to Panama because my one-month experience the previous year had awakened my interest in Latin America and had made me want to learn a lot more about the isthmus and U.S. policy toward Latin America. My fascinating tour lasted a full two years, until July 1986. In my first week in Panama, as I signed a lease on an apartment in El Cangrejo, Panama City's newer business district, the owner of the apartment, a prominent Panamanian who was later elected to the National Assembly, asked me point-blank, "How can your country support a repressive military dictator who is also a drug trafficker?" Needless to say, his question caught me by surprise both because of its boldness and because I was by no means knowledgeable about Panamanian politics at the time. Somewhat embarrassed, I pleaded ignorance and said something quite naïve and noncommittal, like, "I'm sure that if General Noriega was involved in the drug trade, the United States would not support him." Within weeks at my new job, however, I had come across plenty of information that confirmed my landlord's accusations. While the information I was privy to at the time was classified, the popular press eventually published most of the facts about Noriega's nefarious activities. Unfortunately, I never had the opportunity to discuss the matter with my landlord again. By the time I returned to the United States from my tropical assignment in July 1986, the Panamanian government, or PDF, still did not want to renegotiate the base rights portion of the 1977 Canal Treaties. The United States by that year had already decided that Noriega was a liability rather than an asset. Almost three-and-a-half years later, and just before General Manuel Noriega was to appoint a Panamanian as the president of the Panama Canal Commission, the U.S. armed forces invaded the country, arrested the general, flew him to the United States to stand trial on charges of international drug trafficking, and put pressure on Panama's new government to do away with the "nationalistic" PDF. State and Defense Department officials at the time conveyed the notion that the United States had known little about Noriega's nefarious activities. The truth was that U.S. ties with Manuel Noriega were long-standing, seedy and, at times, mutually beneficial. The drama of the "Noriega crisis" and the disingenuousness of U.S. statements about the general piqued my curiosity tremendously.

It wasn't until years later, however, that I applied for a Fulbright Senior Scholar research/lecturing position in Panama, an award that I believed was perfect (and, in my mind, written) for me. I was lucky enough to be selected for the Fulbright, and from July 1997 to July 1998 I researched Panama's political history and U.S.-Panamanian relations, formally and informally interviewing scores of Panamanians at all levels of society. I also had the unique opportunity to teach U.S.–Latin American relations at the University of Panama, right around the corner from the apartment I had lived in as an Air Force officer during 1984–86. My intent upon applying for the Fulbright fellowship was to write a book about the final disposition of the 1977 Canal

Treaties, focusing principally on negotiations to maintain U.S. military bases on the isthmus. As I researched the U.S.-Panamanian "special" relationship, however, I became more and more a student of history, realizing that, to understand the current negotiations fully, I had to understand the bilateral relationship from its inception. The result is a much more ambitious book that took a lot of time to frame and write and that is as much an act of obsession as an act of scholarship.

Many people have helped me write this book. First and foremost, I am indebted to the Fulbright Foundation, which allowed me to spend one year in Panama at a critical period of U.S.-Panamanian negotiations. The Fulbright grant also enabled me to come in contact with many Panamanian students and professors at the University of Panama, all of whom enlightened me on the Panamanian perspective and pointed me in directions I didn't know existed. Loyola University Chicago also made my Fulbright fellowship in Panama possible by providing me with a salary subvention and a one-year leave of absence. I am also indebted to the Department of Political Science at the U.S. Air Force Academy, not only for supporting my assignments in Panama but also for funding my Ph.D. studies at the University of Texas at Austin.

In the three years that I lived in Panama, I spoke with literally hundreds of people, from presidents to domestic servants. They have all had an influence on my interpretation of Panama's political history. Some observers may accuse me of having "gone native," a pejorative term applied to State Department officials who are deemed to have developed too close an affinity toward the "local" perspective. Going native, however, may simply mean that the observer stops looking at the world from the U.S. perspective and begins to understand and empathize with the interests of the "other" country. I am confident that my association with many Panamanians, rather than giving me a biased view, opened my eyes to a more balanced view of Panamanian politics and U.S.-Panamanian relations.

During my Fulbright year in Panama, many people and institutions assisted me with my research. I acquired a great deal of information from two research centers in Panama. Raul Leis's Centro de Estudios y Acción Social Panameño (Panamanian Center for Social Studies and Action), or CEASPA, and Marco Gandásegui's Centro de Estudios Latinoamericanos (Center for Latin American Studies), or CELA, housed a large number of studies and difficult-to-find materials that were essential for my research. The Panama Canal Commission (PCC) opened its doors to me, allowing me to interview and discus my project with a number of people both formally and informally. The PCC's library housed many essential books and documents. The U.S.

embassy also helped me a great deal. I am particularly indebted to Patrick Duddy, director of public affairs, who not only discussed my project with me on numerous occasions (we always disagreed) but also arranged several interviews with key embassy personnel. Belsy Medina at the public affairs office was extremely helpful in helping me with pretty much any problem I had while in Panama and also provided a solid, balanced "Panamanian" perspective.

On a more personal level, many Panamanians opened their homes and minds to me. I am indebted to them not only for the information and access they provided but also for their friendship. Juan Del Busto and Luís Ramón Fábrega Sánchez not only plugged me into Panamanian society but also became good friends. My time with them was intellectually stimulating as well as tremendously enjoyable. I could never have met as many movers and shakers in Panama as I did without their help. They both contributed greatly to the success of this book. Many other people in Panama provided me invaluable assistance and friendship as well, but particularly Miguel Antonio Bernal, Edmundo Gnazzo, Dorita de Reyna, Rubén Reyna, Ester Balíd, and Michelle Labrut. I want to make special mention of Gladys Robles, former *profesora* of history at the University of Panama, who, with great humor, enlightened me greatly, but who died too young, never being able to see her country as a fully sovereign nation.

During the writing process, several individuals helped me tremendously by reading drafts or commenting on my ideas published in other venues. In this regard, I am indebted to Jeanne Hey, Frank O. Mora, J. D. Trout, Carlos Guevara Mann, Ovidio Díaz, Megan Sholar, Anthony Cardoza, and, particularly, Ray Tatalovich for his strong encouragement. I owe special thanks to Steve Ropp, who not only gave me great advice prior to leaving for Panama in 1997 but also served as an excellent sounding board for my ideas and made several insightful suggestions that made this volume much, much stronger.

This book would not have seen print without the perseverance and support of Amy Gorelick, acquisitions editor at the University Press of Florida, to whom I'm greatly indebted. Also at the press, I would like to thank Marthe Walters who expertly guided me through the editing process.

Finally, I want to thank Kathleen Adams, my wife, who not only read and commented on my manuscript but provided invaluable support and love; and my daughter, Danielle, who served as inspiration for me to leave a sort of chronicle of Daddy's past adventures. In the end, of course, I am responsible for what I have written, and I regret that most likely I have forgotten to thank a number of people who deserve mention.

Hegemony and Democracy

Power Distribution at the International
and State Levels of Analysis

The concept of power is central to the study and understanding of politics. This analysis of U.S.-Panamanian relations and the struggle for democracy in the isthmus is for the most part a study of power relations, at both the domestic and international levels of analysis. So that readers can fully appreciate Panama's diplomatic and domestic history, therefore, I will first lay out the assumptions I make about political behavior, as well as the theoretical framework I employ in this study. I will start with the basics to build a foundation for my forthcoming analysis of a small country's quest for political and economic development in a hegemonic international environment.

Panama's importance in the world community belies its small size. This small republic has been a prominent nation-state for two basic reasons. First, its strategic geographic location and size—a narrow isthmus linking North America and South America—has attracted the attention of strong nation-states for five hundred years. These Great Powers have used the territory that is now Panama as a vital location for the movement of people, goods, and resources. Spain's wealth in the 1500s was amassed to a large extent by the quick transport of gold through the narrow isthmus over the *camino real*. Hundreds of years later, in the mid- to late 1800s, the transfer of gold from California and the transfer of people to the American West via the Panama Railroad helped to forge the United States as a continental Great Power. Panama's geography has thus assisted and continues to assist influential nations in developing and enhancing their power. This unique location has also attracted global interest because of its value for world trade, which is increasingly important in the post–World War II world. Second, more recently Panama has been visible internationally because of its importance to the United States, the dominant power in the Western Hemisphere. In the twentieth century, the Panama Canal served vital U.S. commercial and military interests. More than any independent country in the region, Panama represented a symbol for and source of U.S. power and influence. The

United States would undoubtedly have become a Great Power without the Isthmus of Panama. But tiny Panama, more than any other country in the hemisphere, has served as a critical outpost for U.S. power and as a vehicle for U.S. military and economic might. The security of Panama and its canal did and will continue to preoccupy policy makers in Washington who are concerned about vital U.S. interests.

Power and Politics at the Domestic and International Levels of Analysis

A central assumption of this book is that power is the essential element of politics. If the definition of politics is who gets what, when, and how (Lasswell 1936), then those who have power will get the things they want, when they want them, either by persuasion, intimidation, or force. Power is held by key individuals, who in the aggregate make up a society's elite. These elites also lead key social institutions. Thus individuals and institutions wield the power that determines how values are allocated in any society (Easton 1953) or international system. Those individuals, institutions, or nation-states that have power are able to get others either to do something they would not ordinarily do or to not do something they would ordinarily do (Dahl 1957). A second basic assumption I make is that elites and institutions attempt to maximize their interests and to achieve the goals they value most—wealth, power, and prestige (Bartlett 1973). While many individuals and institutions attempt to enhance universal values, such as human rights and social equity, the individuals and institutions that seek political and economic power tend to focus foremost on selfish goals. Likewise, the elites who lead political, military, and economic institutions work to promote their self-interests and the interests of those institutions, goals that often, although not always, overlap. At the nation-state level of analysis, the principal goal/role of decision makers is to promote the interests of their nation-state (Morgenthau 1993, 3–16).

These two assumptions lead us to also assume that individuals behave in a "rational" manner. That is, they attempt to weigh the costs and benefits of each action and decide which course of action will best maximize their values or goals. Human beings, nevertheless, often make mistakes since accurate information is not always available and misperceptions often distort the decision-making process (Downs 1957; Jervis 1976). Rational choice can be clouded also by patterns of human biases, organized into worldviews or paradigms. While serving as shorthand for making choices, these lenses can often distort reality, resulting in what could be called faulty or "irrational" decisions. Elites also tend to focus on the near-term maximization of goals, meaning that long-term interests may be sacrificed to the exigencies of the moment, especially during crises (Allison 1999). Nevertheless, on average, individuals, particularly elites who thirst for power, command more resources, acquire more information, and make choices that over time tend to promote their selfish interests and the interests of the institutions that they lead.

MODERN POLITICAL REGIMES: FASCISM, COMMUNISM, AND DEMOCRACY

The world's countries are governed by formal institutions, which in their totality comprise what is known as "the state." Max Weber defined the state as "a set of administrative, policing, and military organizations headed, and more or less well coordinated by, an executive authority (Skocpol 1986, 29)." By the twentieth century, scholars, political elites, and citizens alike only deemed as legitimate those states that were organized in ways that promoted or at least seemed to promote the interests of its citizens. Prior to the advent of totalitarianism, communism, and democracy, states did not necessarily legitimate their power by claiming that they represented the interests of the people or nation, since monarchy was considered a "legitimate" form of government (Bendix 1978). Throughout the 1900s, while the principle of popular sovereignty displaced other forms of legitimating, political regimes were nevertheless organized in starkly different ways. These differing ways of organizing politics required different legitimating schemes, or different ideologies. Mosca argued that each regime type required a different "political myth" that provided legitimacy to the political system (1939, 115). Fascist regimes organized the state around a single party that claimed to defend the interests of the state, since the state was deemed to be the best reflection of the fatherland. In order to justify this type of regime, political leaders promoted elitist and organic theories of the state, arguing that only the most highly qualified individuals could effectively promote the national interest (Mussolini 1975). While fascist regimes, like those of Germany and Italy, concentrated power in the hands of a revered political elite, the economic elite was allowed to own property and make profits as long as they served the interests of the fatherland or state (Sarti 1971). Fascist regimes, therefore, placed the political elite at the helm but allowed an economic elite to thrive as long as they served vital national interests. Societal power was also highly concentrated in communist regimes. But these regimes considered the political elite as the only true representatives of the masses, thus giving a monopoly of power to one political party that would represent the working class or proletariat. As a result, communist regimes all but eliminated the economic elite through a socialist economy that placed capital, most property, and national resources in the hands of the state. Marxist/Leninist ideology legitimated this politico-economic monopoly by praising the virtues of the political elite (cadre) and by demonizing the bourgeoisie, or dominant economic class (Macridis 1992).

In democracies, on the other hand, political and economic power would coexist and be decentralized. Although even the staunchest defenders of democratic principles admit to the continuing importance of elites, political power in a democratic system is decentralized via competitive elections, competing political institutions, a vibrant economic elite, and private voluntary associations (Dahl 1971). Economic power is also decentralized in a democracy and legitimated via a capitalist ideology that places a premium on property rights and the minimalist state. Democracy, then, is a type of political regime that grants almost equal legitimacy and power to both political and economic elites, while at the same time attempting to limit the power of the state. It is this compromise that has prompted some to label and criticize democracy as bourgeois or elite democracy (Mills 1956) and has led many analysts to view liberal democracy and capitalism as inextricably entwined (Lindbloom 1977; Moore 1966). Despite the power of the economic elite in democratic societies, however, class analysts have recognized that the state, and thus the political elite, can still exercise some degree of autonomy, allowing for some sharing of power between the political and economic elite (Evans, Rueschemeyer, and Skocpol 1985). By contrast, in fascist regimes the state and the political elite were dominant, while in communist regimes the political elite was supreme. In the twentieth century, an era of decolonization, most of the world's nations struggled to find a regime that would best allow for political and economic development. Thus, elites in these newly independent countries had to choose between fascist, communist, or democratic forms of political organization, and Great Powers served as models to be emulated.

As new nation-states emerged in the twentieth century, however, the world's leading democracies defeated the leading fascist and communist nations, thus helping to delegitimate those "totalitarian" regimes. Internal factors also helped to bring down those authoritarian political regimes. Over time, fascism revealed its failure to represent "the people," owing to its elitism, racism, and militarism. Communism demonstrated its antidemocratic and militaristic qualities too and also failed to create an efficient and vibrant national economy that provided citizens with their basic needs. While scholars have tended to characterize these regimes as "totalitarian" and failures, their demise came about not only through internal collapse or contradictions but also through defeat in the international arena. The world's most powerful capitalist democracies destroyed fascist regimes in World War II (1939–45), and most communist regimes in the cold war (1947–91). These regimes would certainly have experienced internal crises and perhaps collapse had they not encountered external resistance, but their quick demise came at the hands of democratic Great Powers that marshaled enormous amounts of resources to protect their economic and political interests from ideological and material assaults by the "totalitarian" nations of the world. The twentieth century then can accurately be labeled as the democratic and capitalist century, what one scholar has termed the end of history (Fukuyama 1992). This international context greatly affected weaker nation-states, such as Panama, that were looking for the best way to organize their political and economic system. Choosing a regime type invariably engaged the weak nation-states in the power politics of the international system.

INTERNATIONAL REGIMES: HEGEMONY AND BALANCE OF POWER

Power is just as important at the international level as at the domestic level, where it can be either centralized, as in a fascist or communist regime, or decentralized, as in a democracy. Our basic definitions of power are also applicable at the international level of analysis. Powerful nation-states more often than not determine who gets what, when, and how in the international system (Lasswell 1936). They are most likely to determine how values in the system are distributed (Easton 1953); and they exhibit power when they are able to convince or coerce another nation-state either to do something it would not ordinarily do or to not do something it would like to do (Dahl 1957). However, there is one fundamental difference between the international and national level of analysis—there is no legitimate central authority to make collective decisions in the international system. Thus, the community of nation-states, as Hedley Bull phrased it, is an "anarchical society" (1977). Under such a system, nation-states provide for their own security and cooperate rarely, only when it is in their perceived national interest to do so. In an anarchical system, nation-states are the dominant actors since no there is no supranational organization to restrain their actions. Naturally, then, nation-states attempt as best they can to preserve such a system by promoting four goals, presented in order of importance: (1) powerful states will attempt to preserve their position in the system and prevent the rise of one dominant power; (2) powerful states will uphold the principle of sovereignty for *all* states in the system; (3) all states will desire peace; and (4) all states will promote international standards of behavior to promote common goals (Rosenau and Durfee 2000, 18–19). Thus, although the primal goal of self-preservation tends to inhibit cooperation, when vital self-interests are guaranteed, states can and do cooperate.

Nevertheless, nation-states want first and foremost to preserve their sovereignty and to prevent the emergence of a dominant power in the system. Self-interest and a preoccupation with national security dominate the actions of nation-states in the anarchical society (Waltz 1959, 73). Decentralization of power is thus a primal goal of nation-states in an anarchical system. When power is decentralized so that more than three nation-states have a significant amount of roughly the same power, the system is said to be multipolar, and a "balance of power" system is said to emerge (Sheehan 1996). The balance of power (BOP) system is the mechanism whereby nation-states prevent the centralization of power in the system. According to Bull, perhaps the most important benefit of BOP behavior is that the international system is preserved since the states in the system work to prevent one power from dominating (Bull 1977, 106–7). Consequently, despite systemic anarchy, a certain degree of cooperation will exist in a BOP system owing to each state's interest in preserving its sovereignty and preventing the rise of a preponderant power. As Hobson points out:

> Although there has been a long line of would-be imperialists who have tried to subvert the anarchical structure of the system to create a hierarchical empire—e.g. Louis XIV, Napoleon Bonaparte, Adolf Hitler— none has succeeded because the others have defensively ganged up through balancing, thereby unintentionally maintaining a multi-state system. (2000, 27–28)

It is important to note, however, that the examples offered above took place in Europe, where a small number of Great Powers performed the balancing. In the Western Hemisphere, independent states have historically not been sufficiently strong to balance the emerging U.S. hegemon. Consequently, in an international system where a dramatic power asymmetry exists, weak states may be unable, perhaps unwilling, to balance a would-be hegemon.

A BOP system thus most closely parallels democracy at the state level of analysis, where power is diffused rather than concentrated. In a BOP system, as in a democracy, alliances are fluid so that power will remain decentralized and checked. The value of a BOP system is that no one state can control the destiny of all the states in the system, just as in a democracy no one individual (dictator), or group of individuals (elite or class) can control the destiny of the society. Democracy derives its legitimacy via the principles of popular sovereignty and limited government, while a BOP system derives its legitimacy from the principles of self-determination and state sovereignty.

The opposite of a BOP system is a unipolar system, where one nation-state has a virtual monopoly on power (Gill 1990). In such a system, the preponderant power is able to impose its will on subordinate states, owing to its overwhelming power capabilities. But unipolar systems are inherently unstable since, as noted above, the other states will at the first opportunity form alliances in an effort to balance the hegemon. As Waltz points out: "A drive for hegemony by any one state may be successful despite the resistance of other states, or for some reason the other states may not resist; but under certain conditions that have often existed in international politics, systems of balance do develop" (1959, 210). So, while a hegemon or dominant power may emerge under certain circumstances, scholars suggest that hegemony will tend to be short-lived either because the subordinate states will eventually form alliances to balance power or because the dominant power will experience decline (Hobson 2000, 41–43). The underlying assumption is that a multipolar system is the desired or default preference of a nation-state, just as decentralization of power is desired at the domestic level.

Under certain conditions, a unipolar system may be said to be *hegemonic*. A hegemonic system is one where one power enjoys a preponderance of military and economic power but is also able to compel or persuade subordinate states to cooperate without employing coercive power. The term *hegemony* was first applied to describe a domestic political system where the dominant economic class controlled society through the application of ideology in addition to naked power. Hegemony, as conceptualized by Marxist sociologist Antonio Gramsci, "involves developing intellectual, moral, and philosophical consent from all major groups in a nation" (Bocock 1986, 37). The term is now commonly used by international relations scholars. However, the term is often loosely applied to any international system where one state has a preponderance of power. International relations scholars first used the term *hegemony* to describe how one dominant power could promote and enforce a liberal economic order in an anarchical system. Increasingly, however, scholars, such as Gilpin and Krasner, use the term more broadly to include military and political hegemony (Gilpin 2001, 95, 99). Owing to the apparent U.S. global dominance at the beginning of the twenty-first century, an increasing number of scholars are using the term *hegemony*, as well as *imperialism*, without its Marxist implications (see, for example, P. Smith 2000). Those who are not inclined to describe a hegemon's ability to persuade as the product of a dominant ideology instead apply either the concept of "soft" power (Nye 2004) or the concept of hegemonic "leadership" (Kindleberger 1981, 242–54). What is most important here is that a hegemonic power differs from a preponderant power in the former's ability to convince subordinate nations to cooperate through noncoercive applications of influence, whether through ideology, leadership, or cultural and political power. A hegemonic power seldom needs to resort to force, owing to its ability to persuade and lead subordinate states.

In this study, I use the term *hegemony* broadly, as Krasner and Gilpin suggest. A hegemonic system exists when one nation-state has achieved a preponderance of military and economic power and has also convinced subordinate states that it is in their best interest to accept the leadership of the dominant power, since the hegemon's ideology will most likely promote the national and collective interests of the subordinate states. In such a system, the hegemon is mostly successful in determining the rules of the game in the international system. The hegemon also assumes the role of enforcing the rules when one or more of the states in the system attempt to challenge the hegemon's leadership or ally with an extrasystemic power. In these situations, the hegemon will often forcefully employ its military and economic instruments of power.

Although realism assumes that nation-states in an international system will attempt to preserve their sovereignty, maximize their power, and join alliances to prevent hegemony from arising, once a dominant state achieves hegemony, subordinate states will yield to or follow the hegemon, resulting in a system of cooperation. Rosenau and Durfee write:

> If a state lacks good external options and has only a limited capacity to build power domestically, it bandwagons with the threat. That explanation accounts for the lack of balancing against U.S. aggressive behavior in Latin America. (2000, 25)

Perhaps, then, in an international subsystem such as the Western Hemisphere, subordinate states will for a long period of time bandwagon with the hegemon, owing to their low power capabilities and their inability to achieve alliances with extrahemispheric states. Rather than being short-lived, as realists assume, hegemony may sustain itself in certain asymmetrical international subsystems. As long as the United States is able to maintain its preponderance of power, the other Great Powers accept that the Western Hemisphere is America's sphere of influence, and the countries of the region are unable to develop their power capabilities sufficiently to challenge U.S. leadership and power, then U.S. hegemony is likely to be the default international power structure in the Americas.

Interestingly enough, then, while nation-states prefer a nonhegemonic system, cooperation is possible and very likely when one state achieves both a preponderance of power and an ideology that is convincing and palatable to the subordinate states. Achieving hegemony, of course, is no small task. While historically many states have amassed large amounts of military and economic power, very few Great Powers have also appropriated and success-fully exported a dominant ideology. The Soviet Union, China, and even Cuba promoted communism and failed. Germany, Italy, and Japan promoted fas-cism and also failed. In the contemporary international system, only Great Britain (nineteenth century) and the United States (twentieth century) can be classified as relatively long-term hegemonic powers, successfully attain-ing preponderance of power and promoting a liberal economic order (Gilpin 2001, 94).

The cooperation and order that exist in a hegemonic system have of course been perceived as positive phenomena in an otherwise conflict-prone, an-archical system. Consequently, while the concentration of societal power in domestic politics (fascism and communism) has been roundly discredited, at the international level hegemony is often lauded rather than disdained. A hegemonic power distribution retains a great deal of legitimacy because, according to some scholars, it provides a valuable collective good—stability. Hegemonic Stability Theory, or HST, developed by Gilpin (1987) and Kras-ner (1976, 1995), asserts that a hegemon can bring stability and cooperation to a system ordinarily subject to uncooperative anarchy. According to HST, a hegemonic power will not act completely selfishly but rather will provide security, promote free trade, establish international economic regimes, and even provide economic development aid to the subordinate states (Hobson 2000, 40). Under such a unipolar regime, the anarchical system is replaced by cooperation, owing to the attainment of collective and national goals by *all* states in the system. The subordinate states accept the hegemon's lead-ership because the hegemon contributes to their security, sovereignty, and even prosperity. Thus anarchy is replaced by the hegemon's willingness and ability to provide what a legitimate government provides at the national level. From the perspective of HST, the hegemon is perceived more as a benevolent dictator than a power-hungry tyrant.

At the domestic level, however, the state (government) provides order and stability, regardless of whether it is democratic, fascist, or communist. Security, a derivative of order and stability, is a valuable human need that for many is a precondition for the acquisition of other needs (Shue 1980). Thus, as long as a minimal level of order is maintained, citizens and elites can argue the merits of various political regimes. Since no legitimate central authority exists at the international level, in world politics order is an even more valuable collective good than at the domestic level, where a national government exists (Schmidt 1998). Hegemony, then, while equivalent to autocracy at the national level, is deemed as the better of two evils, since chaos can be worse than a system where power is highly concentrated. Hegemony also retains legitimacy because the idealism that exists at the national level of analysis does not exist at the international level of analysis. That is, while equality and justice for all citizens are valued at the national level, particularly in a democratic system, at the international level self-interest is still deemed as the best course of action for a nation-state, even if, in the pursuit of those interests, international laws and norms are violated (Morgenthau 1993). Nation-states legitimate their self-serving foreign policies, or realpolitik, by pointing out that, in an anarchic international system, idealism is unworkable and simply allows aggressive states to dominate the system. British prime minister Neville Chamberlain's appeasement of Adolf Hitler prior to the onset of World War II is used ubiquitously as a heuristic example in the study of international relations because it serves as a clear and dramatic justification for the value of realpolitik. The lesson to be learned from Chamberlain's "folly" is that appeasement encourages aggression, resulting in a loss of security. The 2003 U.S. invasion of Iraq was legitimate in the eyes of U.S. foreign policy makers at least in part because of the underlying assumption that appeasing Saddam Hussein would lead to a greater threat to American and global security. In the United States, the prestige of lauded scholar and statesman Henry Kissinger, an oracle of realism, is testimony to the value placed on national self-interest in U.S. foreign policy. While there are strains of idealism, stemming back to the League of Nations championed by President Wilson, realism still has an honored, dominant seat in the chambers of those who design U.S. foreign policy. Scholars, for example, have pointed to the self-interest inherent in the foreign policies of even the most "idealistic" of American presidents, like John F. Kennedy (Miroff 1976) and Jimmy Carter (Dumbrell 1995).

Hegemonic states, such as the United States in Latin America, naturally make an effort to highlight the dangers of anarchy in the international system because they benefit from an international system where power is concentrated in their favor. Anarchy thus becomes part of the political myth that legitimates the notion of hegemonic stability, much as the nasty, short, and brutish state of nature legitimates the powerful state, or Leviathan (Hobbes 1962). Kings went to great lengths to legitimate monarchy via the notion of "divine right." Fascists and communists took similar steps to legitimate their politico-economic systems. Generals who took power in Latin America in the 1960s heralded a national security doctrine that convinced the masses of the urgent need for praetorianism. Likewise, hegemonic powers not only point to the value of security and order they ostensibly provide but also promote the continuation of systemic anarchy by placing barriers in front of international organizations that attempt to control the actions of powerful states and in front of states that promote a BOP system. While anarchy is certainly dependent upon the lack of a central authority in the international system, it is also what states—and, more important, powerful states—make of it (Wendt 1992). The United Nations, while lauded as the triumph of idealism, nevertheless was designed by the victors of World War II in a way that prevented the majority, the poor and weak nations, from acting against the minority, the rich, powerful nations, through the establishment of the UN Security Council and veto power.

I assume, therefore, that while order and stability appear to be features of a hegemonic system, all nation-states prefer a balance of power system, just as citizens prefer democracy in a domestic system. Likewise, I assume that the benefits that a hegemonic power grants to subordinate states are simply overtures to promote the hegemonic system that first and foremost benefits the hegemonic power. In an anarchical system, all states promote their self-interest, so it is folly to think that a hegemonic power would promote the interest of subordinate states at its own expense. If a Philosopher King is an idealist fancy at the domestic level, then the notion of a benevolent hegemon is likewise an illusion at the international level. If you take away a hegemon's economic and military power, it is quite likely that its ideology and leadership will prove to be ephemeral and that subordinate states will attempt to establish a BOP system with alacrity.

Hegemony in the Western Hemisphere: An International Subsystem

The concepts of hegemony and preponderance of power are salient to this study of Panama because they are key characteristics of the international system in the Western Hemisphere. As the United States became a preponderant power in the hemisphere in the late 1800s and early 1900s (Zimmermann 2002), the nation-states of the region did not form alliances to balance America's rise to power. In its quest for regional hegemony, the United States of America exerted enormous influence in the domestic and international politics of the states in Latin America, including the small, weak nation-state of Panama. I will not attempt to explain why the United States became a hegemon while other states in the hemisphere did not (see, for example, Landes 1998). My focus here will be on the characteristics of U.S. hegemony and on the *effects* of U.S. hegemony on Panamanian national development.

CHARACTERISTICS AND MAINTENANCE OF HEGEMONY

How do we know when an international system may be classified as hegemonic? To know when a preponderance of power exists, we must be able to understand and measure power. As noted above, one nation-state can dominate other nations in a system, and therefore seek hegemony, only if it has first amassed a preponderance of power in that international system. For example, if we think of all power in a particular system as constituting 100 percent, a balance of power would exist if no nation were able to acquire 50 percent or more of the power in the system. Fifty percent is a somewhat arbitrary criterion; however, it is logical to surmise that if one nation-state has the majority of power in a system, then it will be able to have a majority of influence within that system. Such an actor would be more successful at promoting its interests and goals than any other actor in the system. Naturally, one particular state will have more difficulty achieving a preponderance of power if there are actors that have substantial power to subvert that state's quest for a preponderance of power. Also, the greater the number of actors in a system, the more difficult it may be for one nation to achieve such a majority of power, particularly if a number of the actors in the system have a substantial amount of power. On the other hand, if one actor has a great deal of power and all the other actors in the system have a limited amount of power, then the preponderant power may be able to continue to amass power and prevent balancing from taking place. Once it acquires at least half the available power in a system, a nation-state is in a position to assert its interests more effectively and perhaps continue to acquire power, eventually establishing itself as a hegemon. A state with a preponderance of power could also more easily employ strategies of divide and conquer, for example, by insisting on bilateral rather than multilateral diplomacy. In a large system with many actors, a state with 50 percent or more of available power will benefit greatly from the problem of collective action, where the many have difficulty organizing against the powerful few in pursuit of their common goals (Olson 1968). In the Latin American subsystem, the United States has attained well beyond 50 percent of power, at least in terms of the elements of power that are easiest to measure—economic and military power.

Chart 1.1 illustrates that in the late 1990s, after the end of the cold war, the United States dwarfed all other countries in Iberoamerica economically.[1] The U.S. gross national product represents 82 percent of the U.S. and Iberoamer-

Iberoamerica
(18%)

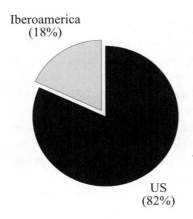

US
(82%)

Iberoamerica
(8%)

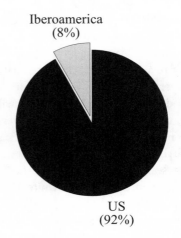

US
(92%)

Chart 1.1. Comparison of U.S. and Iberoamerican GNP in 1998. *Source*: World Bank (2004).

Chart 1.2. Comparison of U.S. and Iberoamerican military expenditures in 1998. *Source*: Stockholm International Peace Research Institute (2002).

ican GNP combined. Not only is U.S. wealth vastly greater than the wealth of all Iberoamerica, U.S. investments provide Washington with a great deal of leverage in the region, since antagonizing the United States could affect each nation's economy (O'Brien 1999). Additionally, U.S. trade in the region also yields leverage for Washington since Iberoamerican nations import mainly vital services and manufactured goods from the United States, while the United States imports nonvital commodities from them. In an international system where such disparity in wealth and economic advantage exists, the dominant nation—in this case, the United States—will almost always be able to determine the economic rules of the game and compel the other nations in the system to abide by those rules (Bergsten, Keohane, and Nye 1975).

Chart 1.2 likewise shows clearly that the United States overshadows Iberoamerica in terms of military power. U.S. military expenditures represent 92 percent of military expenditures by the United States and Iberoamerica combined. Not only does the U.S. government spend huge sums on its military, but U.S. military technology is vastly superior to the military technology of all nations on earth. In addition to the sheer size and sophistication of U.S. military power, Washington, through the Department of Defense, exerts substantial influence in Iberoamerica because of its close ties to the region's military forces, acquired through a long history of U.S. military aid, training, and cooperation (Peceny 1999). Such preponderance of military power allows the United States to determine security interests in the region. The nations of Iberoamerica cannot challenge U.S. military power, must cooperate with America when determining their security policies, are compelled to accept U.S. regional security goals, and are always subject to direct or covert U.S. military intervention. Suggesting an Orwellian logic, while the United States has intervened militarily in the region far more often than any other country in the world, regional security strategies and pronouncements have never identified the United States as a threat to the Latin American countries. Only in a hegemonic system can such an odd reality exist.

These rough economic and military power comparisons demonstrate that in Latin America the United States is indeed a hovering giant (Blasier 1985). Only a truly benevolent giant, à la a Philosopher King, would carry out relations with these subordinate nations in a spirit of cooperation and altruism and in a manner that respects the principles of national sovereignty and the equality of nations. When a nation-state has such a near-monopoly on military and economic power, it will most likely do whatever it wants to do to achieve its perceived vital interests, especially in an anarchic system that justifies realpolitik. A nation-state that has achieved such superiority most likely has done so willingly and purposefully and will act in ways that ensure the preservation of that superiority.

As stated above, however, hegemony cannot be achieved solely by achieving a monopoly over economic and military power. The use of force and economic sanctions and incentives are crude forms of exercising influence; and resorting to force or economic warfare would suggest a weakening rather than a growing hegemony. In fact, hegemony can be said to exist only "when the major institutions and forms of organization—economic, social and political—as well as the key values of the dominant state become models for emulation in other subordinate states" (Gill 1990, 46). As I pointed out above, in a hegemonic system subordinate states will not just tolerate but will also *accept* the leadership of the hegemon. For example, in a hegemonic system, a nondemocratic subordinate state may accept the leadership of the democratic hegemon but may not internalize the hegemon's political and economic institutions. The most effective, powerful hegemon, however, will not only set the rules of the international system and convince the subordinate states to accept those rules but will also convince the subordinate states to emulate its political and economic ideology and institutions. Consequently, if a state has 80 percent of the power in a system but the weak states in the system resist that state's leadership and ideology whenever possible, even if in subtle ways, then hegemony has not been fully consolidated. If, on the other hand, a state has only 60 percent of the power in a system and the weak states in the system accept the leadership of the hegemon and emulate its political and economic system, then hegemony is present and consolidated. Hegemony, therefore, once again, depends upon other, softer types of influence, such as political and cultural power (Slater and Taylor 1999).

Unlike military and economic power, these elements of power are much more subjective and thus difficult to measure validly and reliably. As a surrogate for measurement, we can suggest that ideological, political, and cultural power are weak when subordinate states or sectors within those states resist the leadership or ideology of the hegemonic state. Therefore, if subordinate states look to states other than the hegemon for leadership or if dissident groups within those subordinate states fight to disassociate their nations from the leadership of the system's hegemon, we would then be witnessing a crisis of hegemony. If a hegemon is economically or militarily weak, we would of course expect to see some resistance by the other states in the system. However, if the hegemon has a near-monopoly on economic and military power—as the United States does in the Western Hemisphere—yet the subordinate states in the system reject the hegemon's leadership, then we would be witnessing a diminution of the hegemon's political and cultural power or the rise in legitimacy of a competing power. These challenges to hegemony can occur if the subordinate states come to disapprove of the hegemon's influence or find another state whose influence they prefer. When these situations arise, we can say that there exist challenges to the dominant state's hegemony, either from within the system, from outside the system, or from both directions, which is often the case. Conversely, when subordinate states begin to accept the leadership of the hegemon and to adopt its political, economic, and social institutions, we can conclude that hegemony is in the process of consolidation. In summary, since it would be very difficult to ascertain when a nation has accumulated 50 percent or more of the ideological, political, or cultural power available in the system, we can instead identify instances when a hegemon's leadership and ideology are being either accepted or challenged by the subordinate states. In this way, we can identify when a preponderant power is either achieving hegemony, a hegemonic power is consolidating its hegemony, or hegemony is being challenged.

Whenever subordinate states or a Great Power challenge a hegemonic system, the hegemon can respond in one of two ways. A hegemon either can choose to accept the challenge, taking no immediate action, or it can choose to react quickly to the challenge. When choosing to act, the hegemon can of course attempt to defend its hegemony by use of the "stick," employing threats and force, or by use of the "carrot," providing incentives and concessions. Most policy debates taking place within America's foreign policy establishment focus on these two strategies—carrots and sticks—for promoting U.S. interests in the international arena. Using the 1977 Panama Canal Treaties as an example, the treaty debates centered on whether the U.S. government should play tough with Panama and keep the canal even if by force, or play fair and concede to Panama's demands, even at the risk of losing face and direct control of the canal. At the core of the canal treaty debates, however, as we will see in our case study, was the crucial question of what course of action would best preserve U.S. interests in Panama and in Latin America. At no time did U.S. policy makers, whether from the Democratic or the Republican Party, consider enhancing Panama's power at the expense of U.S. power and interests. The argument here is that doves (often Democrats) are realists who favor the use of "carrots," while hawks (often Republicans) are realists who favor the use of "sticks." Because of this difference, the Democrats have been mistakenly labeled "idealists."

THE "INVISIBLE HAND" OF HEGEMONY

Some analysts have found it difficult to accept theories of hegemony when examining U.S. foreign policy because they assume that hegemony can exist only when a hegemon has the ability to plan and execute imperialistic, coherent, and sustained foreign policies. While hegemony may well have described the relationship between the former Soviet Union and its satellite countries in Eastern Europe, where the USSR exercised almost direct control, some analysts flatly reject the notion that hegemony could describe the relationship between the United States and the nations of Latin America, since U.S. policies promote democracy, are often erratic, defy continuity, and are not driven by key individuals (on the influence of individuals, see Ronning and Vannucci 1987; Challener 1973; Yerxa 1991; and Zimmermann 2002). These analysts often point to the problematic and chaotic aspects of U.S. policy. They contend that the decentralized and democratic decision-making process in the U.S. political system could never result in hegemonic policies, especially when such policies often claim to promote self-determination and democracy. For example, in an in-depth analysis of the conflict between Washington and General Noriega, Kempe writes: "To understand what led up to this [the U.S. invasion], one can make the mistake of looking purely at U.S. interests and how they have shifted in Panama. But U.S. foreign policy is more messy—and certainly not as deliberate" (1992, 1). The actions of a hegemonic power, however, whether democratic or authoritarian, must necessarily have a sustained, logical, and power-maximizing character.

If not, hegemony would be impossible to achieve and sustain. But how could hegemony-sustaining foreign policies emerge and persist in a political system where foreign-policy decision making is decentralized and democratic? We can suggest that if an invisible hand can exist in the realm of economics (A. Smith 1976), it can also exist in the realm of international politics, especially since the international system, like "the market," has no central authority to regulate the behavior of the actors in the system. If the market is sustained by the selfish pursuit of all economic actors in the theorized anarchical capitalist system, then both balance of power and hegemonic regimes in the international system of independent states can be achieved by nation-states and individuals in those nation-states selfishly pursuing the perceived national interest. If all U.S. citizens who influence U.S. foreign policy attempt to maximize U.S. interests, then the aggregate result will be a foreign policy that, while at times messy and bureaucratic in formulation, will ultimately yield power maximization for the United States of America.

History provides evidence for this assertion. In the early to mid-1800s, the United States did not hold 50 percent of military and economic power in the Western Hemisphere. Also, several nation-states in the system could challenge U.S. power in the region, like Britain, France, and even Spain. In fact, the 1823 Monroe Doctrine that warned Europe to steer clear of the hemisphere represented an empty threat since U.S. military and economic power in the region was limited and certainly could not effectively challenge the European powers (G. Smith 1994). In order to achieve hegemony in the hemisphere, the United States would have to develop policies and take steps resulting in a steady accumulation of power. The U.S. construction of the Panama Railroad in the mid-1850s and the U.S. digging of the Panama Canal in the early 1900s represent just two important examples of such policies and actions. By the end of World War II, the United States of America had pushed all European powers out of the hemisphere, dominated the region militarily and economically, and convinced subordinate states that the American model was superior to all others. Certainly a nation-state with erratic, shortsighted foreign policies would have had a difficult time achieving regional hegemony. On the contrary, policies that promoted the imperialist notion of Manifest Destiny along with policies that gave the United States increasing economic and military power in the international arena were common in both the 1800s and 1900s. U.S. policies enjoyed different labels—Big Stick diplomacy, dollar diplomacy, Good Neighbor policy, Alliance for Progress, Caribbean Basin Initiative, to name a few—but in the final analysis, all of these policies were designed and applied to promote and sustain U.S. hegemony in the region. Since U.S. hegemony in Iberoamerica is a current reality, we must find a plausible explanation for its emergence and persistence.

To understand how hegemonic policies can result from the American foreign policy process, we must think logically and in the abstract. Despite the many individuals and institutions involved in U.S. foreign policy making, there is always one underlying constant—all of these actors seek to maximize U.S. interests in the international system. Every time a new U.S. president is elected, he sends a letter to U.S. ambassadors scattered around the globe. These letters have some formal and diplomatic niceties but essentially drive home the point that U.S. embassies are there to promote U.S. strategic, economic, and political interests. Consequently, the worst crime a U.S. diplomat can commit is that of "going native," suggesting that the consul has begun to take into account the interests of the host country. Such an accusation results in either a dismissal, a transfer, or, worse, being ignored. In Panama, General Fred Woerner, commander in chief of U.S. Southern Command, hesitated in supporting the U.S. invasion of Panama, suffered such an accusation, and was summarily removed from his position and retired. When thousands of U.S. government officials and emissaries, from generals to Peace Corps volunteers, promote U.S. interests literally on a 24–7 basis, to use business language, we should not be surprised to discover that in the final analysis, U.S. policies, despite their apparent confusion, result in the accumulation of U.S. power and influence. According to economic theory, when economic actors pursue their self-interests, the resulting market will be efficient and in equilibrium. I suggest, therefore, that when thousands of U.S. government employees and elected officials involved in the foreign policy process pursue the national interests of the United States, the resulting policies will, on average, promote and sustain U.S. power and influence.

Certainly we cannot naively assume that all U.S. officials, agencies, and institutions will interpret U.S. interests similarly. For example, different U.S. agencies may disagree on a particular foreign policy option. The U.S. "drug czar," for example, may want to keep U.S. bases in Panama as a cost-effective way to combat the illegal narcotics trade. On the other hand, the State Department may decide that the U.S. military presence in Panama may produce domestic conflict and anti-U.S. sentiment and thus recommend that the U.S. government move its antidrug operations elsewhere. These positions can and do sometimes change over the course of the decision-making process. Additionally, one senator may insist on U.S. bases in Panama while another may advocate the importance of maintaining good relations with Panama in the future and thus favor the evacuation of all U.S. military personnel. In the complex U.S. foreign policy–making process, individuals in and out of government, elected officials, agencies, institutions, and public opinion are all involved in the process, suggesting the implausibility of some sort of grand plan or hegemonic design. Nevertheless, despite the many possible interpretations of U.S. interests and how to achieve them, all of these actors accept the underlying tenet of promoting U.S. interests worldwide, in this case U.S. antidrug operations. Thus, whether achieved in Panama or elsewhere, U.S. antidrug operations will be carried out. The situation is similar in the economic realm. All actors involved in the foreign policy process promote the economic interests both of the United States and of U.S. companies operating abroad. In fact, many politically appointed U.S. ambassadors are former businesspersons, already inclined to protect the economic interests of U.S. companies abroad. Business interests and national interests often overlap. As a result, cooperation between strategic agencies, such as the DOD and CIA, and U.S. business is common. U.S. companies in Panama, for example, cooperated with the CIA and the NSA in these agencies' eavesdropping operations on Panamanian officials.

Here we must address the issue of egoism and interests. If people are egoistic, why would they preserve the interests of the nation-state? We must realize first that the individuals to whom we refer are, for the most part, those involved in the foreign policy–making process. These individuals are ambassadors, generals, foreign service officers, congresspersons, high-level business leaders, and the like, whose personal interests are tied to the interests of the nation-state. Thus, a diplomat is promoted and rewarded when s/he pursues with determination the interests of the Department of State and the interests of the United States. A U.S. Air Force general is rewarded when s/he advances the interests of the Air Force, the interests of the Department of Defense, and the interests of the United States. The individuals we are most interested in analyzing promote their self-interests by promoting the interests of their institutions and the nation-state. When looking at economic elites and multinational corporations, the link between self-interest and the interests of the nation-state are more difficult to establish. However, the interests of multinationals and economic elites are often similar to the economic interests of the nation-state. For example, the United Fruit Company's paramount goal was to make profits. Since the United Fruit Company's home base was the United States, it was in the interest of U.S. policy makers to promote the interests of UFCO in Panama and Guatemala, since the company's profits repatriated to the U.S. economy, where they enhanced U.S. economic interests. UFCO, on the other hand, benefited from assisting the interests of the U.S. government since Washington often defended the rights of the company in foreign lands. The result is significant

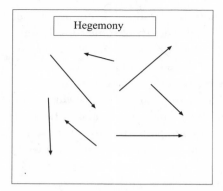

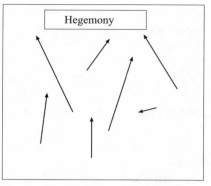

Fig. 1.1. Vector diagram of conflicting policy directions. The sum of these vectors would never lead toward hegemony.

Fig. 1.2. Vector diagram of directed policy directions. The sum of these vectors would always lead toward hegemony.

synchronicity between the policies that state decision makers and multinational corporations promote (see, for example, Gleijeses 1991). While conflicting interests can always be found, in the final analysis the nation-state promotes its multinational corporations, and multinational corporations support their nation-state, even if only indirectly by creating national wealth. Certainly this relationship may change in the future as multinationals continue to globalize their operations.

Some analysts nevertheless assume that U.S. foreign policy is the result of a compromise between a multitude of divergent opinions and policy preferences, the result being vectors that are of different lengths (intensity) and pointing in many directions (see figure 1.1). For any given policy decision, say the Panama Canal Treaties, summing the vectors would often lead the nation in no particular direction or just as likely away from hegemony as toward hegemony. It is more likely, however, that a hegemon's policies consist of vectors that diverge somewhat and have different intensities, owing to bureaucratic differences, but that *mostly* point in the same general direction—toward hegemony (see figure 1.2). There is no master hand at the switch. There are no long-standing cabals. There are no expertly designed long-term grand strategies (although certainly some grand strategies are developed). There is no dominant agency, elite, or class. There is, however, the cumulative effect of thousands of individuals and agencies—backed by a very wealthy and powerful state—that in their own ways all promote the vital interests of that nation-state. The sum of these vectors is a long vector pointing in a direction that serves to establish and preserve hegemony. We could say that all nations attempt to achieve such power and consistency in foreign policy, but only a handful of them are able to achieve the power and influence necessary for its attainment.

Democracy: The Nation-State Level of Analysis

THE MEANING AND LIMITS OF DEMOCRACY

Scholars have been attempting to define democracy literally for centuries, yet the concept remains elusive (Sartori 1987; Held 1987). At present we have two different conceptions of democracy. One version can be labeled *liberal* or *procedural* democracy, while the other may be called *populist* or *substantive* democracy (Riker 1982). Liberal democracy places a premium on electoral procedures as well as on political and economic rights. Populist democracy, on the other hand, places a premium on substantive outcomes and popular participation. Proponents of populist democracy assume that popular participation will yield a more just society, and thus they highlight the results rather than the processes of democracy. In short, from the substantive democracy viewpoint, if a society is highly stratified and resources are concentrated in the hands of a few, then it is assumed that democracy has no substance even if the process is deemed to be democratic. Substantive democracy often requires a populist leader, in Latin America perhaps a modern *caudillo*, or strongman, who can express the interests of the masses that feel shortchanged by the political process. Contemporary democratic theorists, however, have placed more emphasis on liberal democracy since they assume that substantive democracy can lead to a tyranny of the majority and to autocratic populist leaders. We will thus assume that democratic processes, while never ideal, will yield a more just society than nondemocratic processes (O'Donnell and Schmitter 1987). However, as we will see in our analysis, liberal democracy may not be viable in societies where scarcity and vast inequalities exist.

For decades, one parsimonious definition of liberal democracy has dominated the academic literature. Dahl has argued that democracy, or what he labels "polyarchy," is present only when two conditions exist in a society (Dahl 1971). First, the political system must allow citizens to oppose the government and those in power. That is to say, people and interest groups must be able to contest political power and have a reasonable opportunity to achieve political power if they have the support of the majority of the people. Consequently and secondly, virtually all citizens must be able to participate in the political process or it would be impossible to determine the political desires of the majority. In order for these two conditions to exist in a society, the political system must provide for a variety of guarantees, such as the right to free speech, competitive elections, and the right to organize politically, among others. This definition of liberal democracy also allows us to easily express what a democracy is *not*. A nondemocratic system is devoid of contestation and popular political participation. A nondemocratic system exists when one individual, institution, or class is able to control and allocate the values in a society (Sartori 1987, 182–213). Fascist and communist regimes, for example, do not permit contestation because only one political party assumes virtually all legitimacy and power. Popular participation is allowed in these regimes, but such participation never results in a change of political leadership and is mobilized by the state. Dictatorships and military regimes, historically common in many Latin American countries, have limited significantly both contestation and participation. Not only was it impossible to challenge the authority of the dictator or the armed forces, but political parties and popular organizations were routinely proscribed and repressed by these regimes (Collier 1979; Linz and Stepan 1978). Panama's military regimes under Generals Omar Torrijos and Manuel Noriega, as we will see, are clear examples.

While democracy as defined above is appealing for a variety of reasons (Mueller 1999), we must highlight the shortcomings of liberal democracy, since these flaws may affect its long-term survival in Latin American countries. Despite its benefits, liberal democracy is a political system that allows for *limited* mass political participation and chiefly for *elite* contestation. In such a democracy, the masses will never be truly immersed in politics and will thus never directly determine their future. Even though there is good reason to believe that populist democracy can never be practical or possible, it is nevertheless the case that liberal democracy will always leave large segments of the masses and counterelites dissatisfied. Consequently, populist leaders will most likely appear in societies suffering from deep class, racial, or ethnic divisions, even if a democratic regime carries out perennial competitive elections and allows for political rights. Likewise, liberal democracy, despite its homage to popular sovereignty, yields to elites a preponderance of political clout. And the economic elite will always enjoy significant amounts of influence in a liberal democracy since private property and economic rights are sacrosanct (Lindbloom 1977). Unlike in industrialized countries, in developing societies, where class divisions are deeper, populist leaders will appeal to the masses as bulwarks against the power of the economic elite. It should be obvious, then, that liberal democracy's allure, and consequently its likelihood of consolidation, is directly linked to economic development.

Procedural democracy will be maintained much more easily in a prosperous society than in a society where there is poverty and inequality. In poor and divided societies, liberal democracy is less likely to become consolidated and is more likely to slide into populist democracy or even authoritarianism. In these societies, the masses and the middle class may lose their allegiance to procedural democracy more quickly because the societies may not be able to create necessary prosperity. Additionally, less-developed nation-states that find themselves in a subordinate position in the international system will also feel the allure of populism since it will be seen as a defense against foreign dominance and exploitation. The greatest threat to democracy in Latin America, then, may stem not from a lack of support for democratic values but from democracy's own limitations and from the vagaries of the domestic and international economies.

POWER DISTRIBUTION AND DEMOCRACY

Democracy is loosely the domestic equivalent of a balance of power system in the international system in that it reflects a plural distribution of power. The assumed value of separation of powers is that each branch of government will fight to prevent one branch from acquiring too much power—checks and balances thus approximate the idea of balance of power. Dahl's conception of democracy as polyarchy reflects this assertion since polyarchy is a system where the values in a society are allocated via compromises between numerous important actors rather than being determined by one individual, a small elite, or a homogeneous class. Vanhanen, after comparing democratization in 147 countries, concluded:

> Political systems tend to democratize when important power resources become widespread and they tend to remain non-democratic as long as important power resources are concentrated in the hands of the few. . . . The pressure for democratization will increase in all countries where power resources become widespread, and it becomes more and more difficult for the power holders of autocratic systems to maintain their hegemony and to keep the gates of democratization closed. (1990, 194)

The most fundamental precondition of democracy, then, is the existence of a plural distribution of power resources. When an autocratic system begins to lose its monopoly over the means of coercion or over the key resources in a society, then pressure for democratization will begin. Since power distribution is the principal focus of this study, we assume that the civic culture associated with democracy will arise when power in a society becomes increasingly dispersed, since new power holders will naturally promote those values. Consequently, it is likely that authoritarian regimes were prevalent in Latin America after independence in the 1820s owing to the "centralist tradition," where power was highly concentrated in the hands of an oligarchy that was supported by the traditional landed elite, the military, and the Catholic Church (Veliz 1980).

PRECONDITIONS OF DEMOCRACY

Scholars have meticulously attempted to discover the causes or preconditions of democracy in the last several decades (see Lipset 1959, as an early example). In Latin America, democratic development was like a roller coaster, or pendulum, in the last half of the twentieth century. The region experienced a democratic blossoming in the post–World War II period (Porter and Alexander 1961, 3–5) but then suffered a wave of "new authoritarianism" in the 1960s that lasted well into the 1970s (Collier 1979). Then, in the late 1970s, democracy began to emerge anew, and by the end of the century only Cuba and Haiti were devoid of procedural democracy. The most recent democratic transitions in the region spurred a large body of academic work on the causes and preconditions of democracy (O'Donnell, Schmitter, and Whitehead 1986). Once democracy seemed to have taken root in at least a number of countries in the region, scholars shifted their focus to the consolidation of democracy, arguing that the factors that led to democratic inauguration and transition were not always the same as those that led to democratic consolidation (see Diamond et al. 1999, 4–7). We have learned a great deal from this extensive research on democratization and can employ its findings to better understand why Latin American nations transitioned to democracy beginning in the late 1970s and to predict whether these nascent democracies will consolidate. We will keep in mind, however, that at the most basic level, democracy will arise only when power is distributed widely in a society.

National and Elite Unity

For any society to establish an effective political system, a certain degree of unity must be present. National unity therefore is a precondition of any stable political system, including a democracy (Rustow 1970). In a society where there is a lack of cohesion, it is unlikely that a democracy will exist because dominant economic classes, ethnic groups, or interest groups will be reluctant to turn political power over to the majority. In divided societies, unity and order will most likely have to be created by force, and thus authoritarianism will be the most likely form of government. Authoritarian political systems will therefore impose or attempt to create an artificial unity. Totalitarian systems were more sophisticated than most dictatorships or military regimes in that they used ideology to unite the masses and garner support for the state and its policies. Although force was used to prevent dissent, the focus was on creating allegiance to the system and a united citizenry through socialization and propaganda. Autocracies and military regimes, however, relied more on repression than on ideology to achieve unity. While democracies also employ ideology to achieve unity, a great deal of allegiance to the system is achieved through the legitimacy derived from citizens' ability to participate freely in the system and to contest political power. Therefore, support for the system is obtained from the inherent qualities of the system itself. Democratic theorists assume, then, that democratic rule will generate a high degree of unity and allegiance among the citizenry, while authoritarian systems run the risk of eventually losing popular support. The bottom line is that, for a stable political system to exist, citizens must have some common bonds that unite them, such as history and culture, thus leading to the development of a viable nation-state.

A stable political system also requires unity among the ruling elite (see Burton and Higley 1987; and Higley and Gunther 1992). Unity appears to be present in authoritarian systems because a particular elite faction has taken the reins of power and created an environment where contesting power becomes too costly. The outcome is that most elites cooperate with the ruling faction to safeguard their vital interests. Nonruling elites may cooperate and tolerate an authoritarian regime because the authoritarian rulers either did not threaten their interests or actually worked to preserve their interests. The authoritarian military regimes in Latin America in the 1960s and 1970s, for example, received support from nonruling elites and the middle sectors because those groups/classes believed that the generals could best protect their interests. Only after the generals proved to be ineffectual political leaders and threats to stability were eliminated did the abuses of these regimes seem unacceptable and did these nonruling factions begin to challenge the legitimacy of the praetorian regimes they had previously supported.

Democracy then is more likely to emerge when there is national unity and when elites believe that political opposition and participation are principles that are conducive to the maintenance of their interests. As Higley and Gunther argue, "a consolidated democracy is a regime that meets all the procedural criteria of democracy and also in which all politically significant groups accept established political institutions and adhere to democratic rules of the game" (1992, 3). The above preconditions for democracy seem intuitively obvious. The more difficult question to answer is: What condi-

tions lead to national unity and to an elite consensus on democratic principles? National unity is most likely to exist when a population is relatively
homogeneous. When significant racial, ethnic, and economic differences are
present, divisiveness is common, and unstable conditions ensue. Perhaps the
most effective manner in which to create homogeneity in a diverse society
is through state-directed and -monitored socialization. The stability found
in many of the world's developed nations may be attributed to the ability of
a powerful state to socialize its citizens over a long period of time. State socialization, along with a common history and culture, increases the chances
that a society will have a sense of unity and cohesion. Unity and support for
a regime is also enhanced when the state is able to provide what citizens expect from their government. The United States, for example, is a crazy-quilt
of races and ethnicities, yet national unity has been achieved through socialization, prosperity, and responsiveness. Weak and impoverished states,
on the other hand, will have more difficulty achieving consensus. National
unity can also be achieved in the face of an external or common threat and
war, as occurred in Europe (Tilly 1975). And, as mentioned above, unity can
be the product of a democratic system that allows all citizens—regardless of
ethnicity, race, or economic class—to participate in and contest the political
system, whether individually or in groups. An effective state, therefore, is a
sine qua non of any stable political system (see Przeworski 1991; and Linz
and Stepan 1996). An effective state can go a long way toward creating the
national unity and regime allegiance that may not naturally exist in a society,
particularly one that is poor and fractionalized.

Elite consensus that leads to democracy results when all elites are convinced that democratic principles are the best way in which to preserve their
interests. Elites therefore must become convinced that popular participation
and contestation will preserve and not threaten their interests. Democratic
transitions can thus occur when elites believe that democracy is good—or
better than all other alternatives—for them at a particular juncture; but democracy can be consolidated only after elites are convinced that contestation and participation are clearly in their long-term interests. Burton and
Higley have argued that societies move from a primitive condition of elite
disunity to a more advanced stage of elite unity (1987). However, in any society, unity may be disrupted by the rise of new elites. In Latin America, many
nations enjoyed a period of elite unity after independence, when relatively
cohesive oligarchies controlled politics. When mass movements emerged in
the twentieth century, that unity was shattered and oligarchs had to decide
whether to incorporate new elites and groups into the system or whether to
repress them. Long ago, Mosca argued:

If a new source of wealth develops in a society, if the practical importance of knowledge grows, if an old religion declines or a new one
is born, if a new current of ideas spread, then, simultaneously, far-
reaching dislocations occur in the ruling class. (1939, 65)

We will see that in Panama, oligarchic rule was challenged in the 1920s by
the emergence of new social forces that demanded inclusion into the political system. Elite unity therefore is always subject to deterioration and even
collapse. And the nascent democracies of Latin America are more likely to
suffer from elite disunity than the more advanced democratic societies, for
reasons that I will discuss below.

Many factors can contribute to the establishment of elite unity. First, it
should be evident that elite disunity can lead to conflicts that in the long run
hurt elite interests. Burton and Higley argue that intense and unresolved
conflict should be considered as an important precondition of elite unity
since elites learn over time that internecine conflict is detrimental to their
interests (1987). Mass mobilizations also tend to galvanize elites, in that they
respond to pressures from below by unifying their efforts to keep the masses
from demanding too much. Unfortunately for democratic prospects, when
there is mass mobilization, elites tend to unify in order to repress or stem
popular demands rather than to promote contestation and participation.
External threats can also compel elites to work together to defeat a common, foreign enemy. However, external forces can also divide national elites.
In the twentieth century, ideological conflicts between democracy, fascism,
and communism replicated themselves in almost all nations on the globe,
leading to domestic as well as international conflicts. Ideological consensus
will unite the elite since shared values will minimize conflict. In sum, elite
unity will most likely be present in societies where there is little internal
conflict, where the masses are relatively demobilized or pacified, and where
elites share common values. If a foreign threat exists, then the likelihood of
unity will increase. However, if external conflicts permeate a particular society, divisions may emerge. Elite unity, however, does not necessarily have
to result in the establishment of a democratic regime. Other factors must be
present for democracy to appeal to the elite.

At the beginning of the twenty-first century, democracy is almost uni-
versally considered as the most legitimate form of government. As briefly
described above, in the twentieth century both fascism and communism
lost their appeal and were "defeated" by the leading democracies. At present,
most societies are under a great deal of international pressure to establish
democratic forms of government (Diamond 1999). There is no doubt that in

the 1980s and 1990s, U.S. policy promoted the establishment of procedural democratic regimes in Latin America. In the 1960s and 1970s, however, U.S. policy promoted institutional military rule (See Sánchez 2003a). External forces, then, can either unify or atomize elites in their support for democracy, depending on the characteristics of those forces at a particular time. At the beginning of the third millennium, democracy appears to be the only game in town, and formerly authoritarian nations are under considerable pressure to democratize. At the same time, international economic forces calling for neoliberal reform in the developing world are generating conditions that could prove to be divisive if inequality persists in these societies.

Elite unity is also achieved by violence. When threatened by counterelites, especially those who appeal to the masses, elites will most likely lash out to destroy those disaffected factions. Over time, the counterelite may be decimated and eventually disillusioned. During the 1960s and 1970s, when insurgencies were common in most of Latin America, military regimes virtually eliminated Marxist insurgents and "fellow travelers," thus artificially creating a consensus through the elimination of dissenting elites. In addition, socialist countries that provided an alternative model to democracy inspired and assisted those antisystem elites. Once that support evaporated and the socialist model lost its appeal, the consensus toward democracy grew stronger. Similarly, once the communist "threat" was eliminated, military regimes seemed less useful, and praetorianism based on national security doctrine lost its legitimacy. In sum, the elimination of counterelites can assist in manufacturing, albeit brutally, elite and even national unity.

Regardless of how elite unity is achieved, elite consensus over the democratic rules of the game is a sine qua non for democratic consolidation. The elite learn to accept democracy not just because other nations are adopting it as their form of government. Elites over time learn that the adoption of the key democratic principles—contestation and participation—does not result in the destruction of their power and influence, or way of life. They may lose some control in a liberal democracy, but their vital interests are preserved. Contestation allows for rival elites to have a say in public policy and therefore diffuses potential conflict that could hurt elite interests in the long run. As Pareto pointed out, "elite circulation" is vital for the preservation of stability (1935). The elite also learn that popular participation helps to pacify the masses while keeping extremist arguments from winning the day. Dahl has admitted that democracy does not necessarily result in a substantive improvement in the lives of the masses but does result in a feeling that people are having a say in politics (1971). Once elites learn that democracy preserves their interests, while at the same time promoting stability and legitimacy, they will tend to embrace the principles of contestation and participation.

In summation, a stable political system is impossible without at least a minimum level of national unity. An effective nation-state can help to construct national unity. A stable democratic regime can emerge only if an elite consensus over the democratic rules of the game is present. Elites, however, will accept contestation and participation only when power becomes so dispersed that repression becomes too costly (Dahl 1971) and when they are convinced that contestation and participation will not undermine their fundamental interests. If elites retain a monopoly on societal power, then a democratic transition might occur, but repression can continue and the democratic regime stands little chance of consolidation. If the elite have a monopoly on power and a crisis erupts, then they may assert their power, and democracy will very likely break down. The difficulty for the analyst is to determine when the power distribution in a society has reached a point where elites will most likely accept contestation and participation rather than choose repression.

Structural Factors

Developmentalists have repeatedly argued that socioeconomic progress enhances the chances for democracy to emerge (Lipset 1959). Although criticism existed for some time, even scholars who previously attacked the development-democracy hypothesis have recently conceded that socioeconomic development is closely associated with the inauguration of democracy (Rueschemeyer, Huber Stephens, and Stephens 1992). The notion that economic and social development is related to democratic politics is logical for several reasons. First, an expanding and modernizing economy is more likely to generate a plural elite structure and to augur the development of a middle class. Such increased plurality of interests and political power will yield a more diverse society that will begin to demand inclusion in the political system. As Latin America became more differentiated economically in the 1900s, more societal sectors demanded inclusion in the political process, resulting in social movements that manifested themselves in nationalist and populist politics. Likewise, social development, leading to greater educational opportunities, yielded a citizenry that called for more political participation. Thus, new elite factions along with a larger middle class and greater popular political awareness led to a plethora of demands placed upon the traditional ruling oligarchy. At first, the oligarchs tended to resist and repress, but eventually they found that allowing for contestation and participation would calm the masses, the middle sectors, and the emerging counterelite.

Scholars who employed class analysis found an important connection between socioeconomic change and democracy in Latin America. Paige has concluded that democracy is almost impossible to achieve when a traditional landed elite controls a society (1997). Similarly, after studying democratic development in advanced capitalist countries and in Latin America, Rueschemeyer, Huber Stephens, and Stephens asserted that "landed upper classes which were dependent on a large supply of cheap labor were the most consistently anti-democratic force" (1992, 8). Since Latin America's colonial legacy was one of centralized economic and political structures, where the landed elite held a preponderance of power, democratic politics have come relatively slowly to the region (Veliz 1980). However, as the nations in the region developed socially and economically, in many cases leading to the diminution of the traditional landed elite, democratic politics have become much more likely.

The favored societal position of the armed forces has been one of the most important causes of power concentration in Iberoamerica (Loveman 1999). Since independence in the early 1820s, Latin militaries were active politically, but seldom had they ruled directly. Beginning in the 1960s, however, a new authoritarianism ushered in a period of institutional military rule (Collier 1979). The armed forces institutionalized so rapidly in relation to civil institutions during this time that the delicate civil-military balance in the region was severely disrupted (Lowenthal and Fitch 1986). In addition, a new doctrine of national security became pervasive, compelling military officers to become preoccupied with matters of national development and with the maintenance of internal order (Stepan 1986). This historical, and more recent, praetorianism has presented a serious barrier to democratization. Thus, in Latin America particularly, the civil-military balance is of utmost importance for any study of democratization.

Scholars have also pointed out that national divisions militate against democratic development. As pointed out earlier, democracy will take longer to develop when racial or ethnic divisions fracture a society because groups will lack trust in each other, thus making national unity unobtainable. Also, if the elite view themselves as different racially and ethnically from the rest of the population or the masses, then they will be hesitant to allow for participation (Sánchez 1997). Democratic consolidation can occur only when diverse groups have some common bond and have trust in each other. While many observers see Latin America as relatively homogeneous, owing to a shared culture, history, and language, ethnic and racial divisions are strong in this region. Most countries in the region have populations whose racial and ethnic makeup is diverse enough to hinder democracy's chances for survival. Perhaps most important, in most countries a small percentage of the population is of European origin. Even in a country like Cuba, which has experienced a social revolution, the elite tend to be predominantly of European descent. The "Euro-white" elite, found in all countries in the region, hold a preponderance of political and economic power. The majority of the population in the region's countries, by contrast, is of mixed race—mestizo, mulatto, or both. Additionally, many countries have significant portions of the population that can be classified as indigenous, as in Ecuador, Guatemala, and Peru; or of African descent, like in Brazil, Cuba, and Panama. These racial/ethnic divisions not only hinder the chances for national unity but also make the elite fearful of democracy. The small Euro-elite, who have traditionally held the levers of power, have been and will continue to be very hesitant to allow for contestation and participation, lest the "others" desire retribution, power, and wealth. Once they began to understand that liberal democracy could yield greater tranquility and preserve their interests, the Euro-elite began to slowly embrace democratic principles.[2] However, the "democratic" result, as I will discuss below, may be a procedural democracy that is lacking in participation, or what some have labeled as hollow or low-intensity democracy (Diamond 1999; Gills, Rocamora, and Wilson 1993).

In summary, the literature on democratization has suggested that democracy is most likely to emerge when six general conditions exist in a particular society:

1. The citizenry must have a sense of national unity and must embrace democratic values.
2. A viable, autonomous state that can assist in developing national unity must exist.
3. A consensually unified elite must develop whose members are convinced that democracy preserves their interests better than any other political regime.
4. The society in question must have reached a minimum level of socioeconomic development, but, more important, that development must result in the elimination or significant weakening of the traditional landed elite and the enhancement of middle and working classes that call for broader political contestation and participation.
5. The politically engaged armed forces must be transformed into a military that is under the control of civilian political institutions.

6. Ethnic and racial divisions must be minimized so that groups will trust each other and the elite will not feel threatened by the incorporation of "others" into the political system.

DEMOCRATIC CONSOLIDATION

The inauguration of a democracy does not guarantee its long-term survival, or consolidation. We can look at a particular transition and estimate whether conditions conducive to democratic development, such as power distribution and elite unity, are present, but a democracy will have better chances for longevity if other conditions are also present. The literature on democratic consolidation has directed our attention to the importance of institutions and social organizations, such as regime design, political parties, and private voluntary associations (Diamond 1999; Linz and Stepan 1996; O'Donnell 1994). If certain preconditions provide a favorable environment for democracy, these additional features provide the flesh that supports the survival of a democracy. More important, these features help to foster an environment where societal power is more widely distributed. Strong democratic institutions and a vibrant civil society promote what some scholars have termed the "deepening" of democracy (Von Mettenheim and Malloy 1998).

The long-term presence of democracy itself may be the best guarantor of democratic consolidation. That is, a positive experience with democratic politics will reinforce democratic values among both the citizenry and the elite, who will become "habituated" to democratic government and principles (Rustow 1970). Once democracy proves to be useful, its long-term survival is enhanced significantly. The longer a democratic system survives, the higher the degree of elite consensus over the democratic rules of the game and the likelier it will be that the masses will view democracy as the best game in town. But democracy will persist only if democratic institutions are strong and autonomous, allowing a democratic regime to weather bad times and resist sporadic pressures for nondemocratic change.

Most scholars who have studied political systems in Latin America have repeatedly come to the conclusion that political parties in most countries are weak and personalistic (Mainwarring and Scully 1995). Strong political parties alone will not guarantee the survival of democratic politics, but once a democracy is inaugurated, strong political parties will provide organized vehicles through which groups and individuals can contest power and participate politically. A procedural democracy cannot exist without the possibility and actuality of an alternation of power. Consequently, at least two strong political parties must exist for a liberal democracy to have a good chance of becoming consolidated. Peeler suggests that a democracy may be considered stable once the system "has passed through three electoral cycles without the breakdown of its key rules and procedures" (2004, 93). However, the existence of a dominant political party, like in Mexico, will mitigate the chances for stable democracy to emerge since electoral cycles will not necessarily yield alternation of power. Likewise, the existence of many weak political parties, led by individuals with little popular support, will result in a weakly consolidated democracy, even if a series of electoral cycles take place.

Other political institutions are important for democratic consolidation as well. A strong legislative branch that is able to achieve relative autonomy prevents the establishment of *presidencialismo*. Latin American democracies have been heavily criticized for the power of their executives. In fact, assertive presidents in Panama, Peru, and Venezuela have recently attempted to take on greater power through constitutional reforms. Two other institutions are important for democracy's long-term survival: an independent judiciary and an independent electoral tribunal. If these two institutions conduct their business with some degree of autonomy from political and economic forces, then both citizens and elites will have some assurance that policies and elections will be carried out fairly and honestly. Only if laws and elections are reasonably beyond reproach will citizens and elites value procedural democracy for the long haul (O'Donnell 1994).

Democratic theorists have more recently highlighted civil society's importance for the "deepening" of democracy (Von Mettenheim and Malloy 1998). Such a concept acknowledges that a procedural democracy can exist in societies where citizens participate very little in the political process. For example, some scholars have been critical of the recent democratization process in Latin America since the inauguration of democracy has not resulted in positive social changes in the region. Some of this criticism may in turn be criticized as simply the reflection of a naïve assumption that democracy will rid Latin America of its problems once people are allowed the right to participate and contest power politically. But, as stated above, we must keep in mind that procedural democracy allows simply for elite contestation and limited popular participation. Liberal democracy will not necessarily eliminate racism, economic disparities, corruption, and other ills. We must remember that U.S. "democracy" existed for many years with slavery and limits to voting rights that were inimical for a deeper democracy, and that democracy exists in many developed nations alongside racism and other social pathologies. Nevertheless, in Latin America, democracy will benefit greatly from the mushrooming of private voluntary organizations that can serve as vehicles for popular political participation. Thus, the development of a strong civil society will greatly enhance the chances for democratic consolidation since citizens will have more avenues for political participation and power will be more diffused.

A final condition for consolidation is only indirectly related to the characteristics of democracy itself. A newly inaugurated liberal democracy will improve its chances for consolidation if it is able to govern effectively and efficiently (Diamond 1999). This condition, as with others, is intuitive and logical. A new democracy that is able to achieve compromise among principal groups, provide for economic growth, and rule in a fair manner for a relatively long period will experience enhanced legitimacy and thus greater prospects for consolidation. On the other hand, a new democracy that experiences conflict among groups, suffers from economic decline, and becomes bogged down with political strife will run a much higher risk of regime breakdown. Unfortunately, the nations of Latin America will have a more difficult time with democratic consolidation since economic growth is less certain and significant inequalities in those societies increase the chances for social conflict. Additionally, the illicit narcotics traffic in several countries, including Panama, threatens the ability of relatively new democratic regimes to govern fairly and effectively.

For a new democracy to become consolidated, therefore, the following features should be present soon after a democratic transition:

1. At least two relatively strong political parties that reflect citizen interests and are able to effectively contest elections.
2. A viable and relatively autonomous judiciary, legislature, and electoral tribunal.
3. A relatively strong and autonomous civil society.
4. An ability to govern effectively and efficiently for some time.

Anyone who knows even a little about Latin America will quickly come to the conclusion that these conditions will be difficult to achieve fully and effectively. Nevertheless, if the preconditions of democracy are present—national unity, elite unity, minimum level of socioeconomic development, low militarization, and amelioration of ethnic and racial differences—then these other features for consolidation may arise over time, barring the existence of major problems or crises. A severe economic crisis, internal unrest, external manipulation, and the problems associated with the narcotics trade can, however, create conditions under which citizens look to populist democracy or elites look to terminate the democratic experiment.

The Nexus between Hegemony and Democracy

While the above propositions/conditions may apply to all countries, democratic development can also be influenced greatly by the particular historical moment that a nation-state transitions to a democratic regime and by that nation-state's position in the international power structure. Great Britain, for example, began to accept contestation and participation earlier than other nations. External influences were therefore less important for states that democratized early since models that could be copied were not available. Similarly, domestic forces were principally responsible in forging Great Britain's national development since it was the first nation to industrialize. Nation-states that democratized later, like the countries in Latin America, however, have been influenced by the models provided by the countries that inaugurated democratic regimes early and by their subordinate position in the international system. The nations of Latin America in particular have been affected significantly by their subordinate status in the hegemonic international subsystem found in the Western Hemisphere. Most of the nations of Latin America experienced independence in the 1820s. By the early 1900s, U.S. military, economic, and political power was already preponderant in the Caribbean (Healy 1988). Thus any understanding of political development in Latin America must take into consideration this salient feature of the region's international subsystem—late democratization and hegemonic subordination.

As pointed out earlier, hegemony refers to an international system where power is highly concentrated in the hands of one nation-state. In such a system, the hegemon is able to influence the international behavior and domestic politics of the subordinate states. It follows, then, that a subordinate nation-state's democratization may be affected by the actions of the hegemon. Such influence may be direct or indirect. For example, the hegemon can, through its foreign policy, officially attempt to promote the development of democratic politics, as the United States attempted to do with President Kennedy's Alliance for Progress. The Alliance, whether successful or not, was an overt attempt to promote liberal democracy in Latin America, using developmentalist social science theory. Indirect influence occurs when a hegemon's actions create a social context that hinders democratic development. For example, when it assisted the United Fruit Company and Guatemalan economic elites in their struggle against President Arbenz's progressive government, Washington essentially promoted the survival of a feudal economic system led by a traditional landed oligarchy, thus minimizing the prospects for democratic development. Also, when it promoted the armed forces and counterinsurgency in the 1960s during the Alliance for Progress period, the U.S. government helped to disrupt the already weak civil-military balance that existed in countries of the region.

The argument here is that a hegemon may, because of its overarching influence, have a profound effect on those preconditions that promote the transition to and consolidation of democracy. Dahl has noted that "the actions of foreigners may and almost certainly will have some impact on one or more of the conditions" necessary for democracy to develop, especially in "small or less developed countries" (Dahl 1971, 190). A hegemon can affect national and elite unity. A hegemon can affect the ethnic and racial makeup of a society, as the United States did in Panama by importing large numbers of people from English-speaking Caribbean islands. Most important, a hegemon can affect the distribution of power in a society by supporting some groups while attempting to eliminate others. If a hegemon's actions promote the dispersion of power in a particular society, then the inauguration of democracy will be more likely; but if a hegemon promotes the concentration of power, then authoritarian forms of government will more likely emerge. In addition, once a procedural democracy has been inaugurated, the actions of a hegemonic power "may drastically alter the options available to a regime without necessarily altering the form of the regime" (Dahl 1971, 190). When a hegemonic power limits a weak democracy's policy options "the people lose the capacity to govern themselves," reducing that regime's democratic qualities (Dahl 1971, 191). In short, in an international system where the distribution of power is asymmetric, the actions of the dominant power must be considered as an additional, salient factor when attempting to understand the forces that promote or militate against democratic inauguration and consolidation. We can thus add one more general condition for both the emergence and for the consolidation of a democratic regime to our lists above:

> [Additional condition for democracy's emergence]
> 7. In an asymmetrical international system, the dominant power must not take actions that concentrate societal power, weaken the state, or intensify fundamental social divisions in subordinate states.
> [Additional feature for democratic consolidation]
> 5. In an asymmetrical international system, the dominant power must not significantly constrain the policy options of a subordinate democracy.

A hegemonic power will take actions that may or may not be conducive to democratic development in a subordinate state. Clearly, a nondemocratic hegemon would not promote democracy. The Soviet Union, for example, promoted political systems led by one political party, devoid of contestation and free political participation. Studying the actions of a democratic hegemon, like the United States, is more interesting in that we are able to see whether or not a democratic hegemon, despite its desire to enhance and concentrate its power in the international system, will nevertheless promote democratic regimes in subordinate states.

Why Panama Is Important

The Republic of Panama provides a valuable case study for both the study of hegemony and the study of democratization. In analyzing the concept of hegemony, Panama is important because, if U.S. hegemony is not present there, then it is not present anywhere in Latin America. U.S. influence in Panama has been extensive, long-standing, and broad in scope since the mid-1800s. The U.S. government built and operated a major transcontinental railroad and canal, vital for American interests and global commerce. U.S. companies had and continue to have sizeable investments in the isthmus. The U.S. government maintained a plethora of military installations on the isthmus that housed thousands of U.S. troops, and a large U.S. enclave existed on the isthmus in the U.S.-controlled Zone, with its own governor and police force (Major 1993). One study has classified Panama as a country suffering from extreme economic dependence, compared to other countries in the years 1950 to 1973 (Richardson 1978: 103–6). Panama was nearly a U.S. colony, despite the nation's titular independence. On December 31, 1999, however, the canal reverted to the Panamanian government, and the long-standing U.S. military presence finally ended, as stipulated by the 1977 Carter-Torrijos Treaties. These two accords substantially minimized the U.S. presence in Panama and in Latin America. But will the U.S. departure from Panama represent a decline in U.S. hegemony in both Panama and Latin America?

Panama's political history can shed light on the process of democratization as well. We will see below that Panama was one of the last countries in the hemisphere to transition to democracy. By 1990, only Cuba and Haiti maintained a nondemocratic political system, yet Panama was just recovering from a U.S. invasion ending a period of institutional military rule that had begun in 1968. The fact that the nation-state with the greatest U.S. presence and influence was a latecomer to democratization must lead us to wonder about the effects of hegemony on democratic development. Either U.S. policies failed to promote democratic development, or U.S. policies instead promoted conditions nonconducive for the development of polyarchy in Panama. Now that the U.S. presence is smaller, what are Panama's prospects for democratic consolidation?

The Organization of the Book

We now have a general framework for understanding democratic development in an asymmetrical international context. We can therefore examine Panama's political history and its relationship with the United States in some detail to see whether this history can support our theoretical knowledge about democratization and hegemony. In chapter 2, I will look at the characteristics of Panama's political system from independence from Spain in 1821 until its independence from Colombia in 1903. I will focus on the emergence of nationalism and the interests of the elite on the isthmus. I will also examine the U.S.-Panamanian relationship, looking at early U.S. interests, including the building of the Panama Railroad and the U.S. role in Panama's independence from Colombia. Chapter 3 examines Panama's early republic, dominated by an oligarchy that, while liberal in its political orientation, limited political contestation and participation. By the 1920s, however, the middle sectors, along with students and labor organizations, began to demand inclusion and took on a nationalist agenda. At the same time, the United States engineered and built the Panama Canal and expanded its interests both in Panama and in Latin America. In Chapter 4, I consider the emergence of two middle-class institutions that became dominant actors in Panama's political system—the Panameñista Party, led by Arnulfo Arias, and the National Police, led by José Remón. These national forces challenged the oligarchy's dominance, as well as U.S. power and interests on the isthmus. As the middle sectors demanded inclusion, Washington's principal concerns were global security and German influence in the region. Consequently, the U.S. government militated against liberalization in Panama in order to guarantee canal and regional security. In chapter 5, we see that U.S. security concerns continued in the post–World War II period with the rise of the cold war. Increasing nationalism, along with the global move toward decolonization, inevitably clashed with U.S. security needs, and the U.S.-Panamanian "special relationship" came to a violent end with the 1964 anti-U.S. riots. The oligarchy's inability to maintain security and its increasingly nationalistic stance convinced the U.S. government to support the institutional military regime that emerged on the isthmus in 1968. Chapter 6 recounts the Torrijos dictatorship, the 1977 Panama Canal Treaties, the Noriega regime, and the 1989 U.S. invasion. During this hectic period, democracy broke down on the isthmus, while the United States pursued a single-minded goal of preventing a second Cuba and eliminating Soviet influence in Latin America. In chapter 7, we look at the return to democracy in Panama, the elimination of the Panamanian armed forces, the end of the U.S. military presence on the isthmus, and Panama's assumption of control over the famous canal. In the 1990s and into the twenty-first century, democracy flourishes on the isthmus as never before, while the United States achieves hegemony in Latin America. Chapter 8 supplies conclusions and implication from the Panama case study. First, I assess how well the theoretical frameworks explain the U.S.-Panamanian relationship and democratic development in Panama. I also look toward the future in an effort to determine the likelihood that Panama's nascent democracy will become consolidated and to consider the implications of the changes in the U.S.-Panamanian relationship. Finally, I make some generalizations about U.S. policy toward Panama and Latin America based on what we have learned through our examination of U.S.-Panamanian relations.

From the Emergence of U.S. Dominance to the "Taking of the Isthmus"

Colombian Rule and Panamanian National Aspirations, 1821–1903

In this first historical chapter, we will consider eighty years of history, examining both U.S.-Panamanian relations and Panamanian political development. My goal is not to provide a detailed narrative of this fascinating history but rather, as with subsequent chapters, to emphasize watershed events and processes that provide a clear understanding of key aspects of U.S. hegemony, U.S.-Panamanian relations, and Panama's troubled history with democracy in the twentieth century. The late 1800s witnessed the end of a balance of power system in the Western Hemisphere. As European powers lost influence and became preoccupied with other parts of the world, the United States was able to gradually enhance its power and influence in Latin America. This power shift came about not simply because Europe lost interest in the hemisphere, but because the U.S. government took concerted steps to enhance its economic, military, and political power in the Western Hemisphere. This historical period was eventful for Panama as well. After gaining independence from Spain in 1821, the isthmus willingly became part of Gran Colombia, the construct of General Simón Bolívar, *el Libertador*. The isthmian elite, however, soon became disenchanted with Bogotá's rule and attempted to gain autonomy or independence on several occasions. The isthmus eventually separated from Colombia in 1903 with assistance from Washington, which yearned to construct a transisthmian waterway. Panama transitioned from being a Spanish colony, to being an appendage of Colombia, to then being a U.S. protectorate. But Panama's difficulty with democracy was not simply the result of external tutelage. The tight control exercised by a small oligarchy fearful of popular participation also kept democracy at bay. Nevertheless, in the 1800s, nationalist sentiments and desires for self-determination emerged and grew on the isthmus, forging affective orientations that would eventually lead to the creation of a nation-state.

Panama in the 1800s: Destined for Independence

Geography has conditioned the history of Panama with greater force than in other countries.

—Jaime G. Marques, *Panamá en la encrucijada*

As a former colony of Spain, Panama, as part of the Viceroyalty of New Granada, inherited many of the characteristics of Iberian culture and society. Panama's geographic characteristics, however, directed the small isthmus in a divergent path as well. First, long a center of trade and "communication,"[1] Panama's elite developed a cosmopolitan outlook, unlike the more parochial, localized views of *latifundistas* (large landowners) in most of Spanish America. While pseudo-aristocrats whose wealth derived from large land holdings dominated much of Latin America, Panama's urban elite achieved its status principally through commerce and its attendant economic enterprises. As a result, even before 1800, Panama's dominant class adopted a "strong free-trade outlook" (Ropp 1982, 2) and repeatedly called for the establishment of a Hanseatic[2] republic (Soler 1989). Second, owing to its small size and paucity of Indian labor, Panama lacked the strong, dominant landed elite typical of most of the Americas. Spanish gentlemen who wished to create expansive *latifundios* were more likely to settle in Mexico, Nueva Granada (present-day Colombia), or Peru. Third, the Catholic Church was a much weaker political and social actor in Panama than in other parts of the region (Jaén Suárez 1978, 466–69). The Church was attracted to land and souls, and Panama had little territory and few Indians to convert. As a consequence, Spanish America's centralist tradition (Veliz 1980) was relatively weak on the isthmus. Power in Panama prior to and soon after independence, therefore, was much less concentrated than in most other countries in the region. But, similar to the other countries, Panama's *criollo* (homegrown) elite came to resent the arbitrary rule of Spain and its local representatives, the *peninsulares* (born in Spain), prompting them to cry for independence.

On November 28, 1821, Panamanian leaders declared the isthmus independent from Spanish rule and cast their luck with Gran Colombia, the political union of Ecuador, Nueva Granada, and Venezuela. The popularity of Simón Bolívar encouraged this federation, but his leadership style, which tended toward authoritarianism, eventually helped to undermine his grand political designs. When Gran Colombia dissolved in 1930, Panama chose to remain as part of Nueva Granada. The commercial elite on the isthmus had at times gained economically from their relationship with Spain and now assumed they would gain from continued association with Nueva Granada.

Nevertheless, these men of commerce had "always felt that their isthmus was a separate entity with its own political, social and economic philosophies" (Pérez-Venero 1978, ix). Geographic isolation from Bogotá, along with its unique geographic location that invited trade, had created a sense of separateness on the isthmus, if not a strong sense of nationalism. Panama's uniqueness also promoted the appeal of liberal ideas within its upper class, rather than the Old World conservatism more popular in Nueva Granada. Panama's elite tried to walk a tightrope—remaining an appendage of a larger entity for protection while retaining the autonomy necessary for fostering prosperity.

The central government in Bogotá, however, often acted arbitrarily, as Spain had done, and seldom took the interests of the isthmus into consideration. On several occasions in the 1800s, Panama's leaders either declared independence or called for local autonomy. In 1930 and 1931, after both Venezuela and Ecuador had separated themselves from Gran Colombia, some of Panama's elite declared isthmian independence. Nueva Granada successfully put down these separatist attempts, keeping the isthmus under Bogotá's control. Attempts at independence in the 1800s continued, however, most notably in 1840, 1860, and 1899. These efforts were fueled by the fact that Panama's commercial elite felt stifled economically and politically by the Granadine central government, often controlled by Conservatives. Isthmian intellectuals, particularly Justo Arosemena, continued to promote the notion of Panama as a Hanseatic republic, serving as an economic emporium to the world but associated with a powerful state, such as Great Britain, France, or the United States, for protection (Araúz 1994a, 65–72).[3]

Consequently, these calls for autonomy and independence did not truly represent a high degree of nationalism. The isthmian elite viewed themselves as having different interests from the dominant elite in Bogotá, but they did not consistently promote the isthmus's complete independence. And the common citizen, or those of the *arrabal*,[4] had not developed a sense of nationalism, owing to extant racial and ethnic divisions as well as to the large number of foreigners living on the isthmus (Soler 1989). Additionally, the liberalism that existed across the globe in the 1800s did not extend to the masses.

Panama in the Eyes of the Eagle: Destined for Tutelage

Aside from the extent to which it has been carried along by the advance of the Canal operation, the country has made no progress

. . . the people . . . are not at present headed in the right direction, nor possessed of the degree of interest and purpose that the situation demands. In the interior the people have no ambition beyond the needs and pleasures of the immediate morrow. The masses live from hand to mouth—happily enough, maybe, but uselessly. . . . The few well-to-do display no interest in the poorer classes, nor any in the progress of the country, except in so far as it may affect themselves immediately. (Forbes-Lindsay 1926, 416–17)

This 1926 assessment of the Panamanian people is typical of how Americans viewed the Panamanians. Diplomats, businessmen, and travelers from the United States had a penchant for describing the inhabitants of the region in pejorative and racist ways, showing not only a loathing of Latin Americans but a sense of superiority as well. Panama's quest for independence and self-determination clashed not only with Nueva Granada's desire to possess the isthmus but also with America's regional ambitions. U.S. policy makers promptly began to envision a future where only Washington would exploit the unique geographic position of the isthmus for the "benefit of mankind" (*pro mundi beneficio*) since Washington was certain that the isthmians were incapable of such a role. Much has been written about the social Darwinism prevalent in the United States in the late 1800s and early 1900s. This racist philosophy allowed Washington to rationalize its control of the isthmus and its future domination of the Western Hemisphere.

The United States of America, a young upstart in the global arena, began to flex its muscles as early as 1823. President James Monroe promulgated his famous doctrine that warned the European powers that the Western Hemisphere was a separate sphere from the Old World and that they should not attempt recolonization. The Americas were to forge their own destiny; however, that destiny would be determined and guided by U.S. interests and plans. At first, U.S. power and influence were insufficient to push Europe out of the region. But as the century wore on, America[5] expanded westward, gained economic and military vitality, and eventually squeezed European powers—Britain, France, and Spain—out of the hemisphere. The balance of power system, existing in the early 1800s, was replaced eventually by American preponderance of power by the early 1900s (P. Smith 2000, 16–37). While it considered the entire hemisphere as its area of influence, Washington initially focused on the Panamanian isthmus owing to its strategic location.[6] The consequence was that America's interest in the Colombian-controlled isthmus clashed with Panama's quest for autonomy and independence.

In 1846, Benjamin A. Bidlack, U.S. consul in Bogotá, struck a deal with

Manuel M. Mallarino, Nueva Granada's secretary of state, to facilitate mail service from New York City and New Orleans to the western territories. The accord—diplomatically labeled the Treaty of Peace, Amity, Navigation, and Commerce—gave Washington the right to free passage across the isthmus "upon any modes of communication that now exist, or that may be hereafter constructed" (Arosemena G. 1997a, 49)(my translation). In return, Washington agreed to safeguard Colombian sovereignty over the isthmus, leading the United States to intervene militarily fifty-seven times under the accord's provisions between 1846 and 1903 (Pérez-Venero 1978, 56). Such an arrangement essentially precluded the success of any independence movement on the isthmus. The U.S. government, as a result, became the principal bulwark against isthmian self-determination. Washington hoped that the Bidlack-Mallarino Treaty would persuade Bogotá to allow America to build a railroad or canal across the isthmus. In addition, the accord was meant to counterbalance British influence in Central America since London had designs for a waterway through Nicaragua. Only a few years later, potential conflict between Washington and London was stymied by the Clayton-Bulwer Treaty that went into effect on July 5, 1850. The two powers agreed that they would jointly construct a sea route across Central America, would not fortify such a route, and would enforce the route's neutrality, as established by the Treaty of Constantinople (Ealy 1971, 17–26). The United States thus continued to enhance its power in the hemisphere and over the isthmus.

The Gold Rush and the Panama Route

The discovery of gold in California raised to fever pitch American interest in the passage across Panama. Soon after James Marshall successfully found the precious metal in northern California in January 1848, Americans flooded to the isthmus aboard steamships, crossed the narrow isthmus by foot and dugout canoe, and then boarded a steamer at the Pacific terminal for the long sea voyage to California. The journey was arduous, dangerous, and sometimes deadly, owing to a lack of law enforcement, tropical diseases, and the tremendous wealth transiting the region. But the payoff, at least in the minds of those who rushed westward, could be magnificent, making the risks worthwhile. A railroad across the isthmus would make the journey safer, quicker, and more profitable all around. The gold discovery in California also fueled America's imperialist urges, leading Washington to take, at a bargain, huge portions of Mexico's territory, including California, at the end of the Mexican-American War in 1848.

New York City financier William H. Aspinwall and his associates, realizing the potential for profit, negotiated a contract with Nueva Granada to build a railroad across the isthmus. The construction of the railroad, started in 1850 and completed in 1855, was not simply a private venture, however. While Aspinwall and others would raise the money, they insisted on and attained financial guarantees from Washington since they viewed the enterprise as risky and as vital for U.S. economic and military interests. They drew up a contract with the U.S. government that committed the railroad to transporting U.S. military personnel, materiel, and mail across the isthmus for no more than a total of $750,000. The Panama Railroad, therefore, represented a joint venture between men of finance and statesmen who saw a new, more efficient means of communication across the isthmus as vital for enhancing profit and national power. They were correct in their assessment. In 1852, a share of the company sold at just a few cents, but by the 1860s shares sold at an impressive $340 (Schott 1967, 202). The railroad is testimony to the cooperation between the state and the economic elite for the purpose of enhancing state power both domestically and abroad.

The desire for westward expansion, driven by the mantra of Manifest Destiny and the discovery of gold in California, turned Panama into a vital transit point for the United States (Kemble 1943). Two movements were paramount for U.S. economic and territorial expansion: the flow of people from the eastern states to the western territories to look for gold and colonize the West; and the transfer of gold from California to the northeastern states, where industry and banking could turn the fruits of gold fever into profit and industrial development. Between 1848 and 1869, almost $711 million of gold bullion was transported from San Francisco to New York, and almost 410,000 settlers traveled from New York to San Francisco via the Panama route (Kemble 1943, 254–55). Incredibly enough, the Panama route's role in U.S. national development includes even the preservation of the Union. As Kemble asserts: "The effect of the inflow of precious metal upon the development of the United States was great indeed, and its primary importance in supporting the credit of the Union during the Civil War has not often been questioned" (1943, 208). But in 1869, when America's own transcontinental railroad was completed, the Panama route lost its appeal and profitability, and so the economic boom in the isthmus eventually went bust. America had gained greatly, while Panama had served the emerging empire and received little benefit.

The U.S. railroad, while providing some economic stimulus in Panama, came into conflict with the isthmian government's interests. In 1855, the State of Panama was formed as part of the Federal Republic of Nueva Granada. Panama achieved significant autonomy, "with legislative powers in all fields except those relating to foreign relations, the army, navy and war, national postal matters, national debt and naturalization of foreigners" (Pérez-Venero 1978, 42). Justo Arosemena, a leading Liberal and writer, as president of the State of Panama attempted to institute a tonnage fee on railroad transit so that the new government could enhance its treasury. However, the railroad company and the *Star and Herald*, an American newspaper in Panama, vehemently opposed this measure and appealed to Bogotá for help. Arosemena was president for a mere two-and-a-half months. In discussing Arosemena's difficulties, Pérez-Venero writes: "The leaders of Panama were already aware, then, at this early stage following the completion of the railroad, that their relationship with the United States was potentially dangerous, and that the advantages their geographical blessings promised were illusory and disappointing" (1978, 97). The United States not only prevented isthmian independence at this time but also militated against the development of an autonomous Panamanian state. America's power and influence over the isthmus continued to grow. Politically, U.S. influence over the isthmus weakened the Panamanian elite's efforts to achieve independence and financial viability.

The large contingent of Americans on the isthmus during the years of the gold rush also led to a high level of racial antagonism and antigringo sentiment. One of the most bizarre crises in Panama started on April 15, 1856, and is often labeled the "Watermelon War" in the United States. A U.S. citizen, Jack Oliver, intoxicated and bound for California, ate part of a slice of watermelon and continued on his way without paying the vendor, José Manuel Luna. When Luna demanded payment, Oliver loudly uttered, "kiss my arse." The outcome of this insult, typical of Americans traveling through the isthmus, was extensive rioting that left fifteen Americans and two Panamanians dead. The United States landed almost two hundred marines to reestablish order and protect U.S. interests. This incident is important for two reasons. First, it reflected growing anti-Americanism and incipient nationalism on the isthmus. Second, it was testimony to racial divisions in Panama since most of the Panamanians involved in the violent confrontation were reported by U.S. officials to be "black," which meant they were either of African descent, mulatto, or mestizo. Nueva Granada had eliminated slavery in 1852, but it still existed in the United States. Additionally, William Walker, the arrogant U.S. filibusterer, was attempting to take the presidency of Nicaragua, and isthmians believed that Walker might attempt to establish a "southern" American state in Panama. The United States demanded compensation from Nueva Granada and eventually received a settlement of $400,000 (see Chen Daley 1990; and Schott 1967, 194).

The Quest for an Isthmian Canal

The U.S. desire for a maritime route across Central America did not wane with the construction of the transcontinental railroad across the United States. In his 1869 State of the Union address to Congress, President Ulysses S. Grant stated:

> The subject of an interoceanic canal to convert the Atlantic and Pacific Oceans through the isthmus of Darien [Panama] is one in which commerce is greatly interested. Instructions have been given to our Minister to the Republic . . . of Colombia to endeavor to obtain authority for a survey by this government, in order to determine the practicability of such an undertaking, and a charter for the right of way to build, by private enterprise, such a work. (quoted in Ealy 1971, 34)

Despite Washington's continued interest in a transisthmian canal and its ability to reach a modus vivendi with Great Britain, France took advantage of America's temporary weakness during and after the Civil War to vie for a chance to build a canal and flex its muscle in the New World. In 1862, the French occupied Mexico, placing Archduke Ferdinand in power. Although Washington mobilized U.S. troops along the Mexican border in 1865, there was little that America could do at the time to expel the French from its southern neighbor. Benito Juárez and his army drove the French from Mexico, but Paris was able to retain influence in the hemisphere by acquiring the rights from Colombia in 1879 to build a canal across Panama. In a message to Congress in 1880, President Rutherford B. Hays, conveying his fears that the French would build a canal in Panama, stated forcefully: "The policy of this country is a canal under American control. The United States cannot consent to the surrender of this control to any European power" (quoted in Ealy 1971, 35). The United States was bent upon expelling all outside powers from the hemisphere as a necessary step toward establishing American preponderance of power in the hemisphere.

The French nevertheless got their opportunity to build a canal across the isthmus. The venture would be a private one, led by Ferdinand Marie de Lesseps, the "great Frenchman" who had "built" the Suez Canal.[7] To take on this great venture, de Lesseps incorporated the Compagnie Universelle du Canal Interocéanique (Universal Company of the Interoceanic Canal). He drummed up enthusiasm and support for his project by steaming to Panama with his young wife and three of their children. They were an instant hit on the isthmus. Through various means and over an eight-year period, de Lesseps was able to raise an astonishing 1.2 billion francs for the purpose of building a canal that would honor him and France (Howarth 1966, 196). De Lesseps's canal project started in 1881 with great euphoria but ended in 1889 in utter ruin and humiliation. Estimates of fatalities reached as high as 22,000, but the total may have been even higher (Howarth 1966, 197). The workforce on the project grew to a maximum of almost 20,000 men, mostly imported from the West Indies. An alarming 66 percent of the Frenchmen who went to labor on the canal died on the isthmus (Howarth 1966, 197). De Lesseps eventually organized a national lottery to continue to finance the project. To secure government approval, the Universal Company bribed French politicians, actions that eventually helped to end de Lesseps's "second miracle." By 1886, it became clear that a sea-level canal was infeasible, but de Lesseps would not change the project to a lock canal, which would require less earth removal. Since the Universal Company was bankrupt, French investors, both poor and rich, were left holding worthless company shares. Since the project was not even close to completion, the French government began looking for the cause of this grand failure. After an extensive inquiry, the Great Frenchman was charged with defrauding the French nation, found guilty by the courts, and sentenced to a five-year prison sentence that was eventually annulled (his son also received a five-year sentence for fraud and a one-year sentence for bribery). The French government also fell, owing to the wanton bribery of elected officials. The canal project was deemed a failure of such vast magnitude that in the future, large fiascos in France would be referred to with the phrase "Quel Panama!" (What a Panama!). As Americans were apt to do, the French would ascribe failure to the Panamanians (see Skinner 1989; Bunau-Varilla 1913; and Anguizola 1980). A few years after the Panama fiasco, Philippe Bunau-Varilla established a successor company, the Compagnie Nouvelle du Canal de Panama (New Company of the Panama Canal), for the sole purpose of selling the canal rights to another Great Power, while pretending to continue with canal construction.

While de Lesseps was attempting his second miracle, the isthmus was again struggling to get out from under Bogotá's control. In 1883, the newly formed United States of Colombia, under Liberal control, had enacted a new constitution establishing a less centralized, federal government. In just three years, however, another constitution was fashioned, since the so-called Rió Negro Constitution had led to intense conflict between Liberals and Conservatives. The 1886 constitution dashed all of Panama's hopes for autonomy and generated intense frustration and resentment toward the government in Bogotá. Under the new Magna Carta, Panama lost its statehood and became a department controlled by the central government. The new law of the land also gave the Church control of public education, limited press freedom, and reestablished corporal punishment for political crimes. At this point, the U.S. consul on the isthmus estimated that three-fourths of Panamanians desired independence from Bogotá (Meditz and Hanratty 1989, 21). In essence, the 1886 document rolled back the Liberal advances that had been achieved with the 1863 constitution, creating a recipe for Liberal revolts in both Colombia and Panama (Fábrega P. 1991, 33–52).

Small uprisings against the new unitary state occurred in 1893 and 1895. Then a large-scale Liberal uprising commenced in July 1899, eventually labeled the War of a Thousand Days. The principal battleground for this insurrection took place on the isthmus, where the Conservative state had a weak presence and where support for Liberals was strong. The prominent Liberal Belisario Porras led the uprising on the isthmus. Unfortunately for the Liberal cause, the United States sided with the Conservative government in Bogotá and on several occasions thwarted Liberal victories (Conniff 1992, 59–61). Washington wanted to safeguard its relations with Colombia in order to build a canal and, as noted above, was committed by the 1846 treaty to defend Colombia's sovereignty over the isthmus. Washington was also concerned that Liberal efforts to dislodge the Conservative authorities from the cities of Panama and Colón could lead to instability that would potentially threaten the transit of goods and people through the isthmus. Conniff writes: "There is no doubt that the U.S. military interventions occasioned by the Thousand Days War prevented a Liberal victory in Panama and perhaps in the country as a whole" (1992, 61). Washington in effect prevented Panamanians from exercising self-determination and prolonged the power of Conservatives on the isthmus.

At the same time that it was thwarting a Liberal victory in Colombia, Washington was emerging as a preponderant power in the Western Hemisphere and rising to Great Power status globally. The Spanish-American War, lasting just a few months in 1898, forced Spain out of the Western Hemisphere and placed the United States in the position to expand its trade with Asia, by taking possession of the Philippines and Guam. At the start of the war, the USS *Oregon* steamed around South America for ninety days, from the Pacific Coast to Cuba, arriving too late to have an effect on the conflict's outcome. A canal through the isthmus, American imperialists ardently pointed out, would have cut thousands of miles from the trip. It seemed irrelevant to those who promoted a canal that the war was easily won without the *Oregon*'s assistance. On the contrary, proponents of American imperialism, such as Teddy Roosevelt and Admiral Alfred Mahan, used the *Oregon*'s failure to reach Cuba quickly as a key example of America's dire need for a canal through Central America. The war was also a harbinger of Great

Britain's concession of Central America and the Western Hemisphere to the United States. At the end of the 1800s, London was too preoccupied with the Boer rebellion in South Africa and Germany to continue to challenge America's quest for hegemony in the Western Hemisphere. This "splendid little war," as Roosevelt referred to it, also began the American tradition of justifying military intervention in order to protect the rights of people in other countries (Zimmermann 2002, 262). Although U.S. interventions through the years would be motivated by economic and strategic interests, protection of human rights would become a common rationalization, just as saving souls had helped the Spanish to justify their conquest of the New World. By the end of the 1800s, therefore, Washington had forced from the hemisphere all challengers to U.S. power—Britain, France, and Spain. The Latin American states were too weak to balance U.S. power, and potential Great Power allies were no longer interested in forging any anti-U.S. alliances.

As for the French, de Lesseps's grand failure on the isthmus became America's gain. While Paris had been promoting its interests in the hemisphere, Washington had also been looking for a place to build its own canal. The United States had accepted de Lesseps's canal project to a large extent because powerful economic interests in the United States, led by Cornelius Vanderbilt, supported a canal across Nicaragua and because the French canal project was a private rather than state venture. Additionally, as pointed out above, Washington had been preoccupied and weakened by the Civil War. Nevertheless, Howarth has argued that, had any European power taken control of an isthmian canal, Washington would have eventually reacted forcefully (1966, 209). By 1898, America was ascendant, the French were eager to extricate themselves from the isthmus, and conditions were prime for the U.S. government to take over the canal project that French investors were ready to sell to the highest bidder. American preponderance of power in the hemisphere was just around the corner.

Panama's "Independence" from Colombia

By far the most important action I took in foreign affairs during the time I was President related to the Panama Canal. We gave to the people of Panama self-government, and freed them from subjection to alien oppressors.

—Theodore Roosevelt, 1925

The new conditions . . . have so largely modified the nation's [United States'] external policy in the direction of expansion, there is in them nothing to diminish, but rather to intensify, the purpose that there shall be no intrusion of

the European political system upon territory whence military effect upon the
Isthmus of Panama can be readily exerted.

—Alfred Thayer Mahan, 1900

These forceful statements reflect the sentiments of the times in the United States. First, Roosevelt acknowledges that Panama was crucial for America's rise to power. The Panama Canal would enhance U.S. naval power and expand U.S. commerce both abroad and at home by turning the isthmus into America's southern coast. Second, Washington's rhetoric was steeped in the notion that Panama's separation from Colombia was a noble gesture of liberation since Bogotá was curtailing the isthmus's goal of self-determination. The hypocrisy of this sentiment was not lost on those Panamanians who were well aware of U.S. interventionism under the Bidlack-Mallarino Treaty of 1846. Third, Mahan illustrates that the United States was headed down an inevitable path toward expansion and supremacy in the Western Hemisphere. Panama would continue to play an important role in America's regional supremacy.

America's first major step toward Great Power status was the Spanish-American War, while the second would be the "taking of Panama."[8] In 1902, the U.S. Senate ratified the Hay-Pauncefote Treaty, in which Great Britain accepted the abrogation of the Clayton-Bulwer Treaty, thus opening the door for the United States to unilaterally build and fortify a canal in Central America. Although the Nicaragua route was still an option and a U.S. presidential commission had preferred it, President Roosevelt and the U.S. Congress eventually turned to the isthmus to build a canal. While Roosevelt was in the White House, Republicans rather than Democrats would profit from an American canal venture.

Washington quickly turned to Colombia for an agreement that would allow the United States to construct a canal across the Panamanian isthmus. Twice before, in 1869 and 1870, America had attempted but failed to get a concession from Colombia; first owing to Bogotá's hesitance and subsequently because the U.S. Congress balked. This time Washington was ready, willing, and able to forge an agreement with Bogotá for a canal through the isthmus. On January 22, 1903, the United States and Colombia concluded the Hay-Herrán Treaty. The agreement authorized the United States to purchase all of the rights held by the New Canal Company, operate for one hundred years any canal it would build on the isthmus, and control a six-mile-wide zone along the canal route. Colombia, however, would retain sovereignty over that territory. In return, the United States would pay the Colombian government $10 million and a $250,000 annuity beginning nine years after the treaty went into force. Considering what the United States would gain militarily and economically from such a canal, the treaty was a bargain and windfall for U.S. imperialists.

Colombian politicians had slightly different priorities. While believing that a U.S. canal would be to their benefit, Bogotá's political leaders were not in any rush to finalize a deal with Washington. Under the agreement, the U.S. government would pay the New Canal Company $40 million for its canal concession. But the French rights to build a canal would expire in 1904. Colombian leaders preferred to wait until the New Canal Company's concession expired before brokering a deal with Washington so that they could gain the full financial benefits of the isthmus's geographic location. On August 12, 1903, the Colombian Senate, after six months of debate, rejected the accord. Roosevelt was rabid, calling the Colombians "contemptible little creatures" (quoted in Major 1993, 31). Roosevelt would not wait for diplomacy with Colombia to run its course. He acted quickly and forcefully, not unlike a Latin American caudillo (Sands 1944, 11). On September 15, 1903, Teddy Roosevelt wrote to Secretary of State Hay: "At present I feel there are two alternatives. First, to take up Nicaragua; second, in some shape or way to interfere when it becomes necessary so as to secure the Panama route without further dealing with the foolish and homicidal corruptionists in Bogotá" (quoted in Mellander 1971, 17). If Roosevelt had his way (and he did), Colombian sovereignty over the isthmus would not be an impediment to U.S. interests and expansionist plans.

The Roosevelt-controlled U.S. Congress also preferred Panama over Nicaragua since Democrats stood to gain from the Nicaragua route. But the cunning and persistence of two men—the Frenchman Philippe Bunau-Varilla and New York lawyer William Nelson Cromwell—greatly influenced the decision to build a canal through Panama. Bunau-Varilla, the director of the New Canal Company, had three goals: to defend the "honor" of France, to sell the New Canal Company's assets and canal concession, and to make a tidy profit. He had peddled the New Canal Company and its canal venture all over Europe—in Great Britain, in Germany, and in Russia—hoping to sell it for over $100 million, before he turned his sights on Washington (see Bunau-Varilla 1913; and Anguizola 1980). Cromwell had been involved in Panama for years, as attorney for the railroad and more recently as the New Canal Company's representative in Washington. He was in close contact with Panamanians, mostly Conservatives who wanted Washington to build a canal across the isthmus since they were convinced that they would benefit handsomely. Cromwell and Bunau-Varilla may have been helping to protect their respective country's interests, but they also stood to make substantial profits for themselves and for others from the sale of the New Canal Company's rights. The two men had become involved in a scheme to purchase the New Canal Company's shares at a ridiculously low price, cents to the dollar, hoping to then sell the company to the United States for at least $40 million. The scheme brought in a virtual "who's who" of investors, including J. P. Morgan, Charles P. Taft (brother of secretary of war William Taft, who would become president of the United States), and Douglas Robinson (President Roosevelt's brother-in-law), among others (see Díaz Espino 2001).

After the Colombian Senate rejected the Hay-Herrán Treaty, the personal financial interests of key individuals conveniently coincided with the "national interests" of France, Panama, and the United States, leading to the "revolution" that brought "independence" to the isthmus. Cromwell, Bunau-Varilla, Secretary of State John Hay, President Roosevelt, and Panamanians who worked for the Panama Railroad, principally Conservatives, worked together quickly to engineer a revolution on the isthmus. Although Washington was bound by the Bidlack-Mallarino Treaty to preserve Colombian sovereignty on the isthmus and had been doing so since 1846, Roosevelt and his administration now decided that the Colombians had lost their opportunity to have a waterway built on their land, had violated the spirit of the treaty, and represented a barrier to the needs of world commerce. America's leading expert on international law, John Bassett Moore, conveniently supported Roosevelt's machinations against Colombia (E. Morris 2001, 264–65). All that was needed for success was for a group in Panama to call for independence and for the United States to protect the newly established republic.

The extraordinary events surrounding the 1903 "revolution" in Panama are well documented (see, for example, LaFeber 1989, 23–26; McCullough 1977, 361–86; E. Morris 2001, 270–94; and Major 1993, 34–63). Soon after the Colombian Senate rejected the Hay-Herrán Treaty, key individuals began to conspire to separate Panama from Colombia. The men who led the 1903 revolution were Conservative politicians tied to the interests of the Panama Railroad, who stood to gain from a canal through the isthmus and were predominantly "timid" men, not really of revolutionary stock (Sands 1944, 58). A revolution in 1903, coming on the heels of the War of a Thousand Days and led by the individuals involved, was a particularly unlikely political event. However, Cromwell and Bunau-Varilla encouraged and convinced these men that a revolution would succeed because Washington was ready to lend support for such a bold move. Additionally, they promised the revolutionaries financial support and the allure of a prosperous Panama. And so, prompted by several key individuals and by indirect assurances of support from the U.S. government, a handful of Panamanians, concerned that Washington might turn to Nicaragua, announced Panama's independence on November 3, 1903. The principal leaders of the rebellion were José Agustín Arango, an attorney for the Panama Railroad Co.; Carlos C. Arosemena, a friend of Arango and member of the oligarchy; Dr. Manuel Amador Guerrero, medical officer for the railroad; and other members of the oligarchy, such as Nicanor A. de Obarrio, brothers Ricardo Arias and Tomás Arias, Federico Boyd, and Manuel Espinosa (Amador's brother-in-law). Non-Panamanians living on the isthmus who took part in the conspiracy included James R. Shaler, the railroad's superintendent; his assistant, Herbert G. Prescott; and James R. Beers, the railroad's freight agent. Of course, the U.S. consul and U.S. naval officers on the scene became involved as well. These men of commerce and men of state forged an alliance for mutual benefit.

The revolution was quick, inexpensive, and practically bloodless. Although the Colombian government dispatched troops to put down the rebellion on the isthmus, U.S. naval officers, U.S. Marines, and railroad executives effectively stopped Bogotá's counteroffensive. Two steps were taken to prevent the Colombian military from retaking the isthmus. First, the Colombian troops that disembarked at Colón had to be prevented from proceeding to Panama City, where the revolutionaries planned to form a government. On November 2, the USS *Nashville* appeared on the horizon off Colón. On the next day, when independence was announced, a Colombian ship, the *Cartagena*, made port at Colón, carrying about five hundred soldiers, who quickly disembarked. Soon thereafter, the *Nashville*'s commander, John Hubbard, received his marching orders: "Prevent landing of any armed force with hostile intent" (quoted in E. Morris 2001, 283). But the U.S. warship was not needed since the Colombian troops could reach Panama City quickly only by way of the railroad. Colonel Shaler had conveniently moved all railcars capable of carrying passengers out of Colón. The Colombian soldiers and their commanders were thus stranded harmlessly fewer than fifty miles from the heart of the rebellion. More remarkable was the fact that Shaler convinced the two Colombian generals in charge to meet him in a special railroad car that was whisked away to Panama City, where the two duped officers were arrested. The second necessary step was to convince all Colombian troops already in Panama to either support or not take action against the independence movement. This was accomplished rather easily by paying them the wages that the Colombian government had not paid them for months. Their commander, General Esteban Huertas, received around $30,000, his officers got $6,000–$10,000 each, and each soldier received $50 (Mellander 1971, 31). To ensure victory, a total of nine U.S. Navy vessels were eventually on hand to ensure that Colombia did not make another attempt at retaking the isthmus. A Colombian gunboat, the *Bogotá*, anchored outside Panama City desperately fired some shells into the city, killing a Chinese man, the only casualty of the revolution. The U.S. government used force, conspiracy, and bribery to achieve Panama's quick independence in 1903, even though Panamanians for decades had developed a sense of nationalism that Washington had resisted.

The following day, November 4, Panama City's Municipal Council held an open *cabildo* (town meeting). The isthmus's leading figures attended and unanimously supported independence, naming the new country the Republic of Panama. The council granted executive authority to a three-man junta—composed of José Agustín Arango, Federico Boyd, and Tomas Arias—until a government could be elected. Panama's oligarchy, which had supported autonomy or independence for many years, had finally achieved a remarkable victory. It had been able to separate itself from Colombia and could now attempt to control its own economic destiny. The quid pro quo for their independence, however, would come quickly. Bunau-Varilla, who was already in Washington, had convinced the junta to appoint him as plenipotentiary of Panama so that he could begin to negotiate a canal deal with the Americans. The junta agreed since Bunau-Varilla had promised them financial backing and U.S. naval support for the rebellion. They also knew that the Frenchman had powerful connections in Washington that could come in handy. The junta, however, never intended for Bunau-Varilla to sign a treaty on behalf of Panama without their explicit approval.

The revolutionary junta quickly sent Dr. Manuel Amador and Federico Boyd to the United States to negotiate a treaty with Washington that would allow the United States to construct a canal through the isthmus. When they arrived in Washington, D.C., on November 18, Bunau-Varilla informed them that a few hours earlier he had negotiated and signed a treaty with Secretary of State Hay. Bunau-Varilla writes that when he met the two men at the train station in Washington, D.C., and presented them with this fait accompli, "Amador almost fainted at the station platform" (Bunau-Varilla 1913, 378–79). Amador and Boyd tried in vain to re-open the negotiations but quickly realized that Panama's newly won independence depended upon their acquiescence. Bunau-Varilla attempted to get Amador and Boyd to ratify the treaty on behalf of the revolutionary junta, but they balked at this suggestion and decided to take the accord back to Panama for proper ratification. Bunau-Varilla then cabled the junta, threatening that the United States and Colombia might work out an agreement that would put an abrupt end to Panama's independence if Panama did not ratify the treaty. In fewer than twenty hours after arriving in Panama City, Panama's revolutionary leadership ratified the 1903 Hay–Bunau-Varilla Treaty. An important treaty for both the United States and Panama had been negotiated and ratified hastily and without a legitimate process, whether diplomatic or democratic.

The treaty that Secretary of State John Hay signed with Bunau-Varilla was even more generous to America than the Hay-Herrán Treaty signed with Colombia. Instead of a six-mile zone, the U.S. government would control a ten-mile-wide strip of land that would cut the isthmus in two and would separate Panama City from the isthmus's interior. Panama would also forfeit effective sovereignty over the future Canal Zone, since the accord gave the United States authority over the zone as "if it were the sovereign of the territory." Rather than for one hundred years, Washington would now control a future waterway on the isthmus in *perpetuity*. The U.S. government would also have virtual eminent domain over land deemed necessary for the operation and defense of a future canal. And, finally, Washington would have the right to intervene in Panama's domestic affairs. In his memoirs, Bunau-Varilla admits that he made these concessions to Washington unilaterally to ensure that the U.S. Senate would ratify the agreement rapidly. Secretary of State Hay, who had initially proposed a treaty much along the lines of the failed Hay-Herrán accord, nevertheless accepted with alacrity the more enticing agreement offered by Bunau-Varilla, giving little thought to the fact that he was taking a newly sovereign nation's territory forever without the consent of its leaders, let alone its citizens. Hay admitted that the treaty proposed by the Frenchman resembled more a treaty written by an American than a Panamanian. He neglected to mention that the accord also violated sovereignty, the principle of self-determination, and one of the most basic tenets of democracy. America's twin victories in 1903, the isthmus's independence from an uncooperative Colombia, and the Hay–Bunau-Varilla Treaty, however, would quickly create problems for Washington that would last for nearly one hundred years. What is certain is that America respected neither international law nor the isthmus's self-determination in its attempt to build a canal across Panama. Had Panama been a stronger state or had it had an alliance with a Great Power, Washington may have never acquired the concessions it received in the 1903 Hay–Bunau-Varilla Treaty.

While the circumstantial evidence suggests strongly that Washington conspired to "take the isthmus," no smoking gun exists. A former U.S. diplomat who was assigned to Panama as a troubleshooter in 1904, however, describes suspicious U.S. activities. In his memoirs, Sands mentions "the promotion of revolution by the officials of the American steamship and railroad company, the presence of the American consul-general at the secret meetings of the conspirators, the influx of American army officers badly disguised as buyers of native hardwoods and trying hard to speak English with a German accent" (1944, 16). He also points out the suspicious fact that no records of any of the events surrounding the revolution remained at the U.S. legation in Panama City.

The Legacies of the 1800s: Panama's Nationalist Frustrations and America's Rise to Power

During the 1800s, the United States of America achieved important national goals. From 1823, when President Monroe announced his doctrine, to 1903, when the Hay–Bunau-Varilla Treaty was signed, the United States transitioned from being an emerging and developing nation to attaining Great Power status. Washington was able to achieve its expansionist goal of Manifest Destiny through aggression, cunning, and land purchases. Panama played an important role in this process by providing a route for settlers to newly acquired western lands. Only when the U.S. transcontinental railroad was completed in 1869 did the Panama route become irrelevant for settling the American West. During this period, the United States also emerged as an economic powerhouse, reaching a level of industrialization that required trade expansion. Part of the reason for this economic miracle was the California gold rush, which fueled industrialization and domestic development. Again Panama played a role by providing a more convenient and relatively safe passage for the gold bullion transferred from California to New York. America's rise to power was also assisted by Washington's ability to push other Great Powers from the hemisphere. By 1903, the British, the French, and the Spanish had become minor players in the Americas, leaving the United States as the principal power in the region. Washington's ability to acquire the rights to build a canal through the isthmus of Panama was a crucial step for the rise of U.S. military might in the hemisphere and globally since in the early 1900s naval power was the most efficacious way to achieve global influence. As American power rose, Panama as a new republic was incapable of pursuing its vital interests since the United States was simply too strong to challenge and other Great Powers had essentially left the hemisphere to U.S. designs.

America's rise to power in the Western Hemisphere was not a chance occurrence. The ideologies of Manifest Destiny and social Darwinism created an arrogant, racist, and imperialist attitude among America's officials, economic elite, and opinion leaders that almost guaranteed that increased national power would yield increased regional and global influence. The men who led America were guided by these ideologies and thus promoted policies that augmented Washington's influence abroad. Government officials, bankers, diplomats, and even tourists in many large and small ways contributed to American influence abroad, even if at times they disagreed on the specifics. Many individuals and events led to America's rise to power: President James Monroe promulgated a policy initiating an American sphere of influence; James Marshall, a Mormon carpenter, discovered a vein of gold at Coloma, California; James Aspinwall, a New York investor, built a railroad across the isthmus of Panama with Washington's help; and President Roosevelt and Secretary of State John Hay secured a treaty to build a canal across Panama. These individuals and events were essential for what America accomplished in the 1800s.

Can we attribute a grand design or common interest to them? Certainly we can be sure that there was no boardroom where Washington's elite— government, military, and economic—sat down to plan America's rise to power, although a certain amount of cabal-like conspiracy certainly occurred during Panama's 1903 independence. What we can suggest, however, is that ideologies and interests rationalized American imperialist actions. Those actions were carried out by individuals who would gain personally from America's rise to power. The plethora of government officials and private entrepreneurs who sought fame and fortune achieved their personal goals by helping their nation to become a more powerful player on the world stage. Certainly examples of disagreements over policy exist. Cornelius Vanderbilt would have wanted a canal in Nicaragua. If Vanderbilt had succeeded, J. P. Morgan and others would not have benefited from the Hay–Bunau-Varilla Treaty. But other American entrepreneurs would have, and the United States would still have had its canal across Central America with all of its attendant benefits.

Although the United States had achieved a preponderance of power in the Western Hemisphere in 1903, we cannot say that it had achieved hegemony. The nations of Latin America certainly could not challenge Washington militarily or economically, but at that point they were neither emulating the American political and economic system nor necessarily supporting Washington's view of the world. Latin America still had a great affinity toward Europe, its culture, and its principles. Although Panama was already experiencing a significant U.S. presence by 1903, its leaders still looked to Madrid, London, or Paris as much as they looked to Washington and hoped to carve out independent foreign and domestic policies.

While America prospered, the 1800s were bittersweet for the isthmus's political development. Panama struggled for autonomy and even independence while under the control of Bogotá. The Panamanian oligarchy was predominantly Liberal in orientation, desirous of free commerce and more, albeit limited, political liberties. Colombia, however, was divided by the often violent struggles between Conservatives and Liberals. When the Conservatives were dominant, Panama suffered greatly and sought separation. But even when Liberals were in charge, Panama's elite believed that the central government in Bogotá was taking from the isthmus without giving much back. Thus, independence or autonomy became a near-necessity. At the end of the 1800s, in the War of a Thousand Days, Panama's Liberal leaders mounted a significant rebellion against Colombia that had a very good chance of succeeding. Had they succeeded, Liberals in Panama would have led an isthmus with an emerging sense of national unity. But success would slip away since the United States sided with the Conservative government in Bogotá. Thus, U.S. interests stymied a nation's quest for self-determination and prevented the Liberal elite from coming to power on the isthmus.

When the isthmus finally achieved independence in November 1903, the movement was led by Conservatives who had links to U.S. interests in Panama. These leaders were so indebted to Washington that they ratified a treaty that placed Panama under U.S. tutelage in perpetuity and gave Washington control of Panama's greatest asset—its strategic location. As Spence Herrera argues: "In the case of Panama, North American foreign policy has been directed, since the 19th century, toward maintaining control of the geographic position of the isthmus as a vital piece of its scheme of territorial and economic expansion" (1988, 4)(my translation). But while it benefited American interests for many years, the Hay–Bunau-Varilla Treaty, as we will see, would come back to haunt Washington on many occasions. The treaty would also haunt Panama's revolutionaries since they would continuously be charged with *entreguismo* (turning the nation over to foreigners), a theory that has become known in Panama as the Black Legend. Thus, Panama's 1903 independence was not complete, owing to its close association with the United States.

The development of Panamanian national identity during the 1800s suffered from several negative factors. First, division existed between the intramuros and the arrabal, or those who lived inside and outside the city walls. Although to some extent this reflected a class difference, race was a determining factor in the city's geographic divide. The intramuros were of European descent and cosmopolitan in outlook. The arrabal consisted of poor nonwhites, former slaves, indígenas, mestizos, and mulattos. This divisive stratification prevented even the Liberal elite from desiring too much popular participation. Exacerbating this social chasm was the presence of many foreigners who became involved in the life and sometimes the politics of the isthmus. The U.S. presence, of course, was enormously important both politically and economically. These economic, racial, cultural, and national differences made it quite difficult for the nascent Panamanian state to forge a strong, comprehensive national identity.

So, as America was poised for "greatness" at the beginning of the twentieth century, Panama was still struggling for self-determination and national identity, despite its independence. And the Conservatives had usurped the power of the Liberals, making it more difficult for a liberal democracy to emerge. The United States would have its canal and Panama would have statutory independence. The United States would continue to prosper and gain military strength, partly because of the canal, while Panama would struggle to achieve nationhood and democratic politics. The prospects for democracy at the start of the twentieth century were not good even though Panama had a Liberal, constitutional tradition and was devoid of a strong landed aristocracy.

From the Building of the Panama Canal to the Great Depression

Liberal Oligarchic Rule and Rising Nationalism, 1904–29

The early 1900s witnessed the rise and expansion of American power in the Western Hemisphere, as well as Panama's lack of independence and trouble with democracy as a new republic. In this analysis, I am principally concerned with Panama's failure to establish plural politics and its inability to act as an independent nation. While constitutional governments ruled the isthmus, a small, somewhat divided oligarchy controlled the political system. Before 1930, little political contestation took place prior to the casting of votes since in almost all presidential elections the opposition candidate withdrew before the polling started (Gandásegui 1998, 11). The Panamanian republic, nevertheless, began to develop institutions and infrastructure necessary for national integration and political development. Panama had very little room to maneuver, though, since the U.S. presence on the isthmus was imposing and demanding. The new country's leaders were obliged to carry out politics in a manner that did not interfere with Washington's dominant interest—the construction and then operation and defense of the canal. Even during this early period, however, we start to see the emergence of Panamanian nationalism and of nonoligarchic sectors. Panama's oligarchy, for the most part, acceded to Washington's desires, but in 1926 the National Assembly took a bold step by rejecting a treaty with the United States. Acción Comunal, a new, middle-class organization, orchestrated this challenge to American stewardship. Despite this unusual challenge to U.S. power, Washington was able to enhance and secure its interests on the isthmus and expand its power in the Western Hemisphere in the early 1900s by building the canal and employing both the Roosevelt Corollary to the Monroe Doctrine and Taft's dollar diplomacy. U.S. intervention in the Caribbean Basin in the first third of the 1900s was overt and extensive, reflecting Roosevelt's Big Stick diplomacy and economic expansion. The clash between Panama's quest for self-determination and U.S. interests on the isthmus meant that the two countries began to disagree on some important issues even before the U.S. Canal Zone was established in May 1904.

Dual Sovereignty: The New Constitutional Republic and New U.S. Canal Zone

Panama's first constitutional government was established rather quickly after independence. The resulting constitution, however, was neither hastily improvised nor simply modeled after the U.S. Constitution. The new law of the land was the result of a "constitutional tradition" and was crafted by isthmians who had been involved in developing previous constitutional documents (Fábrega P. 1999, 31). On January 15, 1904, a constitutional convention began work in Panama City. Thirty-three delegates were elected, none of whom could be high officials in the new government, a rather commendable effort to prevent conflicts of interest. At this point in isthmian democracy, however, only men over the age of twenty-one who were not domestic servants could vote (Fábrega P. 1991, 327). After promulgating the new constitution, the convention established itself as an interim National Assembly until a permanent legislature could be elected. On February 16, 1904, the convention unanimously elected Dr. Manuel Amador Guerrero, a Conservative, as the nation's first president. The convention also elected three *designados*, or vice presidents, corresponding to Amador's preferences. Liberal Dr. Pablo Arosemena became the first designado. Conservative José Domingo de Obaldía, who would also serve as minister to Washington, won the post of second vice president. The third designado was Liberal Carlos A. Mendoza. Amador had put together a bipartisan government, partly because Liberal ideology was dominant in Panama, even if Conservatives held most elected government posts. At the outset, there appeared to be a high level of elite unity on the isthmus. The constitutional convention dissolved in June 1904, yet a National Assembly would not be elected until mid-1906, leaving Panama with no legislature for two years. Nevertheless, in December 1904, municipal elections were held, providing the nation with some important regional and popular representation. The Liberals routed the Conservatives, showing that, although the Conservatives had led the 1903 independence movement, the Panamanian people were Liberal at heart. The Municipal Council of Panama City served as an early counterweight to Amador's Conservative-leaning government. The stage was set for discord between Conservatives—who felt they deserved to be in power, feared the masses, and had support from Washington—and the Liberals—who had a long history of promoting Panama's independence, endorsed broader political participation, and thus had more popular support.

The most controversial issue at the constitutional convention was whether the U.S. right to intervene in Panama's affairs, as stipulated in the 1903 Treaty, should also be included in the country's new Magna Carta, as had occurred in Cuba with the infamous 1902 Platt Amendment. Mellander points out that the most important mission undertaken by the first U.S. minister (ambassador) to Panama, William Buchanan, who arrived on the isthmus at the end of 1903, was "to make sure that United States interests [right of intervention] were protected in the new constitution" (1971, 49). Washington would not allow any Panamanian government to undermine or challenge U.S. interests on the isthmus. Article 136 would give Washington the right to intervene for the preservation of order and peace. While most of the constitution's articles breezed through the convention, article 136 passed by the narrow margin of seventeen to fourteen votes, showing that even at the time of the republic's inauguration, Panama's elite desired independence. U.S. interests were now secured, and Buchanan left Panama even before the constitution was promulgated. Despite this major blemish—allowing a foreign power to intervene at will—the new law of the land established a unitary government with separation of powers, as well as the direct election of the president and National Assembly. The assembly, however, would elect the three designados. The new Magna Carta also continued a growing Liberal-individualist tradition that dated back to 1841 and provided for individual rights, property rights, direct elections, and separation of church and state (Fábrega P. 1991, 105–6). Conservatives in Panama were more ideologically akin to Liberals than to Conservatives in Colombia. Consequently, Panama's elite was more ideologically and consensually unified at the time of independence than the elite in most of Latin America.

A weak two-party system emerged, but both parties were supportive of free trade; were dominated by an urban, commercial elite rather than by a traditional landed elite; and were relatively secular—a good recipe for the emergence of a liberal political system. The two parties were also connected through family ties, owing to Panama's small oligarchy largely of European origin. Disagreements between the two political parties were based on personal differences and followings more than on ideological platforms (Arias Peña and Quintero 1994, 4–5). Liberals enjoyed more popular support largely because the darker-skinned masses believed they would be represented best by that party since the Liberals supported expanding the electoral franchise. Consequently, the Liberals were often termed the party of the "mulattos" or

"Negroes" by Conservatives and by the United States (Sands 1944, 19–20). The U.S.–Conservative Party alliance that emerged at Panama's independence in 1903 thus hindered Liberal efforts to liberalize politics and to win elections. The balance of power that should have quickly shifted toward the Liberal Party early in the isthmus's political history was tilted toward the Conservative Party owing to U.S. power and influence. Liberals and Conservatives, because of their ideological similarities and owing to a shared fear of the nonwhite masses, nevertheless attempted to establish a political process where contestation could take place behind the scenes and popular participation could be kept to a minimum. Amador's initial bipartisan attempt was the first expression of this tendency.

On May 19, 1904, the United States established the Canal Zone, and with the newly created Isthmian Canal Commission, began the process of building a canal across the isthmus. Washington thus created an American enclave, ten miles wide and some fifty miles long, across the new Republic of Panama. A military governor would autocratically rule the Zone, the first being General George W. Davis. A commander of U.S. military forces would also be stationed in the Zone, since the 1903 Treaty allowed Washington to fortify the canal. And, of course, a U.S. minister would represent U.S. interests in Panama. This American triumvirate would exert enormous influence on the isthmus. At times, however, the triumvirate would bicker over policy and spheres of influence. Conflict emerged almost immediately between the U.S. minister and the Zone governor. At first Washington attempted to end the potential for dispute by fusing the two positions into one. From July 1905 to September 1906, Charles Magoon held both positions. This attempt at unifying U.S. authority on the isthmus did not last. From the time of Magoon's departure until September 1979, U.S. interests in Panama had to be vetted through the U.S. triumvirate—the U.S. ambassador, the commander in chief of U.S. military forces, and the Canal Zone governor. The force of these three powerful posts, along with Washington's might, made it virtually impossible for Panamanian political leaders to operate autonomously. Even if constitutional government and political rights were preserved, Panama's political options would be severely limited, meaning that democracy would be impossible. As Conniff points out, "Canal governors reigned supreme on the isthmus, far more powerful than Panama's presidents" (1992, 80).

In addition to America's overbearing influence, the Zone cut the nation in half, preventing Panama from taking full economic advantage of its geographic location and the canal and hindering rational national development. Since the Zone abutted Panama City, "newer suburbs stretched out like a comet's tail while land in the Zone and close to the city center lay unused"

(Howarth 1966, 267). Panama also found it difficult to attract a labor pool for national development because of the "lure of high wages to be had working for the 'Gringos' in the Canal Zone" (Ealy 1951, 7). To be sure, the U.S. presence brought some benefits to some Panamanians. But overall, Washington benefited more much handsomely than did Panama from the canal venture. And the Zone and the sizeable U.S. presence limited Panama's policies and national development options. But, perhaps more important, the U.S. control of the isthmian canal robbed Panama of its most important national resource—its strategic location.

Initial U.S.-Panamanian Disagreements

It should have come as no surprise that, almost immediately after Panama's independence, disagreement emerged between the new republic and the U.S. government. Complicating matters was the fact that to express their national interests and to carry out diplomacy, Panama's leaders had to deal with the U.S. triumvirate as well as with Washington itself. Howarth notes that, owing to the imposing U.S. presence and the unfair conditions of the 1903 Treaty, "conflict [between the United States and Panama] began at the moment when General Davis, the first American governor, arrived on the isthmus, and it grew for the next sixty years" (1966, 264–65). Thus, even though some observers have attacked Panama's elite for *entreguismo*[1] since cooperation with Washington was the standard operating procedure, isthmian political leaders from the outset attempted to ameliorate the most damaging aspects of the 1903 accord.

In addition to the U.S. "right" of intervention, several provisions in the 1903 Treaty were particularly objectionable to Panamanians, especially since Washington tended to interpret treaty provision in ways that would enhance U.S. interests. Howarth points out: "Initially, every problem was decided in favor of the United States' interpretation, on the basis that might was right" (Howarth 1966, 265). Almost immediately after independence, Washington began to exercise its rights under the 1903 Treaty to acquire more lands or resources in Panama for the purpose of canal construction. This right of eminent domain, as the U.S. government saw it, would generate conflict until well after World War II, since the United States would desire more territory for canal improvements and defense even after construction was completed. Panama's elite did not outright reject Washington's treaty rights but rather objected to the U.S. government's modus operandi of taking land without consultation and without adequate compensation (McCain 1965, 152–53). Washington's position was that the payment of $10 million up front and the annuity of $250,000 that would commence nine years after the ratification of the treaty constituted its total financial compensation to Panama for both the initial lands conceded by Panama, as well as any other lands that the U.S. government deemed necessary for canal operation and defense in the future. Panama, on the other hand, believed that Washington should pay compensation for any additional lands that it appropriated (McCain 1965, 144–45). The 1903 Treaty was somewhat vague on the issues of land appropriation, compensation, and consultation, so treaty interpretation would almost always favor the U.S. position simply because Panama lacked the power to promote its interests.

Numerous economic concerns related to the 1903 Hay–Bunau-Varilla Treaty immediately emerged that would harm the U.S.-isthmian relationship for decades. For example, many Panamanians believed that Washington should pay the isthmus more for the use of the canal and the Zone since the United States would benefit enormously from the waterway. U.S. economic rights and control on the isthmus, rather than creating prosperity for isthmian businesses, resulted in stiff and unfair competition that benefited the Zone and U.S. businesses. Of principal importance was the establishment of commissaries where Zonians (U.S. citizens living and working in Panama) and U.S. military personnel could buy U.S. products at low prices, thus effectively keeping local businesses out of lucrative markets. Zone housing also competed with rental housing owned by Panama's elite. The U.S. government also established a postal service and customs offices, both of which deprived the Panamanian state of potential revenues (see Busey 1974, 19). As a result, Panama's economic elite had to settle for much less than they had hoped. Conniff points out that "the Panamanian bourgeoisie had only a few means of cashing in on the construction boom: they built rooming houses, saloons, brothels, restaurants, and shops along the zone border to cater to soldiers and to the foreign labor force imported to build the canal" (1992, 77). Much of the U.S. economic activity surrounding canal construction and the Zone tended to minimize the Panamanian elite's ability to capitalize on the U.S. presence.

Washington also wanted to control Panama's finances directly. For example, the $10 million that the Panamanian government was to receive in accordance with the 1903 Treaty was turned over instead to J. P. Morgan, who was Panama's first fiscal representative in the United States and who had profited from the 1903 Treaty. Almost immediately, Washington informed the isthmus that $8 million of the $10 million had to be invested in the United States, in order that Panama's finances remain stable (McCain 1965, 104). Soon thereafter, Panama appointed the ubiquitous William N.

Cromwell, who also had profited from the treaty, as its fiscal representative. We can only assume that Panama's appointment of these two individuals had more to do with Washington's wishes than with Panama's interests. Once again, American businessmen were working with the U.S. government to enhance personal and national interests. On June 20, 1904, Panama and Washington signed an agreement pegging Panama's currency, the balboa, to the U.S. dollar. The result of U.S. economic dominance and control was that the economic bonanza that Panama's elite expected after independence and from the canal was not materializing, while at the same time the palpable U.S. influence was a constant reminder of Panama's lack of real independence.

These economic concerns were of great importance, but the issues that would inspire the greatest controversy were those that hurt Panamanian national pride. Thus, while Panamanians accepted shattered economic expectations, they resented arrogance and unfair treatment coming from U.S. officials and citizens—a classic historical case of adding insult to injury. Panamanians found many U.S. actions and policies humiliating and insulting. The racist Jim Crow laws employed in the American South were transplanted to Panama, along with the attitudes that sustained them. The U.S. government established an unequal system of pay in the Zone, whereby U.S. citizens and other "whites" were paid in what became known as the "gold roll," while nonwhites, which included Panamanians, received "silver roll" wages. Under this system, whites received higher wages and enhanced benefits. U.S. citizens who lived and worked in the Zone lived in an engineered tropical paradise, earned 50 percent more than in the United States, were not subject to federal taxes, and benefited from "free furnished quarters, light, fuel and water, health care, and schooling for their children" (Major 1993, 79). Additionally, Zonians enjoyed an idyllic environment, where buildings and nature were meticulously maintained, and where all kinds of activities were abundant and inexpensive. The U.S. government subsidized this colonial, utopian, communitarian existence, likened by some observers to benevolent dictatorship, communism, or both (see Knapp and Knapp 1984). While U.S. citizens enjoyed their paradise, poor Panamanians and imported workers from the West Indies lived in deplorable conditions. The Canal Zone and all of its allure, therefore, survived because of U.S. government largesse and existed alongside squalor and intense discrimination. This was a recipe for generating extreme resentment and even hatred among Panamanians. Additionally, it demonstrated that democracy in Panama was the last thing on the minds of policy makers in Washington. If intense conflict between Panama and the United States did not emerge earlier, it was simply because Panama was in no position to challenge U.S. power and demand better treatment. A more powerful Panama would never have accepted the conditions of the 1903 Treaty and the subsequent application of that treaty by the U.S. government.

Intensifying the initial clash of interests was the fact that Washington was not satisfied with exerting influence in the Zone and Panama and appropriating additional territory but also wanted to take policy actions that infringed on Panama's foreign economic policies. In the first U.S. action of this type, Zone authorities cleared a Chilean vessel at La Boca, in the Port of Ancón, on July 9, 1904. This was Panama's only Pacific port, and U.S. officials were in effect acting as sovereign *outside* the Canal Zone. Panama protested immediately and strongly. Then, on July 15, 1904, Panama City's Chamber of Commerce protested to President Amador because the U.S. government had established tariffs and customshouses in the Canal Zone. The Panamanian government threatened that it would arrest and fine captains of vessels that did not comply with Panamanian laws when making port at Ancón. The Zone authorities and the Panamanian government reached a verbal agreement that in the future Panama could file formal protests that would be addressed at a later date rather than taking immediate action against shipping. Panama immediately filed a protest against the establishment of ports of entry, tariffs, and customshouses in the Canal Zone (McCain 1965, 26–28). Protesting U.S. actions on the isthmus, Panama's minister to Washington, de Obaldía, wrote: "What interest can the United States have in the financial ruin of the Republic of Panama. . . . Is it not rather to the interest of the United States to foster the development of the Republic of Panama and to contribute to its prosperity and aggrandizement?" (McCain 1965, 33). Thus from the very beginning the economic benefit that Panamanians believed they would garnish from the presence of a canal on the isthmus vanished. Instead, the most prosperous nation on earth, which was about to feast on the benefits provided by a canal for its maritime commerce and its navy, decided to take the table scraps as well and limit the small republic's policy options.

Washington also intervened in Panama's domestic politics by playing an instrumental role in abolishing the isthmus's small armed forces. Upon attaining independence, Panama was left with demobilized soldiers and officers and a very popular general, Esteban Huertas. In May 1904, the Conservative-led Amador government sent Huertas abroad with a sizeable sum of money, owing to his Liberal sympathies and his popularity. When Huertas returned in September, he demanded that two Conservative cabinet members be fired, setting off a crisis in the new constitutional government.

Amador asked the United States to get involved. Washington averted a crisis by pressing Liberal leaders and General Huertas not to usurp the legitimate government. Amador then asked Huertas to resign, which the general finally did in late November, after some pressure from the U.S. government (Mellander 1971, 64–66). Huertas's men, however, resisted demobilization to a point where U.S. Minister Barrett made it clear to the soldiers that the U.S. government would not tolerate insubordination in Panama's military and would deal with the situation firmly, handing out the "severest punishment possible" (McCain 1965, 59). Under this pressure, the soldiers quickly decided to accept their meager retirement and enter civilian life.

The army disbanded, and its weapons were stored in the Canal Zone. The young Panamanian government, then, took the important step of eliminating Panama's army and retaining only a police force. By 1905, the United States sent police instructors to train Panama's police, owing to concerns that the force was using unnecessary violence and becoming involved in politics (McCain 1965, 78). Despite Washington's heavy hand, an important barrier to democratic development was eliminated. Washington's motivations, however, were to eliminate any challenge to its military authority, particularly since General Huertas supported the Liberals, who were displeased with the U.S. presence on the isthmus. Washington would also keep Panama's police under surveillance through its "instructors." At the same time, the Panamanian state lost its ability to defend itself and to have complete control of its police.

The U.S. government made an initial effort to address Panama's many concerns by sending Secretary of War William H. Taft to the isthmus. He arrived in Colón on November 27, 1904, on the USS *Columbia*, perhaps as a subtle reminder to Panamanians that their future could still be determined by Bogotá. Immediately, Taft began to mend fences, saying that the United States had "no desire to exercise any power except which it deems necessary under the treaty to insure the building, maintenance, and protection of the canal" (quoted in McCain 1965, 40). William Cromwell accompanied Taft and assisted with his diplomatic effort. The U.S. and Panamanian negotiating teams worked out understandings that were codified via executive orders by the U.S. War Department and executive decrees by President Amador in December 1904. The so-called Taft Agreement was composed of several important understandings between the two governments. The U.S. government agreed that no goods or merchandise would enter ports at Ancón or Cristóbal except those authorized by the 1903 Treaty, those in transit through the canal, or fuel sold by the United States to transiting vessels. Panama would be able to establish tariffs, at low rates, on all other goods that entered the isthmus. Panama would also issue stamps used in the Zone. Free trade would be established between the Zone and Panama, effectively repealing Washington's Dingley tariff for Panama. The United States would retain the ports of Ancón and Cristóbal, however, since Washington argued that, although the 1903 Treaty exempted Colón and Panama City from U.S. jurisdiction, the two ports were not in those cities and were necessary for the construction of the canal (McCain 1965, 43–45; Pizzurno Gelós and Araúz 1996, 30).

Despite limited U.S. concessions, Panamanian leaders welcomed the Taft agreement as a sign that Washington was concerned about the isthmus's economic development and sovereignty. The agreement, however, was not effective in preventing the Zone from becoming a powerful economic entity that continued to hinder Panama's economic development and competed unfairly with Panamanian businesses. The United States established a commissary system in the Zone that by 1908 registered more than $4.5 million in sales. Many of the goods sold at the Zone commissaries entered Panama freely. Zone workers could buy practically everything they needed at these stores, never having to purchase a thing outside U.S.-controlled territory. Panama's businesses simply could not compete (Major 1993, 102–3). The U.S. government also continued to import items that were not essential for canal construction and defense (Castillero Pimentel 1961, 50–55). The 1903 Treaty, therefore, maimed Panamanian sovereignty and self-determination and also constrained economic development on the isthmus.

Early National Elections, 1906–14

Serious political disagreement between Conservatives and Liberals emerged very soon as well. The Conservatives attempted to revoke the citizenship of Liberal leader Belisario Porras, arguing that he had effectively renounced his citizenship by not supporting Panama's independence movement in 1903. Porras had of course criticized the movement as a Conservative appropriation of the Liberal cause that was further tainted by U.S. involvement. The Conservatives, on the other hand, were concerned that Porras would be a major political force in upcoming elections. In November 1905, the Conservative-appointed Supreme Court stripped away Porras's citizenship. Liberal leaders retaliated by organizing an insurrection against Amador's Conservative regime in the interior of the country, assuming that the U.S. government would not intervene in an area far from the canal and the terminal cities. Realizing the risk to the Amador government, Washington issued the Root-Taft Clarification to the 1903 Treaty, asserting that the U.S. government could intervene on the isthmus if asked to by Panama's president or if disorder in the interior threatened to affect the terminal cities and canal construction. Washington was also wary of Porras's political potential since the U.S. minister to Panama, John Barrett, had described the Liberal leader as a "revolutionary firebrand," a "hater of foreigners," and as anti–United States (Mellander 1971, 72). Washington stymied the nascent Liberal revolt and opened the door for Panamanian governments to request U.S. intervention in the future. In effect, Washington agreed and gave itself the right to intervene beyond the bounds of the 1903 Treaty, opening the door for more extensive U.S. intervention.

Liberal and Conservative leaders, in order to avert conflict and perhaps also to keep the voters out of the political equation, decided to negotiate a power-sharing settlement. Part of the scheme involved the distribution of seats in the twenty-eight-member National Assembly. Rather than turning to the voters, the two parties decided they would determine the electoral outcome themselves. Both parties solicited the help of Governor Magoon, who seemed favorable to the idea that both parties cooperate, as they had done during the fight for independence. Needless to say, Magoon did not worry that such an arrangement was patently undemocratic. The scheme flopped, however, because the new assembly, to be installed on September 1, 1906, would choose the three vice presidents, and the first vice president would then have a good chance of becoming president, owing to Amador's advanced age and frailty. Both Liberals and Conservatives wanted to ensure that someone from their party was elected as first vice president. The quest for a power-sharing formula finally ended in early 1906, when the two parties reached an impasse on the makeup of the National Legislature. This lesson would perhaps help to convince the political elite of the value of the popular vote as the act of ultimate legitimacy and political elite selection (McCain 1965, 65; Mellander 1971, 93–96.) If Panamanian political leaders exhibited signs of antidemocratic tendencies, U.S. representatives on the isthmus and officials in Washington shared such tendencies as well, particularly when U.S. interests on the isthmus were involved. We must keep in mind, after all, that democracy in the United States in the early 1900s also suffered from a lack of popular participation and exclusion.

The second municipal elections were scheduled for June 24, 1906. Conservatives, fearing a Liberal landslide, took steps to ensure that many Liberals were kept off the voting rosters and also used policemen, hired just for the election period, to vote early and often. As a result, the Conservatives won the electoral contest, an unlikely occurrence had the elections been free and fair. Unfortunately, some violence also tainted the elections; at the end of the day, gunfights at Santa Ana Plaza, in Panama City, left four men dead and twenty wounded (Mellander 1971, 109). The next day, Charles Magoon dispatched U.S. military officials to Panama City and Colón and let the Panamanians know that the U.S. government was developing contingency plans for the dispersal of U.S. Marines at the upcoming National Assembly elections on July 1. Prompted by Magoon, Conservatives and Liberals then decided to reach a quick electoral agreement, as they had tried to do a few months earlier, to stymie violence during the upcoming election. The two parties also shared a desire to keep U.S. Marines off the streets of Colón and Panama City.

After the violent municipal elections, Magoon decided to take sides. He instructed the Canal Zone police to collect information on Liberal Party activities and then used the information to send written reports to the Amador government (Mellander 1971, 109–10). The Zone governor also instructed U.S. military officers in Panama to be visible while mapping out the terminal cities in an effort to make it clear to the Liberals that the U.S. government was ready to intervene. On the day of the National Assembly elections violence was averted, both because of the visible U.S. presence and U.S. willingness to intervene and because the two parties reached a limited agreement just before the polling took place. Many Liberal supporters decided not to vote since they assumed that the agreement had already sealed the fate of the elections. As a result, the Conservatives ended up with twenty-five seats, while the Liberals won only three. How could the Liberals, even with some conscious absenteeism, do so poorly in national elections when they were clearly the most popular party in the isthmus? Mellander points out that, even though Governor Magoon accepted the government's claims of a free and fair election, "a gross electoral fraud had been perpetrated by the incumbent Amador administration" (1971, 112). The Amador government, despite its claim to represent the people of Panama, carried out blatant fraud. And Washington had accepted the results of an illegitimate election that foiled the popular will because it brought to power the political leaders the U.S. government believed were more sympathetic toward U.S. interests.

Magoon left Panama in September 1906, and, as noted above, Washington abolished the joint post of U.S. minister and Zone governor with his departure. Magoon, who was scheduled for posting in the Philippines, was at the last moment sent to Cuba because instability on that island had led to a second U.S. occupation. Panamanians realized that a similar fate could await them, which may have been an important factor in inhibiting political conflict on the isthmus. Herbert G. Squiers, who also had a pro-Conservative, pro-government bias, replaced Magoon as U.S. minister, while Joseph

Blackburn became governor of the Canal Zone. Under new guidelines from Washington, the governor was to concern himself principally with the Canal Zone, while the minister was to focus on Panamanian politics and U.S.-Panamanian relations. This simple distribution of responsibilities would be difficult to maintain.

President Roosevelt took the historic step of visiting Panama in November 1906, becoming the first sitting U.S. president to travel abroad, a testimony to the importance of the isthmus to U.S. interests. During one of his public appearances, Roosevelt stated that what he hoped for Panama was that it would become a country "whose history reflects honor upon the entire western world" (quoted in Mellander 1971, 120). For Roosevelt, reflecting honor meant that Panama would continue to support U.S. interests and perhaps become prosperous, democratic, and averse to rebellion. Unfortunately, Roosevelt's wish would be a flash in the pan, and Panama's association with the United States would bring it none of these things. While U.S. leaders would call for democracy and prosperity on the isthmus, their policies would often be counterproductive, helping instead to promote authoritarianism and economic and social crisis.

The next national elections, in 1908, demonstrated the amorphous and fluid nature of the Liberal and Conservative parties. The presidential candidates for the 1908 national elections were foreign affairs minister Ricardo Arias and first designate and minister to Washington José Domingo de Obaldía. Oddly enough, the "official" or Conservative government candidate was Arias, a Liberal, while the Liberal candidate was de Obaldía, a Conservative. Ricardo Arias had become so closely associated with the Conservative government that his party did not wish to nominate him for the presidency. José de Obaldía, on the other hand, had forged close ties with Liberals and thus became their presidential candidate. Despite some calls for presidential reelection, the elderly Amador, to his credit, declined, stating that he did not wish to run for a second term because he wanted to support democracy and prevent the *continuismo* (continuation in power) that had been so prevalent in Colombia. This political crisscross of presidential candidates suggests that ideology was not the dominant factor separating the Liberals and Conservatives. In essence, there was significant ideological unity—liberalism—among Panama's political elite.

The U.S. government nevertheless continued to have a preference for Conservatives and to use its power to influence the electoral outcome. In a March 1908 confidential letter, Secretary of War Taft wrote to Governor Blackburn, "I think it is of the utmost importance that we should have de Obaldía as president instead of Arias" (quoted in Mellander 1971, 135). Taft went on to instruct Blackburn to do his best to push Amador toward favoring de Obaldía. Taft's actions not only corrupted the Panamanian political process but U.S. diplomatic procedure as well since he did not confer with Minister Squiers on this matter, who had been instructed to handle relations with Panama. Taft was probably acting on behalf of the U.S. government rather than as a maverick, however. The U.S. government had a favored candidate in de Obaldía, a Conservative who was deemed to be pro–United States. On the positive side, promoting de Obaldía, who had attained the support of Liberals, helped to put Washington in closer association with the more popular Liberal Party of Belisario Porras, who had regained his citizenship in 1907. Roosevelt sent Secretary of War Taft to Panama again in late April 1908, with a detachment of marines. While in Panama, Taft heard rumors that Amador, despite repeated statements of neutrality, had now decided to back Arias for the presidency. Arias could win only if Amador were to support him and allowed fraud to take place as had occurred in 1906. In mid-May 1908, Taft visited Amador, with Squiers and Blackburn in tow. At the meeting, Taft pressed hard to convey to Amador the U.S. insistence on clean elections (principally because clean elections this time would result in a victory for de Obaldía). Taft also instructed Amador to remain neutral and not support any candidate. This advice was rather hypocritical, considering that Taft himself would garner Teddy Roosevelt's strong backing for the presidency in the U.S. election to be held in the same year. Taft then urged Amador to allow two U.S. observers at each voting place in Panama. Taft was essentially asking Amador to violate Panama's constitution, which stated that the Electoral Commission was autonomous and decided all election matters. To get around this, Amador eventually established an Electoral Inquiry Commission that would look into alleged electoral law violations and invite U.S. representatives to take part in the investigation as well as observe the polling on election day.

It is interesting to note, however, that while Blackburn and other U.S. officials were promoting de Obaldía, Arias had the backing of Cromwell and U.S. minister Squiers. Was this a reflection of U.S. foreign policy discord or incoherence? Most likely, this apparent dual position reflects a sound political strategy. If Arias were to be elected, Cromwell and Squiers could then be used as the key U.S. representatives. Suggesting a ploy rather than policy confusion, Blackburn wrote to Taft in May 1908: Cromwell's "close, personal relationship with President Amador and Secretary Arias gave him peculiar advantages in dealing with those gentlemen" (quoted in Mellander 1971, 153). We see in Cromwell a "private citizen" intimately involved in U.S.-Panamanian relations and in the domestic politics of Panama, promoting both personal and U.S. interests concurrently. Despite Cromwell's so-called support for Arias, he wrote to Arias before the election and referred to him and his followers, saying: "Be yourselves the conspicuous leaders in insuring a fair election; it is the surest foundation for maintenance of confidence in your own personality and preservation of the stability of Panama" (quoted in Mellander 1971, 177). By proposing to Arias that he ensure free elections, Cromwell was assuring his "friend's" defeat at the polls. Arias, completely disheartened, withdrew his candidacy on July 4, 1908, and subsequently resigned as foreign minister, perhaps as a signal that he was surrendering to Uncle Sam. His withdrawal would allow de Obaldía to have an easy, uncontested victory. Once again, Panama's political elite showed a preference for determining the electoral outcome prior to voting, suggesting that they supported some contestation but were wary of mass participation. In this regard, the oligarchy and Washington were of like mind—not very supportive of competitive politics and political participation.

The Coalición Republicana (Republican Coalition), composed of Liberals and a few Conservatives who supported de Obaldía, formed before the 1908 election. The liberals supported U.S. monitoring of the elections since they knew that, if not monitored, the Conservative government could steal the election away from them. They also supported monitoring because they feared that without such intervention Washington could intervene more extensively later if fraudulent outcomes led to political violence. To oppose the Liberal alliance, the Amador government established the Partido Constitucional (Constitutional Party) as a vehicle for supporting the existing government and the Arias candidacy. The municipal elections were held on June 28, 1908. Washington had decided not to oversee these elections, but the War Department dispatched over 700 marines to the isthmus in case violence erupted, which of course sent a strong signal to both political parties. Three U.S. Navy vessels were also visible off the coast of Colón with another 600 marines. De Obaldía supporters won decisive victories in the municipal elections, owing to support from the Liberal party.

The national elections followed two weeks later, on July 12. De Obaldía was elected president in a landslide election, owing to Arias's withdrawal from the race. The winner was not democracy but rather absenteeism, elitism, and U.S. power. Despite de Obaldía's impending victory, the U.S. government supervised the peaceful election, as had been planned. Taft sent twelve U.S. Army officers, led by Major William Johnston, to supervise the electoral contest. Interestingly enough, foreign military officers would supervise Panama's democratic process, an odd decision by the world's leading democracy. Although the secretary of war supervised the Canal Zone government and operation, the supervision of elections in Panama by the U.S. government should have been the purview of the State Department and civilians. President-elect de Obaldía had the support of sixteen of the twenty-eight members of the newly elected National Assembly, so he chose all three designates from the Liberal Party. On October 1, he was inaugurated president and thus became Panama's first popularly elected president. Although a Conservative, his designates were Liberals and the National Assembly was controlled by the Liberal Party. This election was a bit more democratic than earlier ones, but contestation and participation were still quite limited, and U.S. power was still palpable. The U.S. government now realized, however, that Liberals were not so different from Conservatives. They supported more popular participation but still represented oligarchic rule and were willing to preserve U.S. interests on the isthmus.

Several presidents occupied the Palacio de las Garzas (Palace of the Herons), the presidential palace, prior to the next elections in 1912, owing to de Obaldía's death in early 1910 and the deaths of other designados who subsequently became chief executives. Liberal Carlos Mendoza became president on March 1, 1910, after de Obaldía's death. U.S. business attaché Richard O. Marsh wrote to the State Department in August 1910 that Mendoza's reelection would be detrimental to U.S. and canal interests. He favored Samuel Lewis, the likely Conservative candidate. Washington supported this position and had informally stated that Mendoza's reelection would be unconstitutional. Marsh ended up getting transferred out of Panama, however, for overt meddling in isthmian affairs. An Argentine newspaper reported that Marsh had threatened U.S. intervention if Liberal leader Porras did not stay out of the upcoming 1912 election. However, Mendoza passed away in February 1910, and in September the National Assembly chose Dr. Pablo Arosemena, who as first designate became president. Arosemena left the presidency for a brief period to run for reelection since many supporters encouraged him to do so. A delegation supporting his candidacy traveled to Washington and met with President Taft to fish for U.S. support. Although informed that the U.S. government would not get involved (denying overt support to Arosemena), Taft strongly expressed to the delegation that universal suffrage in Panama represented a defect in Panama's constitution, since only those citizens who were literate should be allowed to vote (Pizzurno Gelós and Araúz 1996, 61). Washington was now willing to support Liberals but was hesitant to support anyone who was put in office by the "Negro" masses. Arosemena eventually decided against reelection and returned to the presidency on March 7, 1912.

Prior to the national elections in 1912, Conservatives in power formed

Union Patriótica (Patriotic Union) to back Pedro A. Díaz's presidential bid. The Liberal opposition backed the very popular Belisario Porras. Washington sent U.S. military officers to register voters and to oversee both the municipal and the national elections. Owing to U.S. involvement, Panama's government realized it would be unable to manipulate the process, withdrew from the elections, and accused the United States of fraud and of favoring the Liberals. In July 1912, Liberal leader Belisario Porras finally became Panama's president, representing the preference of voters across the isthmus. His election also represented the first time that an opposition candidate defeated the "official" government candidate—an important step toward democratic development. Porras, the oft-labeled "anti-U.S." Liberal, however, achieved Washington's backing and electoral victory only after he expressed solid support for U.S. interests on the isthmus. In January 1912, in a newspaper article, Porras wrote: "The United States constitutes our best friend, whom we should neither fear nor be suspicious of" (quoted in Pizzurno Gelós and Araúz 1996, 63)(my translation). Porras, of course, was very suspicious of U.S. actions and intentions, but he realized that political power on the isthmus could be gained only with U.S. approval. Washington accepted broader electoral participation and even helped with voting registration but did so only after being certain that the president to be elected by the masses was one who would safeguard U.S. interests on the isthmus. Washington's tolerance for contestation and participation on the isthmus depended more on whether U.S. interests would be preserved rather than on genuine support for democratic principles.

Belisario Porras is often described as the first president to begin the "modernization" of the Panamanian nation and state, enhancing public education, erecting national monuments, creating national financial institutions, building roads, railroads, hospitals, and prisons, and inaugurating a national printing press and a nationalized lottery (see Pizzurno Gelós and Araúz 1996, 75–84). Since Porras was the first president to represent the will of the people, we can certainly see him as the first chief executive who had popular legitimacy. But earlier presidents had already taken some important steps toward developing some degree of national unity and integration. President Amador's government began a program labeled *civilización de indígenas* (civilizing the indigenous) designed to Hispanicize and integrate into Panamanian society and culture the Kuna Indians of the San Blas region (Pizzurno Gelós and Araúz 1996, 28). In 1907, the de Obaldía administration passed a law that established the Instituto Nacional (National Institute). The Instituto, inaugurated in 1909, was a national high school that would allow the Panamanian state to socialize and educate those young Panamanians who did not attend private or foreign schools. The Instituto, later to be termed the *nido de águilas* (nest of the eagles), would become the breeding ground for thousands of citizens who would, in the not-too-distant future, clamor for Panamanian sovereignty and the abrogation of the hated 1903 Treaty.

The U.S. Canal and World War I

Panama became an American "prized possession" principally because of the waterway that would eventually link the Atlantic and Pacific oceans (Major 1993). After its completion in 1914, the canal would enhance American military and economic power greatly by allowing U.S. warships and troops to quickly move between the two oceans and by facilitating U.S. trade and commerce. Recall that canal construction was so important that President Roosevelt visited the isthmus to personally observe the progress. Soon thereafter, President Taft journeyed to the isthmus as well, having already been there twice while he was secretary of war in 1904. Even before the canal opened to world shipping, analysts understood the potential of the waterway for America's increasing global influence. It was perhaps inevitable then that Washington would become closely involved in Panama's domestic affairs to an extent that its wishes would normally prevail. The Panama Canal was the largest government project to date in global history, and "American lawmakers backed up the canal diggers in every necessary way" (Haskin 1913, 268). U.S. lawmakers knew that the waterway, despite the immense financial commitment and the U.S. mantra of limited government, would more than pay for itself and allow America to enhance its role as a financial powerhouse. The opportunity for U.S. economic expansion was enormous since trade between America's eastern, southern, and western ports would grow exponentially in the 1900s. U.S. trade with Latin America and Asia would also expand exponentially. Additionally, this growth in U.S. trade would allow Washington to enter into markets where European countries had a monopoly (for the many expected commercial benefits, see Marshall 1913, 210–35). The Panama Canal would eventually pay off handsomely, fulfilling all the above expectations and more.

U.S. canal construction would affect Panama not only via the direct influence that Washington exerted on the isthmus but also through the continued importation of foreign labor. From 1904 to 1914, canal authorities brought into the isthmus "between 150,000 and 200,000 men and women" (Conniff 1985, 29). Most of these laborers were English speakers from the West Indies who were referred to in Panama, often disparagingly, as *antil-*

lanos. For most of these years, about twenty thousand antillanos worked on the canal project. While some workers were repatriated after the canal was finished, many stayed on the isthmus with or without jobs. This immigration was substantial since at the end of the 1800s, Panama's population was only about four hundred thousand. For a small, weak state like Panama, assimilating such a large immigrant population that did not speak Spanish and was racially different was practically impossible. National unity would be difficult at best, owing to cultural and racial differences. Inadvertently, then, Washington intensified Panama's already existing ethnic and racial divisions that already militated against democratic development.

The onset of the "Great War" in 1914 overshadowed the official opening of the Panama Canal. While the world would most likely have marveled at America's enormous engineering feat on the isthmus, global attention was turned to massive military mobilizations in Europe. World War I, however, demonstrated the commercial and strategic importance of the waterway in terms of the amount of goods necessary for the war effort that could be conveyed by ship through the canal. The war also highlighted the military saliency of the canal, both in terms of the flow of warships and soldiers, as well as the imperative to defend the waterway. Consequently, at an early stage, Washington established the key elements of U.S. canal policy—"unilateral control; the right to fortify; and the power to close the canal to enemy shipping" (Major 1993, 22). The notion of the neutrality of international waterways, as established by the Constantinople Convention of 1888, did not strike a chord in Washington. Even though many Panamanian intellectuals wanted the isthmus to adopt neutrality as a guiding principle of its foreign policy, the canal's importance to Washington would prevent Panama from adopting that policy option. Thus, U.S. military installations were soon part of the Canal Zone's dramatic landscape. These military facilities would eventually surround and stifle the terminal cities of Colón and Panama, effectively insulating Panama and its citizens from the canal. Once it decided to end its neutrality toward the European conflict, Washington sent John Foster Dulles to Panama to ensure that the isthmus would break relations with the Central powers. Dulles reported that Panama was quite willing to end its neutrality. "Dulles further indicated that Panama's economic dependence upon the United Sates was the compelling factor in the Panamanian attitude, and disclosed that he had authority to promise the Isthmian Republic exemptions of all income earned in Panama from U.S. Federal taxes in return for cooperation in the war" (Ealy 1951, 43). During the war, Panama gave "the United States carte blanche to undertake any necessary military operation within" the isthmus (Ealy 1951, 44). Geography had blessed the small isthmus, but the U.S. government now fully controlled the country's geographic location, as well as its attendant benefits. And Panamanian foreign policy was also within the domain of U.S. power and influence.

By the time the canal opened, the United States of America had attained Great Power status and dominance in the Western Hemisphere. The Roosevelt Corollary to the Monroe Doctrine rationalized U.S. military intervention in the hemisphere, and Washington did not hold back. From 1898 to 1934, the United States intervened militarily over thirty times in the region, occupying several countries, including Panama, for extended periods. In 1909, President Taft exercised dollar diplomacy designed to augment America's economic might and penetration in the hemisphere. In Panama, U.S. economic activity flourished from the time the Zone was established, when thousands of U.S. investors rushed to the isthmus. By 1914, Panama was awash in U.S. companies, such as United Fruit, Central and South American Telegraph, American Trade Developing, Isaac Brandon and Brothers Tobacco, Caribbean Manganese, among many others. U.S. companies acquired large amounts of land and resources and controlled many public services. The United States had also become extensively involved in banking enterprises on the isthmus (for a description of U.S. economic presence and interests on the isthmus, see McCain 1965, 97–104).

Continued U.S. Intervention and Power

On the eve of the inauguration of the canal, Panamanians continued to resent the Zone's presence and the actions of U.S. Zonians and U.S. military personnel. Minister Magoon explained to Washington that conflict was sometimes exacerbated by the Zonians' attitudes, stating that "natural racial antipathy had been intensified because most of the Americans were Southerners who made no distinction between Panamanians and Negroes" (McCain 1965, 80). The United States on numerous occasions threatened to intervene when clashes took place between U.S. servicemen and Panamanians, both citizens and policemen. Racism and colonial attitudes were clearly part of the cause. In 1908, in an effort to prevent trouble between Panamanians and American military personnel and to forestall Washington's intervention, the Panamanian government allowed U.S. authorities to establish patrols in Panama City and Colón. Most altercations occurred in red-light districts, frequently when U.S. servicemen were drunk or involved in illicit activities like soliciting prostitutes. On July 4, 1912, a riot between Panamanians and Americans took place in a red-light district in Panama City, leaving one American dead and nineteen injured. The U.S. government reacted strongly, accusing Panama's police of brutality and demanding the removal of the chief of police and financial compensation for the aggrieved. Washington threatened intervention unless Panama responded positively to its demands (McCain 1965, 81). The Panamanian government, however, believed that the drunk and obnoxious U.S. servicemen had instigated the violence. After long negotiations, Panama agreed, in April 1915, to allow U.S. police to patrol the red-light districts of Colón and Panama City. On August 15, 1915, the U.S. government asked Panama to disarm its police of rifles and to enforce the law prohibiting citizens from carrying concealed weapons. Panama resisted this U.S. pressure, but the U.S. government insisted, and on May 12, 1916, the U.S. State Department cabled its minister in Panama: "You will immediately inform the Government of Panama that this Government expects immediate compliance with its demand for the complete disarmament of the police in Panama and Colon of high-powered rifles" (quoted in McCain 1965, 85). Panama hesitantly handed over all rifles used by its police. As a result, by 1916 the United States had robbed the isthmus of the fundamental means of preserving its sovereignty and maintaining its internal order. Soon after the canal's completion, Panamanian leaders had lost control of their territory, economic policy, foreign policy, and security apparatus.

Elections continued as scheduled but, as before, contestation and participation were limited. In the national elections of 1916, factions of both parties—Liberals and Conservatives—supported Liberal leader Rodolfo Chiari. This coalition asked the U.S. government to monitor the election as it had done in 1912. But on this occasion, President Porras did not support U.S. involvement in the elections. As usual, the opposition withdrew from the electoral contest. Consequently, the government candidate, Ramón M. Valdés, a Conservative, was elected president without opposition. While some violence erupted in Panama City, U.S. forces that had been deployed along the Zone calmed the situation. A crisis ensued in the municipal and National Assembly elections of 1918, however. Owing to President Valdés's death, first designate Ciro L. Urriola, a doctor and a Liberal, issued a decree postponing the contest. The new legislature, to be elected on July 7, would then choose the new chief executive and preside over proposed constitutional reforms, which President Urriola did not support. The political leadership at the time was divided into reformist and antireformist camps. The dividing issue was whether a citizen who was not born in Panama could become president, allowing Colombian-born Eusebio E. Morales to run for the presidency. Washington, as well as political leaders who favored constitutional reforms, supported a delay in the voting and invoked Article 136 of the Constitution, which allowed U.S. intervention for preserving the constitutional order. On

June 28, 1918, U.S. troops assumed control of Colón and Panama City. Urriola complained to President Wilson, saying: "I protest this interference, which violates the sovereignty of Panama without any justification, inasmuch as the Government of Panama has sufficient means to maintain public order in these cities" (quoted in McCain 1965, 74). Nevertheless, elections, supervised by the U.S. government, were held on June 30 and July 7. Belisario Porras was elected first designate and thus president by the National Assembly on September 11, even though the U.S. government had supported Ricardo Arias. Pedro A. Díaz and Ernesto T. LeFevre became second and third designados. The National Assembly approved several constitutional reforms, including the elimination of the death penalty, the direct election of the president, and lengthening the tenure of legislators from two to four years.

Washington flexed its muscles once more by ordering troops into the provinces of Veraguas and Chiriquí in July 1918, arguing that Panamanians were threatening U.S. citizens and their property. U.S. soldiers remained in Chiriquí until August 1920, making this intervention a two-year occupation. In this case, the United States intervened not to protect the canal or to maintain order in the terminal cities but to protect the interests of private U.S. citizens. After the completion of the canal, a number of Americans had purchased land in Chiriquí, but titles to these properties were under dispute, leading to heated and violent quarrels. One U.S. citizen, William G. Chase, who owned large parcels of land, was accused of killing the governor of Chiriquí, Saturnino Perigault. The Panamanian government satisfied U.S. concerns by establishing a rural guard to maintain order, prompting the U.S. government to withdraw its marines. The U.S. military occupation of territory far away from the canal area was yet another violation of the 1903 Treaty that Panama had to swallow owing to its weakness vis-à-vis the United States. This intervention also demonstrated that the U.S. government and military worked closely with private commercial interests on the isthmus.

In the meantime, Belisario Porras and his supporters wanted the presidency once more, so the popular leader resigned in January 1920 in order to run for the presidency in July of that year, as stipulated by the constitution. The third designate, Ernesto LeFevre, took the presidential sash owing to the death of the second designate. President Urriola opposed Porras's candidacy and asked Washington to monitor the elections. Porras, nevertheless, was easily elected since as usual the opposition candidate withdrew from the contest. During his third presidency, Porras continued efforts to strengthen the Panamanian state and foment national development. His administration's policies focused on industrial, agricultural, and educational development. Porras's government carried out a number of public works during his third administration, but his most important projects included a new home for the National Archives and the Santo Tomas Hospital (Pizzurno Gelós and Araúz 1996, 124–29). Porras's efforts at nation building and state formation, however, were often foiled by a lack of resources and by external forces beyond his control. Panamanian leaders understood what needed to be done to strengthen the state and bolster national unity, but the isthmus's treasury could not support such efforts. Additionally, there was little chance that Panama would be able to attain the benefits derived from their geographic location since the U.S. government controlled the canal and its contiguous territory.

To make matters worse, the new Porras administration immediately faced a serious international crisis that again pitted Panama against the United States. Washington intervened militarily once more in 1920, during the so-called Coto War. In 1900, France, serving as a neutral arbiter in a border dispute, gave Costa Rica a large chunk of land that Colombia had claimed. After Panama's independence in 1903, Panama and Costa Rica could not agree on the precise boundaries set forth in the somewhat ambiguous 1900 decision. In 1910, both countries agreed to arbitration by the U.S. government. The United States was interested in resolving this conflict since both the United Fruit Company and the American Banana Company had economic interests in the disputed territory. In 1914, Panama rejected the decision issued by the chief justice of the U.S. Supreme Court, Edward White, arguing that the ruling modified rather than interpreted the French decision. Panama resisted White's decision since it gave even more land to Costa Rica. Washington hedged its bets since the U.S. government also insisted that both parties respect private property no matter what the results of the decision, to ensure that United Fruit and American Banana Company interests were safeguarded. Belisario Porras, Panama's minister to Washington then, had argued emphatically that the United States should simply interpret rather than amend the French decision. In February and March 1921, Costa Rica sent troops into the contested area, some fighting ensued, and Panamanian police took Costa Rican soldiers prisoner on both occasions. Panama appealed to the League of Nations, but the League hesitated to challenge U.S. dominance in the region. President Harding then insisted that Panama accept Justice White's decision and sent the USS *Pennsylvania*, with marines onboard, to ensure that Panama complied. Porras did not want to resort to war with Costa Rica, but the Panamanian public was raging with aggressive nationalism. U.S. troops were called in to maintain peace when crowds in Panama appeared poised to attack the Palacio de las Garzas at the same time that the U.S. minister was consulting with Porras (McCain 1965, 87–88). Ealy writes: "The fact that this controversy was quieted in 1921 by the overshadowing Yanqui colossus in a fashion so humiliating to Panama and to the League of Nations alike was a very severe blow to the prestige of the World Organization not only in Panama but in all Latin America" (1951, 59–61). The situation became a matter less of international law than of preserving the prestige of the U.S. government and more specifically the U.S. Supreme Court. No "banana republic" or international organization would dare challenge the decision of a U.S. chief justice. In terms of regional power, the Coto crisis demonstrated that U.S. power in the hemisphere was preponderant, accepting no challenges either from within the region, outside the region, or even from any multilateral international organization (Araúz 1994a, 190–93).

In addition to employing military force, the U.S. government continued to take control of Panama's territory for the purpose of canal operation and defense. While the 1903 Treaty suggested that the U.S. government could acquire additional territory for canal operations and defense, Panama, as stated above, argued that such appropriations required both compensation and consultation. Washington, however, eventually instituted a precedent of taking land without even prior consultation, including land that was occupied by Panamanian citizens.

In 1912, Washington asked for control of Gatun Lake, created by damming the Chagres River during canal construction, as well as the land on the lake's shores up to 100 feet above sea level. This territorial appropriation extended well beyond the original Canal Zone and consisted of 167 square miles of land that would come under U.S. control. In 1914, Washington asked for permission to build three roads in Panamanian territory necessary for canal defense. In 1915, however, the U.S. government simply took control of land at the mouth of the Chagres River, stating once again that canal defense justified the territorial acquisition. In May 1918, Panama protested that U.S. troops were occupying almost three acres at Punta Paitilla, a small peninsula close to Panama City, without having asked for the land. Washington responded in July that the outpost was needed for canal defense. In July 1918, Canal Zone Governor Harding asked for over 3,000 acres of land on the Atlantic coast near the Chagres River. Although it agreed to the land concession, as it had in the past, the Panamanian government decided to ask the United States for compensation for taking this land as well as the land taken in 1916 at the mouth of the Chagres. On August 16, 1918, Washington asked for the right to establish coaling stations for its ships along both sides of the isthmus, again for the purpose of canal defense. Panama quickly acquiesced, acknowledging the need to defend against German U-boats. At the end of World War I, Washington asked Panama for most of the island of Taboga, a resort location only a few miles off the coast of Panama City. Once again, canal defense was the rationale. Taboga was not some distant uninhabited territory but considered prime property and a national treasure by Panama's elite. Also, most of the island's inhabitants would have to be relocated. The U.S. government began to relent when in January the DOD stated that it would not need to take possession of the island immediately. Washington then reduced the size of the requested territory. In September 1919, the U.S. government took part of Droque Island and two small islands in Las Minas Bay. These properties were expropriated without any consultation with Panama. Naturally Panama protested Washington's actions. In June 1920, Panama turned over part of Taboga Island to the U.S. government (McCain 1965, 150–53). In October 1923, Washington informed Panama that it would be taking twenty-two square miles of land adjacent to the Chagres River for the purpose of creating a water reservoir. Again Panama protested, arguing that Article 2 of the 1903 accord did not allow the U.S. government to take this action (McCain 1965, 154–55). Panama never fully accepted Washington's "sovereignty" over the Canal Zone, so the latter's continued appropriation of territory angered political leaders, who correctly saw U.S. actions as the baneful exercise of raw power. These U.S. actions demonstrate the enormous amount of power and leeway that the U.S. government had on the isthmus—basically emasculating Panamanian sovereignty and independence.

America's unilateral actions and wanton exercise of eminent domain generated a high level of antigringo attitudes in the early 1920s, even among members of the oligarchy. Panama took steps during that time to narrow the U.S. interpretation of its rights to intervention found in the 1903 Treaty and the Panamanian constitution. First, Panama argued that the 1903 Treaty committed the U.S. government to guarantee Panama's independence, meaning that U.S. intervention could take place only if Panama were threatened by an external enemy. Second, the Panamanian government posited that Article 136 of the constitution allowed for U.S. intervention only if requested by Panama's chief executive. But Washington viewed the 1903 Treaty and Article 136 as documents giving the U.S. government the right to intervene as it saw fit, with or without a request from Panama (McCain 1965, 88). During the post–World War I period, Washington also perceived Panama's interest and membership in the League of Nations as a sign of anti-U.S. sentiment. Ealy writes: "Such prominent men as Julio J. Fábrega, Eusebio A. Morales, and Santiago de la Guardia were found to be openly hostile, and even Ricardo J. Alfaro, who in later years was often to prove himself a fast friend of the United States, was declared in 1922 to be definitely anti-American" (1951, 54). Oligarchs were disposed and willing to cooperate with Washington, but not at any price. Since the canal and U.S. presence did little to serve the interests of Panama's economic and political elite and Washington continued to treat the isthmus as a possession, resentment grew more and more rapidly. But U.S.-Panamanian disputes were not just economic in nature. The pervasive arrogance of U.S. government officials, Zonians, military personnel, and businessmen added fuel to the widespread perception that Americans cared only for themselves. Perhaps as a reaction to anti-U.S. sentiments in the early 1920s, the Zone government requested that the U.S. Congress terminate the Taft Agreement. Congress complied, abruptly abrogating the accord in 1923 and making economic competition from the Zone even stiffer.

Labor Strikes, the Kuna Rebellion, and the Kellogg-Alfaro Treaty

Labor problems emerged in the Canal Zone and Panama as soon as the U.S. Army completed the canal in 1914, owing to the diminishing need for workers. Labor leader Samuel Whyte, a Zone policeman, founded the Isthmian League of British West Indians in 1916, and a year later he created the Silver Employees Association. Owing to anticipated pay cuts, a strike in late 1916 affected both the Zone and Panamanian businesses. Eventually, pay increases were instituted in the Zone. On the Atlantic side, Víctor de Suze, a Panamanian, formed the Colón Federal Labor Union, or CFLU, but the Zone government failed to recognize the organization. The CFLU was relatively successful, getting a land grant for housing from the Panamanian government and bringing in about eight thousand members (Conniff 1985, 53). But the nascent West Indian labor organizations had difficulty with the Zone, owing to racism and the antilabor policies and sentiments of the times.

The rise of the labor movement, while fueled by unjust working conditions and racism, was influenced by the revolutions in Mexico and Russia that promoted the working class and disparaged the bourgeoisie. U.S. labor unions also promoted and helped to create unions in Latin America that were not critical of capitalism. In late 1918, U.S. labor leader Samuel Gompers established the Pan-American Workers Confederation under the American Federation of Labor (AFL), and within six months the AFL began organizing Silver Roll employees. Almost immediately, a strike ensued at the Port of Cristóbal. The Zone government responded by expelling from the Zone Marcus Garvey, a fiery black union leader. In February 1920, another strike took place, even though the Zone governor warned "that strikers would be evicted from Zone housing and stripped of Commissary privileges" (Major 1993, 91). Governor Harding had also warned Panamanian officials that he would send troops into the terminal cities unless they put down the strike. On March 2, 1920, responding to U.S. pressure, the Panamanian government made strike organizing illegal. Zone authorities also took strong action. Major writes: "Several dozen semi-skilled West Indians were dismissed in a systematic purge of the upper Silver echelons which had provided the strike movement with its spearhead" (1993, 92). Nevertheless, strike activity and labor organizing continued, owing to economic hardships resulting from the post–World War I recession. In early 1921, the Federación Obrera de la República de Panamá (Labor Federation of the Republic of Panama), or FOP, was established. A few months later, thousands of West Indians lost their Zone jobs and were forced to move with their families into Colón or Panama City. Samuel Whyte then established the Panama Canal West Indian Employees' Association in early 1924, although no recognition came from Zone authorities. The rise of organized labor in Panama represented a threat to oligarchic control on the isthmus, and thus Panama's political elite resisted labor's efforts. Washington resisted and repressed organized labor on the isthmus as well, particularly in the Zone. If the nascent labor movement represented a rise in political participation and emerging democratization, then Washington squelched participation with at least as much alacrity as did Panama's oligarchy.

In May 1924, Liberal political dominance continued, when Rodolfo Chiari, Porras's official candidate, won the presidency. While continuing Porras's attempts at state formation and national economic development via private initiative, Chiari effectively formed his own personal faction, the Chiaristas, within the Liberal Party. President Chiari would face several important national crises, including a renters' strike, the Kuna rebellion, and a contentious treaty with the United States. During these crises, his administration continued public works projects and road building, established the National Museum, and built a railroad to Puerto Armuelles to transport bananas cultivated in Chiriquí province (Castillero Reyes 1995, 225–26).

Ubiquitous unemployment and an increasing cost of living resulted in a renters' strike in October 1925. Rents had surged by as much as 50 percent, partly because so many West Indians who had lost their Zone employment had moved to the terminal cities. Violent demonstrations left four dead, and during a twelve-day period, U.S. soldiers were deployed to Colón and Panama City (Conniff 1985, 64). The U.S. armed intervention had actually been requested by President Chiari, who feared that Panama's police would not be able to handle the strikers. The Panamanian government urged Zone authorities to employ more Panamanians in the Zone to remedy the dire economic situation. But Zone authorities were more willing to fire than to hire workers at this time. The result was that Panamanian resentment toward West Indians, who were seen as foreigners taking job opportunities from isthmians, increased dramatically. The Chiari government then passed laws preventing non–Spanish-speaking blacks from entering the country and established a poll tax on West Indians. The infusion of English-speaking antillanos generated intense racial and ethnic divisions once the canal-building boom days were over and made the task of fomenting national unity virtually impossible.

The Panamanian state had to deal with much more than strikers and antillano assimilation in 1925. The Kuna Indians living in the San Blas region had for years resisted the government's ongoing program of "civilizing" the indigenous populations. Part of the problem was that, while Panama was trying to Hispanicize the Kunas, U.S. missionaries were trying to Anglicize them. Moreover, former U.S. diplomat John O. Marsh, whom the U.S. government had fired, became intimately involved in a Kuna uprising and even wrote their "declaration of independence." Marsh was partly motivated by his association with Harvey Firestone and Henry Ford, who were looking desperately for rubber plantations to manufacture automobile tires. The Kuna lands of Darien were ideal for this purpose. But Marsh claimed a higher, humanitarian purpose, writing: "I simply can't sit still and see these Panamanian negroids exterminate these wonderful people" (quoted in Howe 1998, 265). On February 22, 1925, Kuna leaders started a small, armed rebellion against the Panamanian government with the goal of establishing the Republic of Yule. The insurrection ended quickly because the Chiari government decided to negotiate a political arrangement with the Kuna leaders. A peace treaty was signed, under U.S. supervision, on March 4. Marsh, who had inspired a rebellion against the Panamanian state, could not be brought to justice in Panama because he was given sanctuary on the USS *Cleveland*. While an independent Kuna nation was not achieved, the insurrectionists attained political autonomy, the right to maintain their culture, and the promise of fair treatment by the Panamanian state. The missionaries and Marsh left the isthmus quietly, and Catholic education resumed its more traditional role. The Kuna were successful for two reasons. First, the U.S. government was helpful in arbitrating the conflict and perhaps indirectly instigating it. Second, the Panamanian state was weak. Howe writes: "Fortunately for the Kuna, the state that confronted them was weak, its military power negligible and its colonial administration perpetually starved of arms, ammunition, paper, and funds" (Howe 1998, 5). While Kuna autonomy and protection from the state were forward steps toward self-determination and democracy, this revolution demonstrated both the Panamanian state's weakness and its susceptibility to U.S. influence.

While various labor organizations were emerging on the isthmus and the Kuna were rejecting state-sponsored socialization, middle-class interests were also surfacing and asserting themselves politically. On August 19, 1923, a group of mostly young, middle-class Panamanians who worked in "Liberal professions" formed a "nationalist-civic" organization called Acción Comunal (Community Action), or AC (Pizzurno Gelós and Araúz 1996, 136). AC's motto was "Patriotism, Action, Equity, and Discipline." The organization was similar to the movement formed in Peru by Víctor Haya de la Torre called Alianza Popular Revolucionaria Americana (American Revolutionary Popular Alliance), or APRA, which inspired like-minded organizations all over the hemisphere. Like APRA, AC was nationalist, promoted social justice and modernization, and was critical of foreign economic penetration, which obviously pointed the finger at the United States. AC leaders chastised the Porras administration for allowing a large number of U.S. citizens to take on important government roles and denounced strongly the 1903 Treaty. They were also very critical of the fact that good jobs in the Canal Zone were taken by non-Panamanians, who in their eyes should enjoy more benefits from the canal's operations. AC would quickly become the organization to most effectively promote nationalism in Panama and challenge the asymmetrical U.S.-Panamanian relationship. AC's political influence would also be tested very quickly.

On July 28, 1926, the United States and Panama signed the Kellogg-Alfaro Treaty in an effort to put in place a replacement for the defunct Taft Agreement. The negotiations for this accord had taken two years, while dissatisfaction over U.S. treaty rights was growing on the isthmus. The new accord committed Panama to a mutual security alliance with the United States. Such a commitment would have ensured that the canal would not remain neutral during conflict in which the United States was involved and would have allowed Washington to carry out any military operation it wished on the isthmus during a conflict (Yao n.d., 16–17). The accord also made no mention of Panama's concern over U.S. expropriation of land, except to say that Washington would consult with Panamanian officials. The United States agreed that commissaries would sell products only to Zone employees and would not establish any new businesses in the Zone. Panama and Washington carried out negotiations in secret, but AC was able to acquire a copy of the proposed accord surreptitiously and convinced *El Heraldo de Cuba* and the Costa Rican magazine *El Repertorio* to publish the document (Piz-zurno Gelós and Araúz 1996, 163–64). Critics of the Chiari administration and of the accord had a field day, particularly AC, which labeled the agreement as "dangerous." On January 26, 1927, the National Assembly issued a resolution stating that it would not consider the accord until the government found appropriate solutions to the nation's problems. The rejection of this treaty represents Panama's first major nationalist victory vis-à-vis the United States. Popular opinion and middle-class interests were raised to fever pitch, forcing the oligarchy to reject Washington's wishes. The political backdrop to this failed diplomatic effort would be a harbinger of things to come. Rising Panamanian nationalism, inspired by the increasing political participation of the middle class, labor unions, students, and teachers, would continue to press the isthmus's oligarchy to challenge U.S. power over Panama. The oligarchy and Washington would see this increased political participation as a threat to their interests and would initially work together to limit and even repress it.

Florencio Arosemena won the presidency in 1928, after the opposition candidate, Jorge Boyd, withdrew from the contest. By this time, Liberal-Conservative distinctions were irrelevant since Liberal factions, the Porris-tas and the Chiaristas, controlled the political system (Leonard 1993, 28). Arosemena would occupy the Palacio de las Garzas during tumultuous times. The Great Depression of 1929 would bring another economic bust to the isthmus, leading to greater dissatisfaction among the masses and emergent middle sectors. These upcoming changes would transform Panamanian politics in ways that would both encourage and militate against democratic development.

The Young Republic: A Liberal Oligarchy with U.S. Tutelage

In the first third of the twentieth century, the United States of America significantly increased its power in the Western Hemisphere. Washington intervened militarily throughout Central America and the Caribbean owing to enhanced U.S. military capabilities, magnified by the canal, while the Roosevelt Corollary to the Monroe Doctrine served to justify these interventions. Washington also expanded its economic interests in and trade with the region, almost always promoting and protecting private U.S. economic interests, as it did on the isthmus (Schoultz 1998, 205–19). During this historical period, however, U.S. government policy was less interested in promoting its political and economic system abroad than in simply promoting its national power. In Panama, the United States was able to act as a protectorate, resulting in near-colonial domination of the isthmus. Although Panama's political elite would have wanted a more just relationship with Washington, they were powerless to compel the United States to change its standard operating procedure. Owing to Washington's ability to expel other Great Powers from the region, Panama had no opportunity to make an alliance that would balance U.S. power and influence. Washington's dominant position not only restricted Panama's foreign policy options, it affected the isthmus's political development as well. Panama's oligarchy was closely tied to the interests of the United States, although they often expressed concerns about Washington's arrogance and economic selfishness. Mellander notes that Panamanian politicians were able very early on to "sniff the subtle whiffs of power which emanated from the United States embassy" and thus "became convinced that no plan of action, whether radical or conventional, could hope to succeed if it aroused the animosity of '*los americanos*'" (1971, 93). But despite these constraints, certain developments and conditions helped to promote democratization.

During Panama's first three decades as an "independent" republic, the Liberal oligarchy controlled the constitutional political system, albeit with U.S. stewardship. While political contestation and participation were restricted significantly, politics in Panama were perhaps more democratic and constitutional than politics in most parts of the world. Power, both economic and political, was concentrated in the hands of very few people. And the political elite were hesitant to allow the voters to determine the winners in elections. Nevertheless, Liberal elite unity was present and growing, the constitutional order was respected, the armed forces were weak, and elections legitimated elite circulation, even if contestation took place prior to the voting and voting restrictions existed. By the 1920s, new political forces began to emerge on the isthmus that demanded inclusion into the political system. Organized labor, indigenous peoples (particularly the Kuna), and the middle class, represented by Acción Comunal, clamored for political inclusion and participation. Consequently, even as early as the late 1920s, some factors favored the development of greater contestation and participation in Panamanian politics.

As mentioned above, Panama's Liberal elite resisted greater contestation and participation, at least partly because the elite considered most citizens as inferior, or the "other." Ethnic and racial divisions thus worked against the forging of a more comprehensive national unity. To compound matters, the Panamanian state was neither viable nor autonomous, particularly considering its subordinate position vis-à-vis the United States. The political elite were unable to fully promote national integration and development owing to their inability to construct a relatively strong state. Concurrently, Washington helped to weaken the Panamanian state by importing large numbers of workers—non-Panamanians and mainly West Indians—into the isthmus for canal construction and by supporting the Kuna rebellion. And, Washington's unwillingness to help promote the isthmus's economic development or to give in on economic issues meant that the Panamanian state could not carry out necessary national projects and services without going into debt. This foreign domination emasculated the political class, making them feel powerless and prompting them to constantly turn to their protector for advice and approval. External dominance also undermined the democratic process since Panamanian politicians turned to Washington for support as much as to the voters and domestic interest groups. The U.S. government supported the oligarchs for the most part because they protected a broad array of U.S. economic, political, and military interests. As a result, Washington did nothing to promote real political contestation and broader political participation. On the contrary, U.S. policy makers helped to maintain Panama's restricted constitutional government. In sum, Panama's democratic development was hampered by a weak state, ethnic and racial divisions, a low level of socioeconomic development, and an oligarchy that, while Liberal, resisted further contestation and participation. Additionally, U.S. influence and actions inadvertently increased racial and ethnic divisions, weakened the state, promoted oligarchic rule, and limited the political elite's policy options. In the late 1920s, therefore, the balance of forces weighed too heavily against the flowering of democracy.

From the "Good Neighbor" to the End of World War II

The Revolution of 1931 and the Rise of the Middle Sectors, 1930–48

This chapter examines the rise of new political forces devoted to nationalism and political participation in Panama. These new social groups and sectors, mobilized partly by severe economic crisis, posed challenges to both U.S. interests and the oligarchy's control of politics. Two new institutions in particular represented the emerging nationalist and participatory urges: Acción Comunal (Community Action) and the Guardia Nacional (National Guard), institutions that to some extent represented the middle or professional classes. During this period, we begin to see the rise of political processes heretofore alien to Panamanian politics—the overthrow of elected governments and the involvement of the armed forces (National Police) in politics. We also witness heightened U.S. security and hegemonic concerns, stemming from German and Soviet influence in the Americas, which prompted Washington to support antidemocratic forces on the isthmus. These salient changes in both the domestic and international environments pitted isthmian goals of sovereignty and self-determination against U.S. hegemonic and security interests.

The Great Depression and Political Upheaval

President Florencio Arosemena began his administration saddled with economic problems that would grow and lead to political transformation. By the end of 1926, Panama's national debt had grown considerably, to an alarming level of $18,686,000 (McCain 1965, 109). Almost the entire amount was owed to the U.S. government or U.S. private banks. The debt was enormously high partly because Panama sustained a significant trade deficit with the United States, by far its largest trading partner. Soon after taking office, Arosemena asked the National City Bank of New York to form a financial committee to look into Panama's dire economic situation. In September 1929, the advisory group presented its findings and recommendations to President Arosemena, but little was done or could be done to improve the situation, which would be exacerbated by the U.S. stock market crash the following month. The economic catastrophe that paralyzed America in 1929 reverberated across the globe. As demand in the United States dried up, production in most of the world decreased accordingly, leading to shrinking economies and high levels of unemployment. In the Canal Zone, employment dropped by 23 percent in just five years, from a total of 15,712 in mid-1929 to a meager 12,020 in 1934 (Major 1993, 203). Unemployment for those on the Silver Roll meant greater social pressure on a Panamanian government already struggling with a plethora of economic ills.

The economic crisis fueled popular resentment toward the oligarchy's unrelenting grip on isthmian politics. The political crisis was exacerbated by President Arosemena's weakness, since ex-president Rodolfo Chiari and his political faction controlled the new administration from behind the scenes. While he had respected the letter of the constitution by not seeking reelection, as other presidents had done, Chiari was not respecting the spirit of the law, particularly since it was rumored that he was planning on running for the presidency once more in 1932. This potential for continuismo, along with attacks from AC and the press charging the government with fraud and corruption, led to a serious regime crisis. A U.S. military intelligence report assessed that the country operated "very much as gang leaders have been running Chicago" (quoted in Major 1993, 250). The Porrista and Chiarista factions of the Liberal Party firmly controlled politics on the isthmus at this time. The ruling class could be characterized as oligarchic and personalistic, with a distasteful amount of patronage and corruption. During the dire economic crisis, it was more painfully clear that the elite and the state were serving foreign and personal interests rather than the national interest. It was only a matter of time until the middle and working classes would rebel.

By 1930, AC had acquired important new leaders who were tired of the status quo. Two new AC members in particular would become fixtures in Panamanian politics for years to come and symbolize a new feature in isthmian politics—expanded political contestation. Arnulfo and Harmodio Arias were born to a middle-class family in the province of Penonomé, in the interior of Panama. They were ambitious, intelligent men who were able to earn advanced degrees abroad. Arnulfo studied in the United States, eventually going to medical school at Harvard University. Harmodio studied law and political science at Cambridge University, England. The two brothers, like other middle-class Panamanians who joined AC, were "frustrated by a political system dominated by elites and supported by the United States"

(W. Robinson 1999, 158) and would become important new players in the political game, leading to the expansion of contestation and participation in isthmian politics.

On January 2, 1931, several hundred members of AC assaulted and took control of police headquarters and the presidential palace at 2:30 a.m., resulting in Panama's first *golpe de estado*, or coup d'état. While Harmodio hesitated over the timing of the rebellion, Arnulfo clamored for action and led the assault on the Palacio de las Garzas. The "bloodless" golpe was quick and successful, forcing Arosemena's resignation. An odd political machination then occurred that took into consideration the interests of both the U.S. government and AC. The Supreme Court invalidated the 1930 election of vice presidents, putting in power the designados elected in 1928, who were acceptable to Washington and not as repulsive to AC as the official winners. However, AC demanded that outgoing President Arosemena appoint Harmodio Arias as provisional president until Ricardo J. Alfaro, as the new first designate and minister to Washington, could return to Panama to take over the presidency. Although it had criticized Alfaro severely for the failed 1926 Treaty, AC leaders felt that they were now poised to attain victory in the 1932 national elections and thus accepted his presidency. As we have seen, Washington had intervened repeatedly in the past, but on this occasion, when a constitutional government was removed from power for the first time, the U.S. government stood on the sidelines and did nothing. Although the Roosevelt Corollary had been disowned by Secretary of State Charles Evans Hughes, McCain suggests that Washington was probably happy to help "remove an administration that was unfriendly" (1965, 91). Washington was also increasingly concerned about the corruption and personalism in Panamanian politics. Regardless of the possible U.S. motivations, before recognizing the new regime, the U.S. government received guarantees that no major changes in policy would follow the golpe.

Although it came to power unconstitutionally, the new regime presented itself as legitimate, owing to the "illegal" machinations of the Chiari-controlled Arosemena administration. President Alfaro dismissed efforts by foreign governments to offer diplomatic recognition, explaining that recognition was unnecessary since there had not been an interruption of the constitutional order. National elections were then held on June 5, 1932, that were considered free and fair. None of the candidates requested U.S. monitoring, reflecting a change in the informal electoral process. President Alfaro refrained from promoting a candidate, thus eliminating the tradition of the "official" government candidate. Three presidential candidates emerged, all from Liberal Party factions. Harmodio Arias became the candidate of the

Liberal *doctrinarios*. Francisco Arias Paredes carried the banner of the *reformistas*, and Augusto Boyd represented the Chiarista National Liberals. Boyd eventually withdrew from the contest, allowing Harmodio Arias to easily defeat Arias Paredes. Panamanian voters had finally elected as chief executive a man who was not from a traditional oligarchic family, even if he aligned himself with a Liberal faction. And the election provided a choice of candidates, albeit from one fractured political party. The middle class wanted change, but most professionals promoted liberalism.

Not surprisingly, at the same time that Panamanians were manifesting greater nationalistic and antigringo sentiments, American products, values, and customs had already significantly penetrated the isthmus. McCain has expressed the degree of U.S. economic and cultural power in the early 1930s quite well:

> The people of Panama used 15,000,000 sticks of American gum annually, newspapers and shop signs were printed in English, one cabinet member admitted that he thought in English, the Panamanians had nineteen [U.S. made] automobiles for every mile of highway, the Chinese legation labeled its official car in English, and the English-language motion pictures found no great handicap when presented in cosmopolitan Panama. The daughters of *altas familias* [elite families] participated in sports, drove automobiles, and even worked. (1965, 242–43)

This extensive cultural and economic influence, magnified by the existence of the Zone with its American colony and U.S. military contingent, while promoting emulation also fomented a nationalist backlash, particularly at a time when the oligarchy benefited handsomely from its close ties with Uncle Sam and the nation was suffering economically.

President Harmodio Arias, although leading a government that brought new hopes to Panamanians, ruled during the height of the Depression—a time of limited options. The new president could do little more than cooperate fully with Washington on economic issues. But Harmodio Arias embarked upon a bold effort to renegotiate the hated 1903 Treaty that generated intense anti-American sentiment. One year after his inauguration, the new president traveled to Washington, D.C., to press for a new, more equitable relationship. His timing was optimal since earlier that year President Franklin Delano Roosevelt had promulgated the Good Neighbor policy. The new American policy rejected the military interventionism of the Roosevelt Corollary and embraced Latin America's yearning for nonintervention. The new policy, however, in no way diminished U.S. economic penetration of

Latin America. The policy was a reaction to the costly U.S. military interventions and occupations in the Caribbean Basin and to America's "isolationism" during the Great Depression (P. Smith 2000, 68–86). Also, by the early 1930s, the United States had little need to intervene militarily in the region. Washington's economic influence was extensive, regimes were to a large extent pro–United States, and order could be maintained by domestic armed forces and National Guards that had close relations with the U.S. War Department. Washington was also concerned increasingly with political developments in Europe and thus needed harmonious relations with its neighbors to the south. In the mid-1930s, then, America could afford, and needed, to be a good neighbor.

Harmodio Arias's diplomatic efforts resulted in the Hull-Alfaro Treaty of 1936, officially titled the General Treaty on Friendship and Cooperation, signed on March 2. This new interpretation of the 1903 Treaty did not include any language on the issue of U.S. sovereignty over the Canal Zone. The United States government, as it had done with the Platt Amendment two years earlier, also made no mention of the right to intervene for the purpose of guaranteeing isthmian sovereignty. Furthermore, the new accord stated that bilateral consultation and action in the future would serve the mutual quest for order and provide compensation for any future appropriation of property for canal operations or defense. Economically, the U.S. government pledged to prevent the Zone from competing with Panamanian businesses as much as possible, an implicit recognition of the unfairness of the existing economic situation. The annuity paid to Panama for the use and operation of the canal increased from $250,000 in gold to 430,000 balboas, Panama's currency that was equivalent to the U.S. dollar. Finally, the treaty gave Panama greater say over immigration, allowing for some control over the entry of West Indians (Arosemena G. 1997b, 289–329). The new treaty, however, while eliminating the most offensive provision of the 1903 Treaty, the right of intervention, did not go far enough to deflate resentment toward the United States. Moreover, the increase in the annuity did not represent a real economic gain for Panama owing to inflation and devaluation. And U.S. promises of economic fairness seldom materialized. One Panamanian scholar has pointed to eighteen separate occasions when the U.S. government promised Panama something substantial but never kept its promise (Castillero Pimentel 1961, 50–55). Many Panamanians, nevertheless, rejoiced at the benefits of the new accord and Washington's apparently more positive spirit of cooperation. The National Assembly quickly ratified the agreement, but the nationalist U.S. Senate delayed ratification until 1939, when Panamanian cooperation in the war effort was needed and the Senate received assurances that the U.S. government could in fact intervene unilaterally if necessary. As early as 1936, Washington had become increasingly concerned with the penetration of the Axis powers in the hemisphere, supplying some motivation for renegotiating a new relationship with Panama in the first place. Thus, although Panama was successful in convincing Washington to renegotiate the hated 1903 accord, the new agreement yielded little of substance.

The new treaty was not President Arias's only success. The new president took steps to strengthen the Panamanian state and worked to enhance national identity. During his tenure, the Panamanian government continued and started numerous state projects throughout the isthmus. Generally, the Arias government, in addition to attempting to deal with the grave economic crisis, tried to foment industry and business and to cast a limited safety net over the neediest citizens. His efforts to reach out to Panamanians at the lower rungs of society "made him the first Panamanian president whose constituency transcended both race and class lines" (Pearcy 1998, 68). Some of his support came from antillanos, a constituency that AC had started to mobilize in the mid-1920s. A notable accomplishment of the Arias government was the founding of a national university, an institution that would allow more Panamanians to pursue higher education on the isthmus rather than studying abroad. Making the promotion of education into a truly nationalist project, the government also established the Pedagogical Institute to prepare the country's teachers and professors. Up until this point, most teachers were either foreign or educated abroad, making it virtually impossible to socialize the population and engender national identity. Now Panama would be able to begin to develop a national cadre of educators who would potentially be more committed to national development and identity.

President Arias and the National Revolutionary Party that emerged from AC, while nationalistic and critical of the United States, nevertheless promoted reformist rather than revolutionary ideas. Arias continued to cooperate with Washington, and Panama's economic elite was able to preserve their interests under his administration. Other political organizations on the isthmus, however, were calling for more dramatic changes, such as recently established Labor parties with socialist and Marxist-Leninist ideologies. These anticapitalist, anti-Liberal parties were inspired by the Russian and Mexican "revolutionary" governments and called for an end to capitalism, bourgeois democracy, and U.S. dominance. Even AC broke with the Arias government, criticizing their former member for promulgating policies that failed to change the status quo, carrying out blatant nepotism, and protecting the interests of the rich and the United States (Pizzurno Gelós and Araúz 1996, 235–36).

New Political Players: Acción Comunal (Panameñismo) and the National Police

While Harmodio Arias was in the Palacio de las Garzas dealing with the economic crisis, promoting national development, and forging a new relationship with Washington, his brother, Arnulfo, was founding a new political movement with its own indigenous ideology. The National Revolutionary Party, after breaking with Harmodio Arias's regime, adopted *panameñismo* as its guiding philosophy. The party's key slogan, "Panama for Panamanians," was a not-so-subtle attack on antillanos and gringos. Panameñismo, like AC, was reminiscent of APRA in Peru, and Arnulfo became a populist leader akin to APRA's founder and leader Víctor Haya de la Torre. Conveniently, the new party and nationalist ideology, in addition to promoting middle-class interests, nationalism, and anti-Yankee sentiment, would serve the political aspirations of the Arias brothers. The various Liberal factions now had to confront real political contestation coming from the National Revolutionary Party and panameñismo. Liberals and the oligarchy would have to decide between incorporating or repressing these new political institutions and ideas.

The ability to repress would soon be enhanced since yet another important political institution was emerging in the early 1930s. Panama's oligarchy and the United States had controlled and monitored the National Police since the birth of the nation. The oligarchy appointed loyal officers to lead the institution, while the U.S. War Department and U.S. forces stationed on the isthmus advised and kept close relations with the police to ensure U.S. interests were preserved. President Arias, however, began to change the National Police by purging Chiarista officers and replacing them with officers from the middle and working classes. In 1932, he appointed José Antonio Remón to a high post in the National Police. Although from a poor family, Remón, incredibly enough, was the only Panamanian police officer who had been trained at a military academy. Arias also asked Washington to end its official police supervisory role (Harding 2001, 33). These changes transformed the National Police by eliminating the oligarchy's tight control of the institution, weakening U.S. influence, incorporating the middle and lower classes into leadership positions, strengthening the institution's power, and fomenting nationalism within the institution. In effect, in the

1930s, Panama's National Police began to achieve "unprecedented institutional autonomy" (Pearcy 1998, 94). But real autonomy would have to wait, since Remón would soon take control of the institution and would use it to become a major political player in the 1940s. Nevertheless, the country's oligarchy would have to deal with yet one more politically active institution in the ever more complex political milieu.

As President Arias's term came to a close, he chose Juan D. Arosemena, his secretary of foreign relations and a member of the National Liberal Party, as the official presidential candidate. Arnulfo Arias's National Revolutionary Party also backed the official candidate. This election, however, was fraught with fraud and vote tampering. The Supreme Court had ruled that Arosemena could not run for president because he had not resigned as secretary of foreign relations in time. To make matters worse, after the election, the president of the National Electoral Board ruled that the opposition candidate, Domingo Díaz Arosemena, backed by AC and the Liberal Doctrinaire Party, had actually won the election. President Arias was nevertheless able to prevent the ruling from affecting the fraudulent outcome. Consequently, Juan Arosemena assumed the presidency on October 1, 1936. Arnulfismo had now supplanted Chiarismo, allowing continuismo to emerge anew. Although some things seemed to have stayed the same, the 1936 election brought to the fore two new political parties, the National Revolutionary Party and the Panameñista Party, expanding both contestation and participation in isthmian politics. While many of the leaders were of Liberal stripe and origin, the new parties represented the slow rise of the middle and working classes into the political arena. President Arosemena's death brought to power on December 18, 1939, first designate Augusto S. Boyd, also of the National Revolutionary Party and son of one of Panama's founding fathers, Federico Boyd.

State-building efforts continued under the Arosemena and Boyd governments. The Ministry of Labor, Commerce, and Industry was established, creating another cabinet position. To a large extent, the government created this new ministry because of growing consensus among Panama's economic elite and nationalists that industry on the isthmus was dominated by foreign interests, particularly by American companies. The goal of the ministry would be to establish and assist Panamanian industries and businesses. Educational institutions continued to grow with the construction of a high school in Santiago, in the province of Veraguas. Prior to the 1940 national elections, the government established the Jurado Nacional de Elecciones (National Court of Elections).

By the end of the 1930s, important international forces were also dramatically influencing Panamanian politics. Worried about Axis influence in the Western Hemisphere, the United States became increasingly concerned about canal and hemispheric security. At the same time, the oligarchy in Panama feared it would lose its political dominance, since anti-oligarchic groups were on the rise. Washington too feared that the influence of popular organizations would challenge U.S. economic and strategic interests on the isthmus. As a result, Washington and Panama's economic elite increasingly turned to the National Police to preserve the status quo and prevent new political groups and forces from gaining power. A clash of interests was inevitable. As political and social mobilization expanded, resulting in new organizations that called for dramatic changes to the status quo, oligarchs and Washington rallied to preserve their status and interests. Axis threats to U.S. preponderance of power in the region and then U.S. entry into World War II added fuel to the heated political cauldron. Panama was still in an economic crisis despite the improving global economy. By 1939, the government had achieved a small budget surplus, but Panama's foreign debt was still hovering around $18 million. William N. Cromwell resigned as the manager of Panama's $6 million investment in the United States, and Chase National Bank took over the portfolio. From that point on, Panama began to have more access to the so-called Constitutional Fund that the U.S. government "paid" to the isthmus as a result of the 1903 Treaty. However, this sum was in no way enough to put Panama on solid economic footing.

The oligarchy had been able to preserve its interests despite the global economic crisis and the rise to power of Harmodio Arias, the National Revolutionary Party, and AC. In fact, AC had splintered since some of its founders believed that the 1931 "revolution" had been betrayed. The 1940 election, however, would prove to be a watershed event in Panama, unleashing nationalist forces that threatened the increasingly precarious status quo. Prior to the election, opposition candidate Ricardo J. Alfaro withdrew his candidacy, arguing that there were abuses against and insufficient guarantees for the opposition. At one of Alfaro's major political rallies, the National Police and government functionaries, who supported Arias, had dispersed the crowds and torn down a large antiregime banner with Alfaro's image. The opposition eventually asked the United States to intervene and monitor the election. Without electoral opposition or U.S. monitoring, Arnulfo Arias Madrid became Panama's tenth constitutional chief executive in a landslide election. Panameñismo would now become the official ideology of the new Panamanian government, representing a challenge to the dominance of both the oligarchy and the United States.

Unlike his brother, Harmodio, and President Arosemena, President Arnulfo Arias was not content with appeasing the oligarchy and Washington by carrying out minor reforms. He and his party were interested in making a "radical turn in Panama's politics" (LaFeber 1989, 75). In order to accomplish fundamental changes, Arias called for the abrogation of the 1904 constitution and the inauguration of a new, more nationalistic Magna Carta. Rather than follow constitutional procedure, which required that two legislative sessions approve a new law of the land, President Arias called for a national plebiscite to determine whether a new constitution should be written. The "yes" vote triumphed at the polls on December 15, 1940, allowing the Arias-dominated legislature to write a new constitution that the president promulgated on January 2, 1941.

In many ways, the new Panamanian constitution represented a "notable advancement" by including articles that modernized and strengthened state institutions, established social rights, implemented limited land reform, gave women the right to vote, and made secondary education free to all citizens (Fábrega P. 1991, 111). But those who opposed Arias pointed to the new charter's most objectionable features as a way to undermine the new president. For example, the presidential term was lengthened to six years and executive power was strengthened, yielding criticisms that the new statute would promote caudillismo and continuismo. Detractors also deemed the new Magna Carta to be racist since it outlawed the immigration of non-Hispanics. Of particular concern to some Panamanians was the presence of antillanos and Chinese shop owners, who had been imported to the isthmus by the United States and France. While racism certainly played a role, the new statute also spoke to increasing fears that Panamanians were losing out to non-Hispanic or non-Panamanian immigrants. Many of these immigrants had not assimilated or become Hispanicized and thus represented a threat to national identity and integration. Nationalism therefore was an important motivating factor in the new anti-immigrant code. But the oligarchy and the United States were particularly concerned about the new constitution's emphasis on social and national rights. Although private property was protected, the new constitution affirmed that "private interest should cede to the public or social interest and legalized expropriations by the state" (Fábrega P. 1991, 111–12)(my translation). The new constitution also allowed the state to become involved in disputes between labor and business and established work as a social right.

Panama's new charter did not go as far in protecting social needs and limiting private property as the Mexican constitution, but the new document put oligarchs and foreign interests on alert. The Magna Carta of 1941 to a large extent represented a challenge to the classical Liberal doctrine that had been prominent in Panama since the 1800s by asserting the power of the state over private interests. In other words, it attempted to ensure that the oligarchy and foreign interests could not use the nation and its resources for their selfish interests only. Panama was not unique since the assertion of the state over private interests was becoming a global phenomenon, to include the New Deal in the United States. Nationalism and panameñismo had now not only asserted itself on the isthmus as a new political force via new political parties, but it had been able to codify its ideology via the new constitution as well. National law now challenged the interest of both the oligarchy and Washington.

In addition to the important changes incorporated in the new Magna Carta, the Arias government conducted itself in a way that engendered fear and concern in Washington. Arias's speeches were typically classified as "anti-Yankee" or "pro-Axis" by U.S. government officials, who worried that the new president would not defend U.S. interests (Ealy 1951, 110). Prior to Arias's victory, Washington had asked the Panamanian government for over one hundred defense sites outside of the Canal Zone for the purpose of protecting the canal against Nazi incursions in the hemisphere. Arias hesitated in allowing the United States to acquire more territory, however, and, favoring canal neutrality, presented Washington with a series of conditions and demands. Arias then refused to allow the arming of U.S.-owned merchant vessels flying under the Panamanian flag. Curiously enough, the Panamanian merchant marine fleet was extensive because in 1916 U.S. shipping companies began registering their ships in other countries to escape the requirements of the Seaman's Bill, passed by the U.S. Congress to improve the pay and working conditions of U.S. merchant marines. The Panamanian "flag of convenience" prospered again just prior to U.S. entry into World War II. The U.S. government had declared the canal neutral in September 1936, thus preventing U.S. companies from selling goods to, and U.S. ships from supplying, the Allies. Washington then promoted the use of flags of convenience to skirt neutrality and help the Allied war effort (Ealy 1971, 88). As far as Washington was concerned, Arias now represented a major obstacle to the maintenance of U.S. regional power and to the preservation of U.S. interests in Panama. The U.S. government would not tolerate such a leader in Panama. By spring 1941, U.S. Naval Intelligence opined, "the present conditions are considered dangerous to the security of the canal and it is believed that they should be corrected as soon as possible" (quoted in Pearcy 1998, 93). Although U.S. intervention would not be ruled out, Washington preferred that a domestic golpe remove Arias from power.

While it may be valuable and interesting to know whether or not Arnulfo

Arias was a fascist, what is most salient for our analysis is that Arias's actions and attitudes were inimical to U.S. interests at a time when Germany
was challenging U.S. power in the Western Hemisphere. Racism existed in
the United States, and U.S. diplomats would certainly not fault the leader of
a country for attempting to minimize the power of nonwhites. But Arias's
racist nationalism went beyond admiration of *Der Führer* or *Il Duce*, since
it coincided with Spanish Falangist ideology that came into direct conflict
with American interests. Arias's embracing of Hispanidad meant that pro-
Anglo sentiments in Panama would suffer. As William Robinson points out:
"Panameñismo clashed with US strategic military interests" (1999, 164). And
Arias's "revolutionary" direction also clashed with Washington's economic
interests—the protection of U.S. private investment and property on the
isthmus from government interference. If U.S. power were truly preponderant, no leader in a small republic who challenged American economic
and security interests could remain in power, particularly at a time of Great
Power conflict.

The Resurgence of U.S. and Oligarchic Interests

Arnulfo Arias's rhetoric, combined with his threat to oligarchic and American interests, meant that "el Hombre's" days in power would be numbered.
The last straw occurred when Arias threatened the institutional interests
and leadership of the National Police (Harding 2001, 34–35). Arias had attempted to form a separate security force called the Policía Nacional Secreta
(National Secret Police) with a Guatemalan officer as its inspector general.
Leaders of Panama's National Police were also concerned about Arias's re-
fusal to cooperate with Washington on security matters since such cooperation would naturally raise the status of, and funding for, the institution. The
fiery José Remón also resented the Arias brothers since they had on two
occasions attempted to limit his powers (Guevara Mann 1996, 62–63). Two
prominent leaders, Remón—at the time police chief of Panama City—and
soon-to-be-president Ricardo de la Guardia conspired to oust the president.
Arnulfo Arias provided the perfect opportunity for the plotters by flying to
Havana, Cuba, on October 7, 1941, supposedly to visit a mistress, without
following constitutional procedure that required presidents to inform the
Supreme Court when traveling out of the country. U.S. intelligence officials
tipped off the golpistas, and almost immediately the National Police and disgruntled ministers moved against "el Hombre." The Supreme Court deemed
the presidency as vacant. The first designate, Dr. José Pezet, immediately
resigned, sensing the obvious movement to remove Arias from power. The

second designate, Ernesto Jaén Guardia, was then appointed president, but he resigned as well. The third designate was in Peru, so the minister of government and justice Ricardo de la Guardia, who also supervised the National Police, became Panama's new chief executive (Ortega C. 1965, 67–69).

De la Guardia was like a breath of fresh air for both the oligarchy and Washington. He was a pro-U.S. businessman from an oligarchic family, a true *rabiblanco*.[1] Owing to his close association with Remón, de la Guardia could also count on support from the National Police. Once in power, the new president elevated Remón to second in command of the police, making a countergolpe nearly impossible. Panama quickly gave Washington all the military installations it wanted, a total of 134, and allowed U.S. merchant ships to be armed. In violation of the neutrality principle, Panama also allowed the U.S. government to use Canal Zone ports to supply the Allies in the war effort against the Axis powers (Ealy 1951, 106–7). Soon after the Japanese attacked Pearl Harbor, the Panamanian government declared war against the Axis powers and allowed the U.S. government to increase its military presence and activities on the isthmus dramatically, both in and out of the Zone. The U.S. government acquired important installations, such as the Río Hato air base, comprising 20,000 acres and a 9,000–foot airstrip, radar stations throughout the county, and a navy PT-boat installation on Taboga Island. Panama also gave the U.S. Rubber Development Corporation monopoly over its rubber production (Ealy 1951, 118). Panama rounded up suspected Germans (as it had done in World War I) as well as Japanese and Italians living on the isthmus, seized their property and businesses, and shipped them off to America (Ealy 1951, 89–90). While the United States was at war with the Axis powers, Panama cooperated with Washington completely, ignoring the neutrality principle and its quest for independence.

Despite unprecedented cooperation, the U.S. government kept a very close watch on the new government. To be fair, as with many other oligarchs, de la Guardia was pro–United States, but he nevertheless expected some gratitude and concessions from the United States in return. Panama received a variety of benefits for its cooperation and generosity. The U.S. government, for example, turned over to Panama some land close to Panama City and Colón that the Panama Railroad had controlled; built a road to Río Hato and one linking Panama City with Colón;[2] provided some economic concessions; and carried out a variety of other public works (Castillero Reyes 1995, 253). De la Guardia's cooperation was also not without limits. Washington wanted 999–year leases on the new defense sites, but de la Guardia insisted that the new facilities remain under U.S. control for no more than one year after the end of hostilities. By this time, the oligarchs knew that popular opinion and nationalist sectors would not stand for unbridled Panamanian generosity toward the United States. Although the middle sectors had failed to keep control of the political system, panameñismo was emerging as a viable force on the political landscape.

On the home front, however, de la Guardia ignored the most nationalistic Arias policies associated with panameñismo, which gained him support from the National Police and Washington but led to some popular unrest. He also called for the establishment of a constituent assembly with the goal of replacing the 1941 constitution with a less strident and controversial charter. On December 29, 1944, a presidential decree suspended the 1941 statute and authorized the election of a constituent assembly in which all political parties would participate, a notably more democratic manner through which to produce a new law of the land. But de la Guardia did not discard the Arias constitution until after taking advantage of the new six-year presidential term. The National Assembly had anticipated selecting an official interim president in 1943, but de la Guardia, backed by Remón and Washington, maintained himself in power. To ensure stability and protect U.S. interests in Panama in time of war, Washington provided assistance, equipment, and training to the National Police. Such support gave the police even more power and allowed Remón to enhance his influence. Although de la Guardia had a small constituency, the National Police, strengthened by U.S. aid, effectively "stifled the president's opponents and perpetuated his presidency" (Pearcy 1998, 97). The oligarchy and Washington would not allow contestation and unlimited political participation when vital interests were at stake, thus militating against democratic development. With de la Guardia in charge, Panama's oligarchy "regained control of the nation's government," albeit precariously (Pearcy 1998, 94). At the same time, however, the golpe against Arias had the effect of placing nationalistic students into the fore of political activism and opposition. In 1944, disgruntled students in Panama City formed the Federación de Estudiantes de Panamá (Federation of Panamanian Students), or FEP. Even though Arnulfo Arias had gone into exile, panameñismo had become a strong force on the isthmus, and segments of the middle class were fuming at the loss of the "revolution of 1931." De la Guardia's government came under increased and intense opposition, forcing the National Assembly, on June 15, 1945, to select Enrique A. Jiménez as provisional president. Jiménez was a member of the Partido Liberal Nacional (National Liberal Party) but had the support of most major political groups. Like de la Guardia, however, Jiménez was a man from the traditional oligarchy upon whom Washington could rely. The change of presidents was a means to appease the opponents without really changing the status quo.

The canal, and thus Panama, was a key asset for the United States during World War II. The waterway not only facilitated the movement of troops and ships to the war effort but served as a critical line of communication for supplies and goods. In 1947, the Zone government estimated that the U.S. government had saved approximately $1.5 billion in maritime costs during the war years by using the canal (Pizzurno Gelós and Araúz 1996, 302). Owing to the war effort, U.S. businesses on the isthmus also prospered. The number of U.S. business enterprises between 1929 and 1943 increased by more than 3.5 times, to a total of seventy-nine (LaFeber 1989, 78). World War II also helped to stimulate the Panamanian economy, thus ameliorating somewhat the negative effects of the Great Depression. Between 1939 and 1946, some of Panama's principal exports almost doubled (LaFeber 1989, 78). Expanded U.S. activities on the isthmus also brought profits to local businesses since the Zone commissaries could handle only so much commercial activity, particularly during wartime scarcity. The U.S. defense facilities scattered throughout the isthmus also brought some increased economic activity to several areas in Panama's interior. The canal was so important during World War II, in fact, that the U.S. government began work on a third set of locks, requiring the importation of thousands of workers but also providing jobs for some Panamanians. The economic growth and activity prompted by World War II gave the new government some much-needed breathing room, particularly since nationalist forces were still alive and kicking on the isthmus. Nevertheless, Panama continued to suffer from the commissary and base exchange systems that purchased almost all of their goods and merchandise from the United States. Part of Panama's economic bonanza during the war years derived from the scarcity of goods and merchandise imported from the United States and Europe, thus forcing isthmian elites to purchase more domestic products and goods. In effect, the war was generating some degree of industrialization and thus socioeconomic development. As the oligarchy regained its brief loss of power, with U.S. help, Panamanian society was changing to an extent that repression would become increasingly costly. The strengthened National Police would help to repress more effectively, but social mobilization quickly outpaced the weak state's repressive capabilities.

In October 1945, Arnulfo Arias returned from exile, and the political situation on the isthmus entered a unique period during which presidents came and went almost every year. The traditional oligarchic system lost the scant legitimacy it retained once World War II imperatives ended. The middle class, however, did not constitute a unified force, and none of the new sectors was sufficiently powerful on its own, save the National Police, to take control of the political system. Owing to the dramatic decolonization that occurred globally after World War II, nationalist forces on the isthmus increasingly viewed the United States as an imperialist, colonial power. Despite the emerging postwar instability, Washington had to keep Panama at arm's length, particularly since the Good Neighbor policy proscribed direct military intervention. Washington thus turned to the National Police, now led by Remón, to ensure that order and stability reigned on the isthmus. As long as Remón, a "pro-Yankee opportunist" (Guevara Mann 1994, 53), protected U.S. interests, Washington would work with him to ensure domestic tranquility, regardless of the deleterious effects of militarism on democratic development. Washington in effect helped to maintain the concentration of power and the militarization of politics during a time when emerging middle sectors should have been incorporated into the political system. In the immediate post–World War II period, democracy was stymied on the isthmus by an alliance between the weak oligarchy, the National Police, and the United States.

In December 1945, an attempt by a youth movement in Colón to take over military barracks prompted the government to arrest Arnulfo Arias, despite his claims of innocence. Arias remained in prison for over seven months. To ensure that Arias did not reenter the political arena while a new constitution was drafted, the U.S. government placed FBI agents as advisors to the secret police and at the U.S. embassy for the stated purpose of preventing the rise of "subversive elements" (quoted in Major 1993, 270).

On March 1, 1946, with "el Hombre" conveniently out of the way, Panama's third constitution was finally promulgated. The new charter retained some important reforms incorporated in the 1941 constitution but eliminated the most contentious provisions of the Arias Magna Carta, particularly the centralization of authority in the hands of the chief executive and the controversial anti-immigration provisions. The changes were sufficient to relieve the anxiety of the Panamanian economic elite and the United States. The new constitution modernized and liberalized the state by promoting separation of powers and judicial independence. Like the 1941 charter, the new constitution gave women the right to vote. The new law also brought back the four-year presidential term and instituted the direct election of vice presidents, as part of presidential slates. To appease Washington and the oligarchy, the new charter attempted to balance individual property rights with social rights. The 1946 constitution enjoyed a great deal of legitimacy since it was the result of a legal project under the direction of three leading Panamanian jurists: Ricardo J. Alfaro, Eduardo Chiari, and José D. Moscote. Additionally, the new law of the land was extensively debated and ratified by a constituent assembly that was freely elected by an expanded electorate (see Fábrega P., 1991, 118–75). Panama could now boast a modern constitution steeped in liberal ideas but also providing social guarantees. Unfortunately, at the same time such a document went into effect, the economic and political situation on the isthmus once again became increasingly problematic and volatile, leading to less rather than more democracy.

Postwar Depression, Political Discord, and Cold War Geopolitics

The economic boom engendered by World War II turned into a bust with Germany and Japan's surrender in May and August 1945. The quick decline in U.S. commercial and military activity on the isthmus led to a commensurate decline in jobs and prosperity, eventually resulting in economic depression. Although the Jiménez administration had inherited an unprecedented budget surplus, by the end of the 1940s, Panama entered into a severe economic crisis that fueled high levels of nationalism and resentment toward America. The isthmus had cooperated fully during the war against the Axis powers, but now Washington was turning its back on its good neighbor. Despite economic woes, Panama continued to expand the state. During the Jiménez administration, the campus of the University of Panama was built; Tocumen National Airport was constructed; customshouses in the ports of Colón and Panama City were established; and the Colón Free Zone was inaugurated. The new Labor Ministry established a modern labor code; and the National Economic Council was founded for the purpose of advising the National Assembly and the president on economic policy. Ropp has pointed out that after World War II, as with many other countries, including the United States, Panama's state experienced a period of "rapid expansion" (1982, 29). Prior to this period of government expansion, Panama's state was extremely weak, since the national elite were followers of classic liberalism, the military had been eliminated, and U.S. influence hindered the development of autonomous state institutions (Ropp 1982, 29). As it grew, the state bureaucracy's interests would increasingly coincide with the interests of the middle and nationalistic sectors.

Almost immediately after the end of World War II, Panama and the United States became engaged in a conflict over the 134 defense installations that the de la Guardia government had offered Washington in a 1942 agreement. Owing to increasing concerns about the Soviet Union and international communism, the United States wanted to renew the leases on many of these installations, particularly the Río Hato air base. In August 1946, the U.S. government informed Panama of its desire to renegotiate the 1942 base agreement that required the United States to vacate those facilities one year after the end of hostilities. The Jiménez government rejected the proposal since Washington wanted long leases, some as long as ninety-nine years. The Panamanian position, promoted by foreign minister Ricardo J. Alfaro, was that the leases should last no longer than one year, as was becoming the norm internationally. Negotiations continued for over one year, during which time U.S. defense experts became less convinced of the necessity of the Panama bases for canal defense (see Major 1993, 319, 323). Nevertheless, Washington's tenacity and pressure won out, but only after the U.S. government relented on the length of the leases. The Jiménez government eventually accepted the Filós-Hines Agreement that allowed the U.S. government to keep only fourteen defense installations. Consistent with Panama's constitution, however, the new base agreement had to be ratified by the National Assembly that was increasingly responsive to public opinion. As expected, nationalist groups rallied in opposition to the accord, including the University of Panama, the National Institute, the Federation of Panamanian Students, the Youth Patriotic Front, the Association of National Educators, and the National Union of Women, among others. Prominent Panamanians also supported these groups, including ex-presidents Ricardo J. Alfaro, who had resigned as foreign minister, and Harmodio Arias. The National Police repressed several demonstrations against the agreement but could not intimidate the large numbers of nationalistic, anti-U.S. demonstrators. This popular mobilization compelled the National Assembly to unanimously reject the new base agreement on December 22, 1947. Participatory democracy, it seemed, had won the day. The U.S. government announced quickly that it would vacate the defense sites immediately. Washington most likely realized that the defense sites were less important to canal defense than the potential for an anti-U.S., anti-oligarchic social explosion on the isthmus.

Panama's rejection of the 1946 Filós-Hines Agreement occurred at a time when the United States was charting out a new foreign policy consensus centered on the containment of communism. The Soviet-communist threat had quickly replaced the fascist threat. Arias had been seen by Washington as a possible promoter of fascist ideology on the isthmus, but he was ushered from power quickly, and now fascism had been roundly defeated at the global level. The Soviet Union, however, now represented not only a challenge to U.S. military superiority in the post–World War II world but threatened to promote an ideology that was the direct antithesis of democratic capitalism. Domestically, the Russians promoted centralized political systems controlled by a communist party and the replacement of capitalism by a socialist economy controlled by the state. The Soviet Union thus represented a clear threat to the U.S. quest for hegemony since the Russians were attempting to establish a preponderance of power in certain spheres of influence and promoting an ideology that would undermine the U.S. model of capitalism and democracy. With the Truman Doctrine, Washington took up the leadership of the "free world" and committed itself to stalling any further Soviet advancement worldwide.

Even though in the early stages of the cold war the Western Hemisphere seemed to be relatively free from Soviet influence, America took no chances. Washington organized the first post–World War II mutual defense treaty in the Americas with the signing of the Rio Treaty on September 2, 1947. The twenty-one nations of the hemisphere promised to defend each other if attacked by an external aggressor, namely the communist Soviet Union. Soon thereafter, on April 30, 1948, the nations of the region signed the charter establishing the Organization of American States (OAS) in Bogotá, Colombia. The Bolivarian Dream would ironically be led by the colossus to the north. While the nations of the hemisphere understood that the OAS would be dominated by the United States, they nevertheless were reassured by the inclusion of the principle of nonintervention in the founding charter. Panama, still under oligarchic control, was a willing participant in and signatory to both the Rio Treaty and Bogotá Charter.

On May 9, 1948, Panama held the first direct presidential election since 1940, when Arias was elected but quickly ushered out of the Palacio de las Garzas by the oligarchy and the National Police. This first election under the 1946 constitution pitted several candidates against one another, owing to the increase in nonoligarchic political parties. The oligarchy's candidate was Domingo Díaz Arosemena, a businessman educated at Seton Hall College in New Jersey and a member of the Liberal Doctrinaire Party. Despite his rabiblanco credentials, Díaz had participated in the 1931 revolution. Arnulfo Arias ran under the banner of his new party, the Partido Revolucionario Auténtico (Authentic Revolutionary Party). Candidates were also fielded by the Partido Renovador (Renovation Party), the Partido Nacional Revolucionario (National Revolutionary Party), the Partido Socialista (Socialist Party), and Union Popular (Popular Union). The expanding contestation was overwhelmingly nationalist, anti-oligarchic, and anti-imperialist. For the first time, the vice presidents would run as part of the presidential slate rather than being elected by the National Assembly. Panama seemed poised to finally establish a more inclusive polyarchy. Despite poverty and financial and economic crisis, Panamanian society had become considerably more complex, educated, and organized by the end of World War II. This socio-economic development had given rise to numerous middle- and working-class organizations that demanded inclusion into the political system. The new political actors wanted both to participate politically and to contest political power. While they did not share a common ideology, they were all nationalistic and thus anti-U.S. and anti-oligarchic at heart.

Owing to greater contestation and participation, distrust, the politicization of the National Police, and the cold war environment, the election was marred by violence and irregularities. Since the National Police had become an autonomous political actor, the political parties had responded by organizing their own security forces, commonly referred to as shock troops. In early July, the National Election Board provided preliminary election results that put Arnulfo Arias in the lead by about 1,500 votes (Pizzurno Gelós and Araúz 1996, 341). Fearing that the oligarchy would steal the election, Arias and his followers organized a golpe against the Jiménez administration. The government, with support from Remón and the National Police, responded by suspending constitutional guarantees. The National Assembly then attempted to carry out a legislative golpe by electing a new president and vice presidents, but the Supreme Court ruled that the legislators had acted unconstitutionally. While Arias feared that the election would be stolen from him, pro-oligarchy legislators feared that the government would honor the electoral outcome, thus bringing "el Hombre" back into the Palacio de las Garzas. The big surprise came on July 30, when the National Election Board announced Díaz as the winner with just over 2,300 votes more than Arias (Pizzurno Gelós and Araúz 1996, 343). Arias fled quickly to Costa Rica. The political situation did not improve. In the next four years, five presidents would occupy the Palacio.

The Imperatives of Regional Security and the Rise of New Sectors

The Great Depression represented an ideological blow to capitalism and liberalism. The Western industrialized democracies declined in both power and prestige. The rise of fascism posed a challenge to democracy and capitalism as dominant global ideologies. While some countries in Latin America, particularly Argentina and Chile, looked to Italy, Spain, and Germany as potential models for their societies, Panama continued its unnaturally close association with the United States. Although Panama's oligarchy and new middle sectors called for changes to the U.S.-Panamanian relationship, Washington still unduly influenced isthmian domestic and foreign policy. America continued to enjoy its preponderance of power in the hemisphere, but owing to the rise of fascism and the looming cold war, a consolidated, regional U.S. hegemony would have to wait until a time when capitalism and democracy could capture the hearts and minds of the region.

In the two decades after the Great Depression, democratic development was both strengthened and undermined. Perhaps one of the most important lessons to be learned in the study of democratization is that the causes or preconditions of democracy do not always co-vary positively in an eventual stop at polyarchy. Beginning in the 1920s, nascent socioeconomic development led to the rise of stronger middle and working classes. These nationalistic sectors became sufficiently strong to challenge the oligarchy's monopoly over the political process, beginning with the 1930 "revolution" and culminating in Arnulfo Arias's election to the presidency in 1940. Nationalist forces also pressured the government to reject the 1947 Filós-Hines Agreement with the United States, representing at least some degree of political independence in foreign policy. These were very positive changes since both contestation and participation were enhanced. Nationalist groups like Acción Comunal also contributed to the development of greater national unity, but Arias's presidency at the same time exacerbated ethnic and racial divisions in Panama.

As Dahl suggests, when those in power are pressed to allow for contestation and participation, they can either accede or repress (1971). In Panama, the oligarchy, with U.S. assistance, decided to repress and to oust the middle sectors from power. Arias's brief presidency in 1940–41 provides the ultimate example. Although Arias was by no means a revolutionary, the oligarchy and the National Police feared that "el Hombre" would undermine their privileges, while Washington dreaded that Arias would not cooperate with U.S. strategic interests. Panama's oligarchy was still Liberal at heart, but the rise of middle- and working-class sectors frightened them to such an extent that they called for the National Police and the United States to help them control these new forces. Consequently, an unfortunate turn of events for the development of democracy was the rise of a stronger, politicized National Police led by a dominant personality, José Remón. The balance of power, therefore, shifted toward the oligarchy and the concentration of political power owing to the increased repressive power of the state that was encouraged and assisted by Washington. At the same time, state institutions other than the police were significantly weakened by the economic depression and the emerging political conflict.

From the Cold War to the End
of the "Special Relationship"

Twilight of the Oligarchy and the Onset of Military Rule, 1949–68

The initial years of the cold war witnessed the end of the oligarchy's political control in Panama, an end to the "special" U.S.-Panamanian relationship, and the absolute breakdown of democracy on the isthmus. The cold war period, beginning officially with the promulgation of the Truman Doctrine and National Security Directive 47, was a time of superpower conflict, with global resonance. Naturally, Panama could not escape being caught in this conflict, principally because of its strategic importance and close association with the United States. First, under the policy of containment, Washington became preoccupied with national security and anticommunism. Heightened security concerns prompted Washington to establish unnaturally close ties with the armed forces of Latin America, providing them with equipment and training and promoting a security doctrine that focused on the maintenance of internal order (Sánchez 2003a). Although Washington saw the Western Hemisphere as relatively safe from communist influence, the reformist Arbenz government in Guatemala in the early 1950s, and then the more radical Castro regime in the early 1960s, brought the cold war to the Americas. Because the cold war was also an ideological conflict, the political decay that was already emerging on the isthmus was exacerbated as some counterelites who rejected U.S. leadership began to look toward Cuba and socialism as models. After the 1959 Cuban Revolution, those who questioned America's leadership were provided with an alternative model of political and economic development that eschewed U.S. dominance. Anti-U.S. groups were inspired, and Washington worked harder to maintain order through closer ties with the region's militaries. In this polarized and militarized context, democratic development was practically impossible, and democratic breakdown became the norm. Within this bitter global dispute, Panama's already troubled democracy suffered a monumental setback in 1968, when the National Guard took control of the political system directly. Since the oligarchy was unable to ensure social order, Panama's armed forces took the reins of power, much to the eventual delight of Washington.

The Díaz Arosemena Presidency and the Chaotic Aftermath

Domingo Díaz Arosemena was president for less than one year, owing to his declining health. During his short, chaotic tenure, he approved a civil aviation agreement with the United States that nationalistic sectors roundly criticized. The accord, signed on March 31, 1949, established ground rules and reciprocity between the United States and Panama and governed the use of the new Tocumen Airport east of Panama City. The agreement would allow U.S. commercial flights to operate out of Tocumen rather than out of Albrook Field, a U.S. Air Force facility. While the aviation agreement was not particularly injurious to the isthmus, popular mistrust arose because the negotiations were conducted in secret. Student demonstrators, led by FEP, took to the streets and clashed with the National Police, resulting in two deaths and dozens of casualties (Pearcy 1998, 138). The National Assembly nevertheless ratified the accord on April 12. The "Usurper," as Díaz became known, also had to deal with several conspiracies to oust him from power. In one attempt, the secret police discovered a shipment of weapons and accused Harmodio Arias of sedition. The Díaz government acquired the incriminating evidence from the National Police, which had received it from U.S. Army Intelligence. At this point, the U.S. embassy in Panama surmised that relations between the U.S. military and the National Police had "never been better" (quoted in Major 1993, 85). On April 25, 1949, the National Assembly declared a state of siege and suspended constitutional guarantees, paving the way for Harmodio Arias's arrest. Making domestic matters worse, the post–World War II economic crisis forced the Díaz administration to make large cuts in government spending and to reduce the salaries of government workers, including teachers. As a result, it was virtually impossible for the government to carry out any major public works projects.

Díaz's declining health brought the first designado, Daniel Chanis, a medical doctor, to the presidency on July 28, 1949. President Chanis attempted to bring the nation back to constitutional order, but in less than four months Colonel Remón forced him to vacate the presidential palace. The National Assembly had begun to investigate a variety of business dealings in the country, including the beef industry, in which Remón had acquired a monopoly in beef slaughtering. A special legislative commission found numerous violations and problems with the industry, prompting the new president to call for Remón's resignation as commander of the National Police. Instead, the colonel was able to force Chanis to resign the presidency after the police besieged the Palacio de las Garzas. Remón was already demonstrating his personal power and the increasing influence of Panama's strengthened police force. Although some have argued that militarism has always been a characteristic of Panamanian politics (see, for example, Harding 2001), it was not until the rise of a stronger National Police under Remón, aided by Washington, that the police/armed forces became highly politicized and a decisive political actor.

Remón's aggressive move against Chanis put the colonel's cousin and second designado, Roberto F. Chiari, into the Palacio as the new interim president. But he lasted a mere five days since Remón's political machinations were becoming so blatant that the Supreme Court and even Chiari supported a move to return Chanis to the presidential palace. A group of legislators and "citizens" accompanied Chanis in a march to reclaim the presidency, but the police confronted the marchers, leaving behind a dead six-year-old boy and thirteen injured, including two legislators (Pizzurno Gelós and Araúz 1996, 362). A strike was called, and many sectors demanded the resignation of Colonel Remón and his second in command, Bolívar Vallarino. The National Police was now too powerful, however, to be dislodged from power. In a surprising move, Remón pushed for Arnulfo Arias to become president. The strongman hoped that bringing back "el Hombre" would deflate several nationalist sectors and lead to more popular support for the National Police. To legitimize Arias's presidency, Remón reconvened the National Election Board, which then made the unexpected announcement that Arias had in fact won the 1948 election. The hasty recount put Arias ahead of Díaz by just over 2,500 votes (Pearcy 1998, 139).

The second Arias presidency, beginning on November 25, 1949, like the first one, was troubled and ended earlier than scheduled. But Arias had acquired some valuable experience since his earlier stint as president. Initially, some countries, including of course the United States, hesitated to recognize his government. U.S. ambassador Monnett B. Davis was angry at the startling political outcome and was sure that Arias once again would prove to be a problem for U.S. interests. The ambassador warned the U.S. secretary of state: "His [Arias's] dictatorship can be expected to be absolute and I am confident he will cooperate with our enemies to our embarrassment" (quoted in Major 1993, 86). But by now Arias was aware that antagonizing Washington was not conducive to a long tenure, so he quickly announced his anticommunist credentials. In April 1950, his cabinet went as far as issuing a decree outlawing the communist People's Party as well as prohibiting any communists, loosely defined, from acquiring government jobs. The decree stated: "All propaganda, activity, or agitation of a Communist character is contrary to the democratic regime of the Republic" (quoted in Ealy 1951, 168). Arias also supported the U.S. government at the outbreak of the Korean conflict, in June 1950, by volunteering to send a Panamanian military contingent and offering the use of the Río Hato air base. Arias agreed as well to pay some indemnities to the U.S. government for claims that went as far back as 1915. It seemed that Arias, the ardent nationalist, had finally succumbed to U.S. power and influence or at least learned how to appease the colossus to the north. But Washington was still leery and would wait to see how Arias would continue to behave.

Even though he had temporarily placated Washington, serious domestic problems besieged Arias. The economic-financial situation had not improved, meaning that the government could not satisfy demands for public services. Public opinion was no longer on his side as it had been during his first presidency, principally because Remón had placed him in power by dubious means. And his political party no longer controlled the National Assembly. It was virtually impossible in this context for the Arias government to put in place significant reforms and an economic development program. Arias was able, however, to pass legislation that ended the monopolistic practices in the beef-slaughtering industry in which commanders Remón and Vallarino were involved. He also reestablished an independent secret police responsible directly to the president. These successes were perhaps part of a deal that Arias had made with the two commanders, since the National Police did not move against him (Pizzurno Gelós and Araúz 1996, 363–69).

Arias's undoing came after he tried once again to change the rules of the political game. He argued that drastic changes were necessary to generate economic development and to refinance the national debt. On May 7, 1951, President Arias abrogated the 1946 constitution and put his 1941 Magna Carta into force once more. With this decree, he also closed down the National Assembly and the Supreme Court. Opposition was instant and from all quarters. Arias had also been jailing opponents, using subversion and anticommunism as reasons for his repression. Scores of Panamanians, even students and teachers who in the past had been ardent panameñistas, took to the streets. Demonstrations and rallies deteriorated into violence, since at first Colonel Remón and the National Police backed Arias. At one conflagration, a shoot-out ensued between a group of legislators and the Secret Police. Eventually a civic work stoppage was called, and teachers and students went on strike. The public seemed to have lost their support for Arnulfo Arias.

The crisis ended with Arias's ouster from power and his public trial. The

National Police once again demonstrated its critical role as powerbroker on the isthmus. Colonel Remón finally turned on Arias after opposition to his government was nearly universal and when Arias's men shot two National Police officers who had been dispatched to the presidential palace to let him know that the National Assembly had removed him from power. Remón then sent the National Police to the Palacio to arrest Arias and succeeded only after a lengthy exchange of gunfire that left nine dead, hundreds wounded, and over one thousand arrested (Pizzurno Gelós and Araúz 1996, 372). As Arias was escorted out of the Palacio, he shouted defiantly, "*volveremos!*" (we shall return!). El Hombre was tried by the National Assembly for murder and abuse of power. During the trial, Arias showed his contempt for the proceedings by reading the book *Kon Tiki*. Arias was jailed and banned permanently from public office, but, true to his word, he would return again and again.

Alcibiades Arosemena, the first designado and a businessman, took over the presidency on May 10, 1951, while Arias was still in the Palacio trying to hang on to power. Much of Arosemena's term in office was dominated by the upcoming presidential election. His government was manipulated by Remón, who had amassed not only military and political power but economic power as well. Arosemena finished out a four-year presidential period that saw five chief executives in the Palacio de las Garzas, so the nation was now principally concerned with seeing who would be the next elected chief executive. Despite turning to the International Monetary Fund (IMF) and International Bank for Reconstruction and Development (later to become the World Bank), Arosemena was unable to resolve Panama's dire economic condition. Likewise, the new president did not have the political support or autonomy to resolve the chaotic political situation, despite the fact that his cabinet represented all political parties, save for Arias's. To pacify popular opposition, Arosemena announced a political amnesty in February 1952, allowing Arnulfo Arias to return to the political scene.

Indeed, the political scene had changed dramatically in the last decade. The National Guard headed by Colonel Remón had ascended to the pinnacle of political power, an uncharacteristic militarism on the isthmus. The oligarchy had lost most of its legitimacy and political dominance. The middle sectors had attempted to rule but had failed to achieve any kind of consensus, political program, or cohesive political organization. Arias, who could perhaps best represent the middle class and professionals, had failed to rule in a way that increased his mass following. The United States, while still meddling in Panama's affairs, mostly covertly and economically, had remained on the sidelines at least in terms of direct military intervention. Such a chaotic political context invited the rise of a strongman.

To add fuel to the political fire, toward the end of 1951 the United States government was increasingly concerned about communist influence in the Western Hemisphere. Communist political parties were gaining momentum, and Washington was concerned about the "leftist" nature of the Arbenz government in Guatemala. In December, U.S. ambassador John C. Wiley had concluded that the U.S. government should back Colonel Remón as president of Panama since he was "the sole anti-Communist leader in the entire political panorama" (quoted in Major 1993, 275). Remón was also the only individual who could presumably ensure social order, so important to U.S. interests on the isthmus. In October 1951, the colonel resigned as commander of the National Police and put together a coalition of political parties, Coalición Patriótica Nacional (National Patriotic Coalition) that included the National Revolutionary Party, the Authentic Revolutionary Party, the Renovation Party, the Liberal Party, and the Popular Union. Washington not only helped to promote the rise of Remón's influence in Panamanian politics but supported his ascendance to the presidency as well. Likewise, the oligarchy preferred Remón over the possibility that revolutionary forces would take control of the political system.

The Remón Presidency

The 1952 presidential election pitted Colonel Remón against his cousin Roberto F. Chiari, who had fallen out of favor with the police commander. Chiari's coalition, named the Coalición Civilista (Civil Coalition), brought together the National Liberal Party, the Independent Revolutionary Party, the Patriotic Front, and the Socialist Party. Despite Remón's brute power and some support for his political coalition, his electoral victory was partly the product of his overt control of the National Elections Board. Arias had given support to Remón's candidacy at first but bowed out before the election, forcing the colonel to use his clout with the Elections Board to ensure victory. The political fault line was clear at this time—those who favored Remón and those who opposed him. When the colonel's candidacy was announced, three government ministers resigned in protest. Despite the polarization, the election was devoid of major violence, and on June 1, the final results gave Remón a resounding victory, 133,208 votes against only 78,094 for Chiari (Pizzurno Gelós and Araúz 1996, 381).

On October 1, 1952, Colonel José Antonio Remón Cantera became Panama's twelfth constitutional president, sworn in by his brother, Alejandro Remón, president of the National Assembly and a lieutenant colonel in the National Police. The colonel would become an interesting and perplexing president. As the commander of the National Police for many years, Remón had a definite nationalist streak. Commenting on the colonel's values, the distinguished statesman Ricardo J. Alfaro wrote: "He always knew how to sustain the Panamanian point of view with admirable lucidity and energy" (quoted in Zentner 1984, 102)(my translation). He tried to become a populist like Argentina's Juan Perón, and his wife, Cecilia, even took on an Eva Perón–like role by catering to the downtrodden. But Remón's populism went only so far since he was tied by marriage, money, and some lineage to the nation's oligarchy. And he served Washington's cold war interests well by maintaining order, preserving key American interests on the isthmus and keeping anti-U.S. and progressive groups out of the political game, often using repression. In fact, after he was elected, Washington "immediately cranked up aid programs" to Panama (Conniff 1992, 106). Colonels, like oligarchs, were good for U.S. business and U.S. security needs. While Remón's nationalism appeared minimal compared to other nationalists, the colonel would nevertheless feel uncomfortable constantly sacrificing the nation's interests to the interests of the oligarchy and Washington.

One year after becoming president, Remón strengthened and militarized the National Police. In December 1953, the National Assembly passed a law establishing the Guardia Nacional (National Guard), a pseudomilitary organization that subsumed the existing National Police, with a force of about 2,500. The law also divided the isthmus into military zones. The loyal Colonel Vallarino became the Guardia's new commander, but as commander in chief, Remón retained ultimate control. The new institution received more financial attention, with higher salaries and greater benefits, such as disability pay. In addition, Remón's government made it a crime to insult a member of the Guardia. Although it had promoted Panama's demilitarization since 1904, Washington now supported this move toward militarization with alacrity, and most likely even pushed for such a change. Remón was from the same mold as other Latin American dictators that Washington had carefully groomed, such as Fulgencio Batista in Cuba, Anastasio Somoza in Nicaragua, and Rafael Trujillo in the Dominican Republic. These military strongmen took control of their respective political systems, with Washington's blessings and assistance, at a time of social mobilization and agitation from leftist groups, since American interests zeroed in on maintaining the pro-U.S. status quo and keeping anti-U.S. leftist groups out of the political process. To guarantee its interests on the isthmus, where political decay could emerge at any moment, Washington established close and friendly links to the country's security forces, which were "the key to the political situation" (quoted in Guevara Mann 1994, 71)(my translation). Washington had kept a close eye on Remón for many years, since he received training in the United States as early as 1941. So, in 1953, Washington gave the newly established Guardia $100,000 under the Military Assistance Program (Harding 2001, 40). In the years to come, Guardia personnel would increasingly get their training in the Canal Zone or in the United States, thus solidifying the ties between the U.S. military establishment and the Guardia's corporate leadership. These arrangements were deemed essential by John Foster Dulles, the rabid anticommunist who became U.S. secretary of state in January 1953. These actions of course severely undermined democratic development by trouncing upon civil authority, shifting the political balance of power on the isthmus away from middle- and working-class sectors, and increasing the power and politicization of the armed forces.

The Remón administration's domestic program focused on regaining financial solvency through fiscal discipline, and reviving the economy by increasing national production, both industrial and agricultural. This economic modernization scheme would be accomplished with limited state intervention in the economy. As with other populist dictators, however, Remón favored using the state as a way to strengthen national development. Tax reform laws were passed to raise government revenues by taxing the rich and minimizing tax evasion. Remón sold off the properties where Panama's Constitutional Fund was invested, finally ridding the isthmus of the Cromwell financial legacy. Remón saw himself both as a reformist and a nationalist. At the same time, however, the colonel-turned-president never threatened the economic interests of the oligarchy and actually "reduced the power of organized labor" (Harding 2001, 39). In the political arena, Remón weakened opposition parties through a variety of strategies. A new law required any political party to achieve a minimum of 45,000 votes in an election before it could gain formal recognition. This electoral change made it impossible for small parties to become major players and meant that only the Liberal Party could mount any viable opposition to Remón's coalition. The Remón government also outlawed the communist People's Party and purged suspected "communists" from the National University, the country's schools, and government bureaucracies. His policies fell in line nicely with U.S. interests and urgings. Washington desired a pro-U.S. regime on the isthmus that would be able to maintain stability, protect U.S. interests, and stymie any potential communist influence but, at the same time, achieve some degree of popularity and legitimacy. José Remón—a populist, pro-U.S. anticommunist who controlled the armed forces—was just the man to accomplish these tasks.

Naturally, President Remón would eventually want something tangible for cooperating with America's anticommunist crusade. So, in late September 1953, he traveled to Washington to discuss with President Eisenhower a new bilateral relationship that would amend the 1903 Treaty. Even before his inauguration, Remón had visited several countries in Latin America to garner support for a new U.S.-Panamanian relationship. And in April 1953, Foreign Relations Minister José Ramón Guizado informed Secretary of State Dulles that Panama wanted to negotiate a new relationship with Washington. The Panamanian delegation, led by Octavio Fábrega, requested important changes to the 1903 and 1936 accords, including eliminating perpetuity and creating mixed tribunals that would limit America's claim to jurisdiction in the Zone. What the Panamanian team eventually got, however, was a series of economic concessions that, while not appeasing the isthmus's nationalist aspirations, nevertheless satisfied some of the economic aspirations of the oligarchy (See Araúz 1994b, 307–14). The Treaty of Mutual Understanding and Cooperation, commonly known as the Remón-Eisenhower Treaty, signed on January 25, 1955, represented an important victory for the Remón government. Under the new accord, Panama's annuity from the canal increased to $1,930,000. As before, this figure did not represent a real increase in inflated dollars but nevertheless brought more money into Panama's treasury. For the first time, Washington allowed Panama to tax Panamanians who lived and worked in the Zone. Since around 40 percent of the isthmus's workforce lived in the Zone by the end of the 1940s, this change represented a major source of revenue for the government (Ropp 1982, 30–31). The United States also agreed to let Panama take some advantage of the canal enterprise by authorizing isthmian companies to sell more products to the Zone and to transiting vessels. Washington also agreed to end its monopoly over transisthmian rail and road construction. Panama, however, could not allow another country to build a waterway across the isthmus without Washington's approval (Arosemena G. 1977b, 357–85). Washington therefore rewarded Remón for his cooperation, hoping to increase the strongman's popularity.

But even before the diplomatic victory celebration was over, Panama had already entered into another political crisis. On January 2, 1955, President Remón was murdered by two men firing machine guns while he was at a racetrack, creating an immediate political vacuum. His first designado, José Ramón Guizado, assumed the presidency and called for an immediate investigation. Remón's assassination, however, remains a fascinating, unsolved

mystery (see LaFeber 1989, 94–95). The Guardia arrested suspects number-
ing in the hundreds instantly and early on suspected Arnulfo Arias (who
was not arrested because he was out of the country). Within a few days, one
of the suspects, Rubén Miró, a lawyer and nephew of Harmodio Arias, confessed to having been the mastermind of the crime. Days later Miró shocked
the nation when he also confessed that President Guizado had actually initiated the assassination plan. The National Assembly removed Guizado
on January 15 and then installed itself as a special Justice Tribunal for the
purpose of trying the former president. The tribunal found Guizado guilty
but handed him a sentence of less than seven years. Eventually a Popular
Tribunal absolved all implicated individuals from guilt, including Miró and
Guizado. Theories about the crime abound and implicate the international
drug trade (in which Remón and the Guardia were allegedly involved); the
CIA (which had already overthrown nationalist and progressive President
Arbenz in Guatemala); the U.S. mafia (which wanted to further penetrate
Panama as it had done in Cuba); the oligarchy (which wanted to regain po-
litical and economic control); and even some elements within the Guardia
(led by Alejandro Remón, the commander's own brother).

The Return of the Oligarchs

Ricardo Arias Espinosa, the second designado, assumed the presidency on
January 15, 1955. Arias Espinosa, born in Washington, D.C., was another
true rabiblanco, a businessman and Georgetown University graduate who,
along with Remón's brother Alejandro, was also seen as a potential mastermind of the colonel's assassination. The Arias Espinosa government, with
Guardia support, quickly reversed the Remón reforms that most hurt key
members of the oligarchy—mainly taxation. The new commander, Colonel
Bolívar Vallarino, also cooperated fully with the new government. Vallarino
came from an oligarchic family that had lost its wealth, so he chose the military route to power, not atypical of Latin America's oligarchs, attending the
Peruvian military academy and rising quickly through the National Police
hierarchy. Vallarino moved the military away from the political center and
allowed the economic elite to have greater control in the government. The
result was that after Remón's death the oligarchy came back into the driver's
seat in isthmian politics. But Panama was still awash with anti-oligarchic
nationalism that had already permeated even the Guardia.

Panamanian nationalism was stirred again when Egyptian president Ga-
mal Nasser abruptly nationalized the Suez Canal on July 26, 1956, after Britain and the United States refused to help fund his Aswan High Dam Project.

Nasser was able to expel the British and take control of canal operations. This assertive action by Nasser "fired some zealots and even the moderates on the isthmus with the idea that Panama should do the same" (Ealy 1971, 84). Panamanian pride was quickly hurt when Secretary of State Dulles announced that Panama was different from Egypt and that the United States had authority over the Zone and the canal through its treaties with Panama. When it was then excluded from an international conference to address the Suez Canal's nationalization, the Panamanian government protested and took the matter to the United Nations. By 1956, Panama's long-standing concerns about the U.S.-Panamanian relationship, particularly as it pertained to the canal, resonated with the international community's support for self-determination and anticolonialism. These ideals, together with the emerging activity and popularity of socialist and communist parties, began to create serious problems for American leadership in the Western Hemisphere, as anti-American sentiments swept the region. When Vice President Richard Nixon visited South America in April–May 1958, angry mobs greeted him. Certainly many people in Latin America continued to have positive attitudes toward the United States, but increasing numbers were convinced that Washington's predominant goal in the region was exploitation and control. America was losing its soft power and legitimacy since fewer people and governments were viewing the United States as a leader worthy of support and emulation.

National elections were held as scheduled, and Ernesto de la Guardia Navarro became Panama's thirteenth constitutional president on October 1, 1956. He had attended the Instituto Nacional and earned a master's degree at Dartmouth College. De la Guardia was part of Remón's Civilista coalition, but the oligarchy through the various Liberal parties had strong influence in his administration. Beginning with the de la Guardia administration, Panama entered a period of tenuous oligarchic rule, backed by the Guardia and the United States government. The difference with the pre-1931 period was that the oligarchy had lost all legitimacy; nationalism was even stronger and augmented by international sentiments of self-determination and decolonization; the middle sectors demanded more participation; and the Guardia had emerged as a strong, relatively autonomous military-politico institution. Additionally, Washington, unsure of the oligarchy's ability to maintain order, was increasingly looking to the Guardia to maintain its interests on the isthmus. When the government came under attack from nationalist sectors, the Guardia was ready and able to protect its institutional interests, the economic interests of the oligarchy, and U.S. interests. De la Guardia placated the Guardia, building *cuarteles* (barracks) and providing more benefits to the institution. The new government was able to carry out public works and continue efforts at state and national development. Although the national and external debt grew, revenues and production had increased since the serious post–World War II economic crisis had passed. Efforts in education continued, and the government allotted as much as 20 percent of the national budget to build and fund schools (Pizzurno Gelós and Araúz 1996, 418). The government also worked to better penetrate the interior of the country by building roads, funding educational programs for indigenous communities, and working to enhance agricultural programs. One problem for the country had always been the physical divide created by the canal and the Zone. In the 1950s, however, work progressed on the Inter-American Highway, and a bridge across the canal on the Pacific side was completed, eventually called the Bridge of the Americas. The isthmus finally had relatively easy, yet limited communication, both human and commercial, between the interior and the capital.

Panama's ruling oligarchy was still besieged by fervent nationalist sentiments on the isthmus, however. Students and teachers—who demanded more from the state and were critical of the cozy relationship between the oligarchy and Washington—exhibited the most intense nationalism and anti-oligarchic sentiments. In the late-1950s, students took to the streets, inevitably clashing with the Guardia, the principal defender of the status quo. The economic recovery after the post–World War II depression was fleeting, and unemployment had already reached high levels. In May 1958, several clashes took place as students directed their anger at both the de la Guardia government and the United States. The Guardia used tear gas (provided by Washington) and force against students who demonstrated in front of the Palacio, leaving a sixteen-year-old student dead. Numerous student groups demanded that the government improve the condition of the nation's schools. De la Guardia's response was not sympathetic, however. He addressed the nation saying that the National Guard had been provoked by professional "agitators."

Indeed, "agitators" of all kinds were active throughout the isthmus. While communists were often singled out, conservative forces and the political opposition were also skilled and willing participants. Many of the students were coaxed by opponents of the government, and groups that opposed the U.S. presence and the oligarchy also seemed to want a social and political explosion. The U.S. Central Intelligence Agency also used "agitation" and disinformation to discredit anti-U.S. groups and to achieve political goals. Guatemala provides one glaring example of Washington's ability to create chaos and regime change. Without convincing evidence, it is very difficult to really know who was doing what during these tumultuous cold war years. While agitators could certainly lead a demonstration to violence, there is no denying that student concerns about the plight of public education in Panama and the unequal relationship with the United States were well-founded. The mobilized students eventually demanded the dismissal of the Guardia commanders and an investigation into the death of the young student who had died at the hands of security forces. Since the government did not comply with these and other demands, the students, aided by labor groups, called for a national strike for May 22, 1958. Panamanian students could practically control the capital since they were able to barricade major roads at will. When the Guardia responded, obviously eager to carry out their institutional mission of maintaining order and assuming this was the work of agitators, violent clashes ensued, resulting in eight deaths and more than seventy wounded. The government, in addition to the curfew it had established, suspended constitutional guarantees. The Guardia took control of the city, and students retreated to the university campus. Prominent Panamanians and government officials increasingly called for a peaceful resolution to the crisis and volunteered their time and energy. Eventually, on May 29, student leaders and the government reached a settlement. Labeled *el pacto de la colina* (Pact of the Hill), the government committed itself to addressing quickly the country's dire educational condition. The government would also make reparations to those who were injured and to the families of those who had lost their lives. All those arrested would also be released. Incredibly enough, the government made a commitment to reform the Guardia by making it more responsive to civilian control and less political and by precluding it from engaging in economic enterprises. It seemed that Panama's civilian leaders were reasonably amenable to compromise and willing to take steps to minimize the Guardia's political power. However, the government's promises never materialized, prompting students and teachers to continue to protest and oppose the government. Panama was not alone; the social unrest that existed on the isthmus in the late 1950s and early 1960s plagued most of the countries of the region, most notably Cuba.

The Cuban Revolution and Hemispheric Security

Fidel Castro's triumph over the dictatorship of Fulgencio Batista, on January 1, 1959, had profound regional ramifications. As in most countries of Latin America, Panama's nationalists celebrated Cuba's "nationalist" victory over a U.S.-supported dictatorship. Likewise, Panama's socialists and revolutionaries were emboldened and inspired by Castro's toppling of the Batista mafiacracy and by Cuba's revolutionary regime. Consequently, in 1959 Panama experienced increasing numbers of student protests, nationalist manifestations, and acts of subversion. After forming the Movimiento de Acción Revolucionaria (Revolutionary Action Movement), radical students attempted to replicate the Castro revolution by taking to the mountains in Cerro Tute, in the province of Veraguas. Captain Omar Torrijos would become involved in fighting this small domestic insurgency. Several other groups attempted to establish a *foco* insurgency (a military strategy devised by Che Guevara that focused on the military, rather than the political, organization of small bands of guerillas) in other parts of the country, and the 22 of May Youth Revolutionary Movement carried out acts of sabotage in Colón and Panama City. Some of these subversive activities, however, were supported by those who opposed the de la Guardia government, particularly the Arnulfistas.

In April 1959, the de la Guardia government became aware that a group of Cubans and Panamanians were planning to "invade" Panama to replicate Castro's guerrilla war on the isthmus. How this information came to the Panamanian government is a mystery in itself, although historically such information came from U.S. intelligence sources. Despite assurances by the Cuban government that it would not export subversion, a group of ninety-seven mostly Cuban would-be rebels landed in the province of San Blas and established a revolutionary foco near the town of Nombre de Dios. De la Guardia appealed to the OAS, invoking the Rio Treaty. Owing to diplomatic assistance from a variety of countries in the region and of course the United States, the Panamanian government was able to defuse the international crisis and orchestrated the return of the Cubans to their country. The Cuban "invasion" highlights the influence of the international context on isthmian politics. Castro was attempting to spark revolution in other countries of the region, for the purpose of creating new friends, challenging U.S. hegemony, and diverting U.S. attention from his revolutionary regime. At the same time, Castro's example inspired Panama's leftist opposition groups. As a result, Washington quickly created and implemented policies designed to preserve U.S. hemispheric power. The cold war context at the international level trickled down to the domestic level, leading to polarization and political crises.

After Castro's rise to power, Washington created a dual-pronged strategy toward Latin America for the purpose of preventing another Cuban revolution. First, the Kennedy administration fashioned a major policy initiative named the Alliance for Progress, unveiled in March 1961 to the delight of governments throughout the region. The Alliance called for reforming Latin America through socioeconomic development and political change toward democracy. The United States committed itself to providing large amounts of economic aid in order to promote such reform and development. However, while socioeconomic development was touted as the solution to the region's problems, Washington also provided the militaries of the region with unprecedented levels of military assistance and promoted a military doctrine of internal defense. After 1959, the U.S. government through the DOD established very close relations with the armed forces and promoted internal security as the primary military mission in the region. Under the Alliance, Panama—like most countries in the region—received increased U.S. economic and military aid. For example, U.S. economic assistance to Panama increased by 500 percent during the three-year period beginning in 1961, to $41 million (Harding 2001, 46).

The increased focus on regional security also prompted Washington to bolster and upgrade the network of military installations in Panama designed to protect vital U.S. strategic interests in the region and to safeguard the efficient operation of the canal. All U.S. defense installations in Panama came to be directed by the U.S. Southern Command (SOUTHCOM), led by a commander in chief (CINCSOUTH), and headquartered at Quarry Heights, on the Pacific approach to the canal and adjacent to Panama City. The CINCSOUTH, initially a two-star U.S. Army general, came to exert a great deal of power on the isthmus. The U.S. Army had the bulk of the troops stationed in Panama, roughly ten thousand, as well as most of the larger installations. The most important U.S. Army posts were Ft. Clayton, home to U.S. Army South, on the Pacific side; Ft. Sherman, home to the U.S. Jungle Operations Training Center; and Ft. Gulick, home to the School of the Americas, where thousands of Latin American military personnel were trained for over three decades, on the Atlantic side. As for the U.S. Air Force, on the Pacific side it operated Howard AFB, home to most air operations, including many intelligence-gathering flights, and later headquarters to the U.S. counter-narcotics effort in Latin America; and Albrook Air Force Station, home to the Inter-American Air Forces Academy. The U.S. Navy controlled Rodman Naval Station on the Pacific side, where Latin American naval personnel took a variety of courses on small-craft operations. Two other prized military possessions were Galeta Island, which housed a number of important intelligence operations, and the Tropic Test Center, which allowed the U.S. military to test the effects of a tropical environment on all sorts of weapons and combat equipment. This extensive defense complex in Panama was vital for an array of DOD missions throughout Latin America and even for global U.S. strategic activities (see Gurdián Guerra 1998; U.S. Southern Command 1997d; and Leis 1985).

This intensified U.S. militarization in Panama led to increased resentment and even hatred on the part of many Panamanians, who accurately saw their nation as a strategic U.S. garrison. Had the United States been faithful to the 1903 Hay–Bunau-Varilla Treaty and simply maintained fortifications to defend the isthmian waterway from external attack, Panamanian anti-Americanism may have been kept to a minimum. However, the United States now maintained defense facilities in Panama increasingly for reasons other than canal security. By the 1960s, in fact, defense experts agreed that the waterway was virtually indefensible. The United States could stop neither a strategic attack (nuclear missiles) nor an insurgent attack directed against the canal. It was increasingly clear to Panamanians that Washington stationed U.S. forces on the isthmus principally to protect the canal from *domestic* turmoil in Panama that could spill over into the canal operating area and disrupt U.S. military operations. This aspect of canal defense essentially meant defending against Panamanian nationalism that often had an anti-American edge. It was increasingly clear that Washington also maintained bases in Panama to achieve its regional strategic missions, such as power projection, denial of canal access to adversaries in times of war, intelligence collection, and maintenance of military-to-military ties with Latin America, activities that were not authorized by any bilateral treaty. In a nutshell, Panama served as a large aircraft carrier in the Latin American "area of operations" for U.S. strategic planners (Pedreschi 1987; Ryan 1977; C. Morris 1989). Increasing numbers of Panamanians saw this presence as nothing more than naked colonialism.

The Cuban Revolution and the resultant increase in U.S. military presence on the isthmus sparked more student and nationalist demonstrations. In November 1959, on Panama's day of independence, increasingly radicalized students (Goldrich 1966), led by two prominent leaders, attempted to plant small Panamanian flags in the U.S.-controlled Canal Zone. Operación Soberanía (Operation Sovereignty) targeted the United States and the Canal Zone rather than the Panamanian government. Students had already carried out a similar event on May 15, 1958, when they entered the Zone and planted Panamanian flags. At that time, the Zone police quickly removed the isthmian colors without much fanfare, perhaps because the students were focused principally on attacking the de la Guardia administration. But in 1959, Operación Soberanía was repeated by a group of prominent Panamanians, including Aquilino Boyd, former foreign relations minister and a deputy in the National Assembly, and Ernesto Castillero Pimentel, a well-known university professor. When students attempted to plant Panamanian flags this time, they clashed with Zone police, who used tear gas and water cannons to disperse the demonstrators. These events led to public protests and further clashes, including attacks against U.S. facilities, prompting Washington to call in U.S. troops. Although no one was killed, the chaos left sixty-four Panamanians and more than forty-five U.S. citizens injured (Pizzurno Gelós and Araúz 1996, 438). U.S. ambassador Julian F. Harrington sent a strong protest to the Panamanian government, demanding reparations. The "special relationship" between the United States and Panama was finally unraveling. From the U.S. perspective, Panamanians were hypernationalistic. From the Panamanian perspective, the United States was behaving like a colonial power, unwilling to recognize Panama's inherent rights over the Zone. U.S. analysts have often characterized Panamanians as hypersensitive over symbolic issues, such as displaying the flag. However, it is clear that the Zone government and Washington also saw the display of national colors as an important symbol of sovereignty. Consequently, the Zone authorities and Washington resisted Panama's attempts to display the national colors lest it suggest an inherent right of sovereignty. After this crisis, President Dwight Eisenhower decided that, to prevent a nationalist uprising, Panama should be allowed to display its flag in the Canal Zone. The nationalist U.S. Congress, however, stood firm in its position that Panama's flag not be displayed at all in the Zone. Eventually, in September 1960, Eisenhower resorted to executive privilege and ordered that both nations' flags be flown together in specified locations in the Zone (LaFever 1989, 101). It is clear that, while economic, political, and military power are the primal national interests, symbols of power are also important both to Great Powers and subordinate countries.

Incredibly enough, the de la Guardia administration managed to survive the political tumult of the late 1950s and turned power over to another elected president on October 1, 1960. In the presidential campaign, the candidates represented political coalitions, as had become the norm; but now many more political parties adhered to these coalitions since the law of 45,000 had been repealed, and only 5,000 votes were needed for official recognition of a political party. Former president and presidential hopeful Roberto F. Chiari represented the Union Nacional de Oposición (National Opposition Union); Ricardo M. Arias Espinosa headed the Coalición Patriótica Nacional (National Patriotic Coalition) that had been founded by Remón; and Víctor Florencio Goytia led the Alianza Popular (Popular Alliance), representing the middle and nationalist sectors. Arnulfo Arias's newly created Panameñista party, however, turning away from its popular base, supported Chiari in return for a law allowing "el Hombre" to enter the political arena once more. Chiari thus won the peaceful election handily, signifying the oligarchy's and Liberal Party factions' victory over the Guardia's political base.

The relative calm of the 1960 election, particularly coming on the heels of the crises of 1958 and 1959 and the Cuban Revolution, is perhaps testimony to the truly nationalist character of Panama's middle and popular sectors. Anti-oligarchic and anti-U.S. sentiments were not principally the creations of foreign influence, communism, but were the manifestation of popular sentiments that longed for a state that represented the "people" and a foreign policy that defended the nation's sovereignty. While many Panamanians lauded Castro's victory over U.S. interests, universal support for emulating the Cuban Revolution was not present on the isthmus. Communism, while somewhat popular in Latin America and even in Panama, never represented a major challenge to the U.S. model of democracy and capitalism. Washington, however, would not take any risks at a time of Great Power conflict and did everything possible to destroy nationalist, anti-U.S., and leftist movements, whether attempting to come to power via the barrel of a gun or via the ballot box. During the cold war, more contestation and participation was not conducive to the preservation of U.S. strategic interests, and Washington behaved accordingly.

As with previous presidents, Chiari inherited a government devoid of funds and saddled with a large debt. Within a year, however, his administration began to benefit from increased U.S. economic and technical assistance under the anticommunist Alliance for Progress. Washington's newly acquired generosity allowed the Panamanian state to carry out more public works than would have been expected given the country's dire economic situation. The government built schools and roads throughout the country while making important strides in public health programs. The Chiari administration also constructed some low-cost housing and established a minimum wage. The isthmus benefited from the arrival of fifty-seven eager Peace Corps volunteers (LaFeber 1989, 104). The efforts of the Chiari administration and Washington did not produce sufficient prosperity and jobs, however. Consequently, the Panamanian government found itself having to deal with continued social unrest from student and labor organizations. In November 1960, banana workers in Bocas del Toro province went on strike, demanding that the U.S.-owned Chiriqui Land Company provide higher wages and better living conditions. Chiari intervened, successfully defusing the dispute. In the meantime, workers at Puerto Armuelles also went on strike. In this case, the strikers clashed with the Guardia, resulting in one death. The banana workers denounced the Guardia and its leaders, as students had done in previous years. In late 1962, university students, supported by students at the Instituto Nacional, went on strike. The strikes in the early 1960s, while stemming from valid concerns, were often dismissed by the government, business groups, and U.S. authorities as the work of "communists" and "agitators." Panama became an increasingly polarized country to a large extent reflecting the bipolarity of the global system.

The 1964 Flag Riots: Death Knell of the "Special Relationship"

Despite increased U.S. aid and attention, in January 1964 serious conflict with the United States emerged anew over the issue of flags. The Zone governor had decided not to fly an American flag outside schools in the Zone so that the Panamanian flag would not have to be concurrently flown, as President Kennedy had now ordered. The governor took this step believing that it would be better to fly neither flag than both flags since patriotic Zonians were adamantly against flying Panama's flag. On January 7, 1964, students from the Canal Zone Junior College decided to raise the Stars and Stripes up the flagpole at Balboa High School, in defiance of the governor's orders. Students in Panama quickly learned what had happened and requested permission to enter the Zone and fly the Panamanian colors. The Zone police allowed only six of about two hundred willing students to enter the Zone. Six Panamanian students, therefore, were about to raise their nation's flag in the Zone as hundreds of patriotic Zonians looked on. Some of the Zonians who were present became angry and chased the students out of the Zone, tearing the Panamanian flag in the process. When word spread that Panamanian students had been roughed up and insulted in the Zone, thousands of people took to the streets in a cathartic display of nationalism and anti-Americanism. After three days of chaos, twenty-one Panamanians and five U.S. citizens had lost their lives, while scores were injured.[1] Panamanians quickly assumed that their death toll had resulted from the use of deadly force by Zone police and U.S. military personnel who were dispatched to protect the Zonians. Since the Chiari government was hesitant in this instance to repress its own population, the crisis did not end until Major Omar Torrijos and Lieutenant Manuel Antonio Noriega flew in from the province of Chiriquí and established order (Janson Pérez 1997, 63). President Chiari, outraged at how the U.S. government and Zone authorities handled the situation, broke diplomatic ties with Washington on January 10 for the first time in U.S.-Panama relations. The Chiari government took the extraordinary step of invoking the Rio Treaty, as de la Guardia had done a few years earlier with the Cuban "invasion," arguing that the United States had attacked Panama. The OAS Council eventually reprimanded Washington for using "excessive force" but concluded that it was not guilty of committing aggression against Panama. The Panamanian Bar Association requested the

International Commission of Jurists to carry out an independent investigation of the tragic events. This commission, however, found that the U.S. and Zone governments did not use excessive force, owing to the threat posed by rioters (International Commission of Jurists 1964). According to the report, though, the United States could have taken alternative measures that would have ameliorated the violence.

The 1964 flag riots represent a watershed event in U.S.-Panamanian relations in that it led to a national consensus in Panama on the 1903 Treaty and the "special relationship." Until then, Panama's oligarchy had simply wanted Washington to accept some, principally economic and symbolic, changes to the hated 1903 Treaty. Before the 1964 riots, Goldrich pointed out that Panama's political elite and oligarchy "while frequently using antiyanquism to pry concessions from the U.S. government . . . have never sought to change the basic rules of the game" (1962, 8). The tragic events of January 1964, however, brought Panama's oligarchy and nationalists together into an alliance demanding that Washington abrogate rather than amend the 1903 accord. America's hesitance to give an inch had led to a unified Panamanian call that Washington give a mile. A clear foreign policy consensus had finally emerged—a consensus that would bring Panama's interests in direct conflict with U.S. interests on the isthmus. The Chiari administration took a strong stance, refusing to restore diplomatic relations until the U.S. government agreed to renegotiate the 1903 Treaty. The Johnson administration thus faced a dilemma: wanting to keep the basic tenets of the 1903 agreement but at the same time desiring to defuse the social powder keg in Panama. President Johnson quickly announced that the United States would begin talks with Panama to alter fundamentally the relationship established by previous treaties. After some intense diplomacy, on April 3, a joint declaration by ambassadors Ellsworth Bunker and Miguel Moreno stated that the two nations would restore diplomatic relations and begin negotiations to eliminate the causes of the conflict by reaching a new, more equitable and just agreement (Moreno 1999). But this new diplomatic initiative diminished neither Panama's surging nationalism nor Washington's proprietary sentiments about the canal and the Zone. It did, however, allow for a relatively smooth national election. It fell upon the new administration to broker a new deal with Washington.

The 1964 Elections: Oligarchic Finale

The oligarchy was successful in maintaining their precarious grip on politics in the May 1964 elections. Once again numerous political parties (a total of nineteen), alliances, and presidential candidates competed for votes: the Alianza de Oposición (Opposition Alliance) backed Marco Aurelio Robles; Arnulfo Arias led the Panameñista Party; the Coalición Patriótica (Patriotic Coalition) supported Juan de Arco Galindo; Acción Radical (Radical Action) was led by Norberto Navarro; José Antonio Molino was the Demócrata Cristianos (Christian Democrat) candidate; the Partido Socialista (Socialist Party) supported Humberto Harris; and José de la Rosa Castillo was the Partido Reformista (Reformist Party) candidate. Although Arias's Panameñista Party gained more votes than any other political party, Robles, who was backed by his cousin, President Chiari, received a narrow plurality of the vote tally. In addition to receiving official backing, Robles's victory was also due to the abundance of candidates, the strong stance the oligarchy had taken against Washington, and the fact that he acquired his secondary education at the strongly nationalist Instituto Nacional. The elections, nevertheless, also showed some signs of fraud and irregularities. Numerous acts of sabotage occurred and formal accusations were lodged, but Robles was successfully inaugurated on October 1, 1964. Although the oligarchy maintained its tenuous grip on power, the political spectrum in the last several decades had broadened significantly, making it practically impossible for any president to hold together a national consensus.

Upon taking office, President Robles faced numerous challenges. In addition to the usual economic problems, there was generalized dissatisfaction with the government, continued nationalism, increased radicalism inspired by the Cuban Revolution, and the daunting task of forging a new relationship with the United States. On the positive side, the new administration enjoyed some political capital gained from President Chiari's staunch stance against the United States and received some economic benefits from Alliance for Progress programs. The Robles government, acknowledging the desperate state of education in the country and recognizing the increasing power of students and educators, allocated a substantial portion of government revenues toward education. The Panamanian government continued to carry out public works throughout the country, and in 1967 the Pan-American Highway, running along the length of the isthmus, was completed. Ironically, while Panama's gross domestic product grew more rapidly during the 1960s and industry's share of that product continued to expand, the fiscal crisis continued and inequality increased (Zimbalist and Weeks 1991, 27–30). The economic growth of the 1960s was aided by foreign direct investment and by numerous programs of the Alliance for Progress, Inter-American Development Bank, and U.S. Agency for International Development. The government's increased involvement in the economy meant that it controlled a greater share of the country's GDP, thus increasing state power. But demands upon the political system were continually increasing and political polarization yielded greater dissatisfaction with the status quo.

The economic "gains" of the 1960s, therefore, did not suppress public discontent. The Robles government had to confront numerous protests from students, workers, and peasants, as well as acts of sabotage. The Panamanian government and Washington continued to dismiss these activities as manifestations of communist infiltration and instigation. As a result, the Guardia asserted itself and repressed many legitimate student and labor protests. In January 1965, students celebrated the first anniversary of the 1964 flag riots, eventually marching toward the U.S. embassy. The Guardia dispersed the demonstrators using tear gas, but student demonstrations continued. Student protests flared again in Colón and Panama City after a student leader, Juan Navas, was found dead along a road close to Colón in June 1966. The murdered student was Luis Navas's brother, secretary general of the politically active and antigovernment Federación de Estudiantes de Panamá (Federation of Panamanian Students), or FEP. Students accused agents of Panama's secret police, the Departamento Nacional de Investigaciones (National Department of Investigations), or DENI, of the crime, which of course implicated the government. The Guardia repressed demonstrators on various occasions using clubs and tear gas mostly, but occasionally firing weapons. Two more students were killed during clashes with the Guardia. Both sides used the death of Juan Navas as a political issue: leftists accusing the Robles government or the CIA, and anticommunists pointing the finger at leftist agitators. As a result of the increasing violence in Panama, President Lyndon Johnson stated: "The United States cannot allow the security of Panama to be imperiled. . . . We have a recognized obligation to operate the Canal efficiently and securely and we intend to honor that obligation" (quoted in Ealy 1971, 126). President Johnson was in essence preparing Americans and Panamanians alike for the employment of U.S. force if the situation in Panama continued to deteriorate. In the polarized cold war context, Washington would not risk American national security and power in order to defend the sovereignty or self-determination of another country.

Students were not the only ones to challenge the Robles administration. In 1965 and 1966, the government was besieged by labor problems. Public workers organized rallies calling for increased wages and carried out a number of strikes. As it had done with the students, the Guardia used tear gas to keep labor unrest under control. Workers at a sugar refinery in Aguadulce went on strike for better wages and collective bargaining guaranties. Owing to resistance from the National Sugar Company, government officials, and the Guardia, the Industrial Syndicate of Sugar Workers then organized a march to Panama City, labeled the March for Justice, in an effort to meet face-to-face with the chief executive. Also, the Peasant Agrarian League protested at the Foreign Ministry because peasants who had acquired land through the government's land reform program could not access that land and Zone officials were threatening to displace them (Pizzurno Gelós and Araúz 1996, 490–98).

While dealing with increased domestic dissatisfaction, the Robles administration had the difficult task of negotiating a new relationship with Washington. Realizing that a new treaty was virtually inevitable, in September 1964 the U.S. Congress established the Atlantic-Pacific Interoceanic Canal Study Commission to look into the feasibility of building a sea-level canal and to recommend a location for such a waterway. In December 1964, President Johnson announced that the United States would enter into a new relationship with Panama and also begin plans to build a new sea-level canal with Panama and "other interested governments" (quoted in Lindsay-Poland 2003, 87). The establishment of the Interoceanic Commission and Johnson's words would send a strong signal to Panama—that, if it asked for too much, the U.S. government could possibly build a new waterway elsewhere. Building a sea-level canal was now feasible and potentially less expensive by using nuclear detonations to move massive amounts of earth. One potential problem with this plan already existed, since the United States had signed the Limited Nuclear Test Ban Treaty with Moscow in 1963. The fact that a government commission looked into the use of nuclear detonations for building a large, sea-level canal through the isthmus, or elsewhere, seems ludicrous now, but at the time there was great optimism about the potential uses of atomic power.

From the U.S. perspective, the Panama "problem" required high-level attention. President Johnson put together a Panama Review Group to iron out the U.S. position on a new accord. The group was led by Assistant Secretary of State Thomas Mann, a hard-liner who advocated U.S. support for dictators and military regimes that could effectively prevent communist revolutions. The initial U.S. position would allow Panama to take over all territory not necessary for canal operations but would allow the United States to defend the canal and retain a military presence in perpetuity. The U.S. government would also have control of any new waterway for at least fifty years (Major 1993, 336). The Panamanians, of course, wanted to control the canal and desired to end the U.S. "right" to operate and defend the canal. In June 1967, after many months of difficult negotiations, the two governments announced that they had reached an agreement and that signing ceremonies would follow quickly. Three treaties would, if ratified, govern the new, improved U.S.-Panamanian relationship. The first accord dealt with the existing canal. This agreement was historic in that it replaced, thus abrogated, the infamous 1903 Treaty, as well as its 1936 and 1955 amendments. The Zone would become a Canal Area that would be governed jointly, but Panama would retain legal sovereignty. Under this agreement, Panama would also receive higher annuities and would benefit from any excess revenues the Canal operation accumulated. This accord would expire, with a termination window of ten years, beginning on December 31, 1999, upon which Panama would take control of the canal. The second treaty granted to the U.S. government the right to build a sea-level canal, to be operated jointly. The third agreement, while making canal defense a joint responsibility, allowed the United States to protect the canals in perpetuity and thus would allow U.S. military forces to remain on the isthmus (Arosemena G. 1977c, 35–218).

The so-called Three-in-One Treaties generated immediate controversy in both countries. The news media acquired copies of the accords before they could be officially presented to the public by the two governments. Intense criticism emerged, both in Panama and the United States, from sectors opposed to any form of compromise. Nationalists and key political leaders in Panama rejected the notion of a continued U.S. military presence and defense rights in perpetuity, as well as any delay in Panama gaining complete sovereignty over its territory. The news media in Panama attacked the agreements on many fronts and Arnulfo Arias's Panameñista Party formed the United Front in Opposition to the accords. In the United States, two groups emerged dedicated to fighting against any concessions to Panama: the American Emergency Committee on the Panama Canal, with over one hundred prominent sponsors, including writers, military officers, commentators, and scholars; and the Committee for Continued U.S. Control of the Panama Canal, consisting of seventeen prominent professors, attorneys, editors, and businessmen (Busey 1974, 32–33). The Johnson administration also had to face strong opposition from members of Congress who opposed "giving away" the canal (Busey 1974, 32–33). With presidential elections just over one year away in both countries, the new treaties were doomed to failure. Both chief executives decided to delay ratification until new administrations were in power.

The new treaties created serious problems for President Robles. Opposition to the treaties was so intense that, when controversy arose over the official presidential candidate for the next election, the government's political coalition collapsed, and the National Assembly impeached Robles on grounds of electoral coercion, among other constitutional violations. Max

Delvalle, the first designado, assumed the presidency on March 24, 1968. Immediately, the Guardia publicly expressed its support for President Robles. When Delvalle decided to attend a session of the National Assembly, the Guardia, led by Lieutenant Colonel Omar Torrijos, used tear gas to disperse the crowd—made up mostly of Panameñista assemblymen—who accompanied the new president. The Supreme Court eventually ruled that President Robles's ouster was unconstitutional, and Delvalle stepped down. Once again, the Guardia had served as final arbiter at a time of political crisis and prevented a nationalist challenge to U.S. interests at a critical time.

Arnulfo Arias's Third (Brief) Presidency

One month after the constitutional crisis, national elections took place. Three presidential candidates were on the ballot: David Samudio, the official candidate, represented the People's Alliance, comprised of the Liberal Party and three others; Arnulfo Arias led the National Union, consisting of the Panameñista Party and four others; and Antonio González Revilla represented the Christian Democratic Party. Perhaps the most notable feature of this election is that Arias was supported by some elements of the oligarchy, owing to his traditional nationalist stance, which now attracted segments of the oligarchy. Prior to the voting, the opposition charged the government with numerous electoral violations in support of Samudio's candidacy. On May 9, an unsuccessful assassination attempt against Arnulfo Arias occurred as he campaigned in the province of Darién. Political violence intensified, resulting in several deaths. The president of the Electoral Tribunal resigned owing to threats against his family. As the votes were being counted, Guardia commander Bolívar Vallarino met with Arias to ensure that if elected the latter would not retaliate against, and respect the hierarchy of, the military. Arias's assurances were enough for the Guardia to allow his victory, realizing that stealing this election could lead to political and social mayhem. A civic-religious movement, headed by Archbishop Tomás Clavel, called for an honest count of the ballots and thus also promoted a fair vote tally. In the wake of the Cuban Revolution and the 1964 anti-U.S. demonstrations, Arias's panameñismo became the rallying cry of most Panamanians.

The Electoral Tribunal, under the leadership of a new president not beholden to President Robles, then recounted the votes. Arnulfo Arias and his National Union emerged victorious and gained a clear majority in the National Assembly. Arias's victory was possible for several reasons. First, it became clear to Washington, the Guardia, and many Panamanian political and economic leaders that stealing this election could lead to a political and social explosion, that is, a potential second Cuba. Second, Arias now appeared less hostile to the Guardia and to U.S. interests. Arias had come to a gentleman's agreement with Commander Vallarino, and, by 1968, Washington was convinced that the Panameñista leader had turned "pro–North American, particularly in matters concerning the Canal" (LaFeber 1989, 122). Prior to taking office, Arias traveled to Washington, assuaging fears that he would threaten U.S. interests. Third, some oligarchs had become estranged from Robles and Samudio because of their coziness with Washington but also because Robles and Samudio were pushing for tax reforms that would be financially costly for segments of the oligarchy. Consequently, "el Hombre" returned to the Palacio de las Garzas, taking the presidency away from the oligarchy once more.

Arias's third presidency, however, was even shorter-lived than his first two. He took power on October 1, 1968, and only ten days later disaffected Guardia officers ousted him, with support from segments of the oligarchy, in Panama's first-ever military golpe. Panama's caudillo could get the votes but was either unwilling or unable to guarantee the interests of the isthmus's key powerbrokers—the oligarchy, the Guardia, and the United States. Even before his inauguration, some elements of the oligarchy had approached key officers in the Guardia to discuss preventing Arias from taking power. After entering the Palacio de las Garzas, however, Arias ignored his pact with Vallarino and moved to marginalize Guardia officers who opposed him and promote those who were sympathetic to him and panameñismo. Consistent with the agreement, on October 11, Commander Vallarino was scheduled to retire and Arias would reward him with a government position in Washington. Colonel José María Pinilla, Vallarino's deputy, would assume command and Arias would faithfully respect Guardia hierarchy. But on October 10, the government announced that both Vallarino and Pinilla would retire. The new Guardia commander would be Lieutenant Colonel Bolívar Urrutia, and his second in command would be Lieutenant Colonel Aristides Hassan, both of whom were pro-Arias Panameñistas. Arias then moved to weaken officers who were known to oppose him. Two powerful officers who had plotted against him prior to his inauguration, Colonel Omar Torrijos and Major Boris Martínez, were principal targets. To marginalize Torrijos, Arias appointed him as military attaché to Guatemala and El Salvador, a not-so-subtle political exile.[2] Then, on the morning of October 11, Arias decreed that the Presidential Guard would come under the command of the presidency, effectively taking control away from the Guardia. That same day, Major Boris Martínez led a successful rebellion against Arias, who quickly went into exile in the Canal Zone and eventually gained asylum in the United States.

Uncharacteristically, there is no evidence that the U.S. government was involved in or even aware of the events of October 11. Washington, however, after turning a cold shoulder to the golpe, eventually recognized and supported fully Panama's military regime and General Omar Torrijos's eventual dictatorship. In the 1960s, authoritarianism was good for U.S. interests, even if it meant undermining a nascent liberal democracy.

The End of Oligarchic Control and of the "Special Relationship"

While several countries in Latin America began to democratize after World War II, the popularity of socialism and to a smaller extent communism soon undermined U.S. leadership in the region. By the late 1950s, democracy seemed to be on the rise in several countries in the region and the influence of dictators appeared to be waning (Porter and Alexander 1961, 1–5). Several countries had eschewed militarism and established democratic regimes— Costa Rica in 1948, and Colombia and Venezuela in 1958. Some dictatorships had been eliminated—Cuba's Batista in 1959 and the Dominican Republic's Trujillo in 1961. Additionally, countries in the region were looking more and more toward the United States than toward Europe for leadership, to a large extent because of increased economic ties and strategic cooperation during World War II, when Washington established the Inter-American Security system. This brief period of U.S. ascendancy, and perhaps incipient hegemony, in the Western Hemisphere, however, was replaced quickly by the cold war conflict that introduced a new challenge to U.S. leadership. Once Cuba experienced its revolution in 1959 and the Castro regime challenged U.S. economic, military, and political leadership, large numbers of Latin Americans put their hopes on the nationalist, anti-imperialist goals of Cuba's revolutionary regime. The reaction from Washington and conservative forces in the region was almost unanimous support for militarism in what became known as new authoritarianism or institutional military rule. In the 1960s and 1970s, Latin America adopted a new, more brutal, and long-term form of military rule, quickly moving away from a brief post–World War II period during which emulation of the American model of liberal democracy seemed to be on the rise. The United States remained a preponderant power, economically and militarily, but emulating America's political model swiftly went out the window.

As the cold war conflict infected Latin America, Washington, Panama's oligarchy, and the Guardia were unwilling to further liberalize the political system, fearing that more democracy could lead to a second Cuba. These fears were somewhat misplaced, however, since most Panamanians simply demanded sovereignty and self-determination via nationalism rather than a turn toward socialism and alliance with Cuba or the Soviet Union. As nationalist forces reached a crescendo in 1964, fears of communist infiltration in the hemisphere convinced conservative forces that repression rather than liberalization was necessary since a national consensus or elite unity that would yield a stable democracy seemed impossible. The oligarchy had finally lost its ability to control the system. Arias, as the most popular representative of nationalist and middle-class interests, was unable or unwilling to fashion a national consensus. Although students and labor also represented popular and nationalist forces, these sectors were in no position to forge national unity or to take over the political system. Only one institution, the Guardia, had the resources, power, and U.S. backing to impose order and govern the isthmus. While Washington may have desired a democratic Panama, the Mann Doctrine, employed unofficially by Washington, favored supporting authoritarian regimes that could maintain order and keep communism from coming to power over democratic regimes that could not effectively accomplish these tasks (P. Smith 2000, 157–59). Panama's oligarchy would have preferred to maintain its hegemony, but like Washington, they preferred that the Guardia, rather than socialists or Panameñistas, take power. During the cold war, U.S. and oligarchic interests were expressed as anticommunism, but at the root was the fear that the status quo would change, whether via socialism or via nationalistic panameñismo, which were viewed as too inimical to their vital interests. Washington's primordial goal was preserving U.S. regional power by keeping nationalism and communism out of the region. As a result, the Guardia took power in Panama with support from the oligarchy and Washington, putting an end to the isthmus's frail and limited polyarchy. While democracy had been weak in the past, it was nonexistent once the Guardia took power—the National Legislative Assembly was closed down, political parties were proscribed, civil liberties were trounced, and the Guardia ruled by decree. But nationalism had not died in Panama since, after 1964, Panama's oligarchs were still insistent that the U.S.-Panamanian relationship required a dramatic restructuring. Panama's poor and rich alike now demanded the abrogation of the 1903 Hay–Bunau-Varilla Treaty. For the moment, however, this national goal would have to wait.

From U.S. Support of Dictatorship
to the U.S. Invasion

The Demise of Democracy and the 1977 Canal Treaties, 1968–89

For two decades after the 1968 golpe, Panama was gripped by personalistic, institutional military rule, lasting until 1989, when the U.S. government invaded the country to remove from power General Manuel Antonio Noriega. Political and economic divisions within the oligarchy, the increasing strength of the middle sectors that clamored for nationalism, and Arias's mercurial nature all led to the almost inevitable takeover by the Guardia Nacional. The golpe and the military regime that followed were also facilitated by Washington's close ties to the anticommunist Guardia officers, and U.S. fears that nationalism could get out of hand on the isthmus, potentially leading to the dreaded "second Cuba." Despite being mostly anticommunist, the Guardia was still steeped in nationalism. Consequently, General Omar Torrijos, who by 1969 controlled the Guardia and thus the nation, eventually demanded a price from Washington—a new canal treaty—for having forestalled a social revolution in Panama. After some extensive pressure from the Torrijos regime, Washington relented, and in 1977 both countries signed and ratified the Panama Canal Treaties. But the euphoria of the new relationship quickly turned sour. After Torrijos's untimely death in 1981, General Manuel Antonio Noriega, in classic Machiavellian fashion, took control of the Guardia. The return to democracy that Torrijos had promised became a farce, both because Noriega wanted to retain the Guardia and himself in power and because Washington felt it needed the new caudillo for its strategic goals in Central America. Eventually, as a strategic partnership with Noriega became less important, Washington came to the conclusion that U.S. interests were better served by the elimination of both the general and the Guardia itself. After many concerted but failed attempts to oust the dictator, on December 20, 1989, President George Bush ordered the U.S. military to invade the isthmus. The United States invaded the country only ten years after the new treaties had gone into force. Panama, once again, understood the extent of U.S. power and its precarious place in the international system.

The Military Junta's Initial Troubles

Once it ousted Arnulfo Arias, the Guardia immediately established the Provisional Governing Junta, led by Colonel José María Pinilla. The junta very quickly appointed a civilian cabinet with ties to the oligarchy and business elite and stated that it would soon hold national elections. But the Guardia trampled upon democracy, closing down the National Assembly, suspending constitutional guarantees, and proscribing all political activity (Velásquez 1993, 1–4). By January 1969, the key civilians in the government resigned, accusing the Guardia of attempting to establish a military government similar to the one that had recently taken power in Peru.[1]

Despite the superficial unity, a struggle for power within the Guardia soon materialized. At the outset, Major Boris Martínez was the leading officer since he had troop loyalty and had led the golpe against Arias. Lieutenant Colonel Omar Torrijos Herrera, however, outranked Martínez and had also taken part in Arias's ouster. While the Provisional Junta provided the façade of power and unity, a General Staff was created, led by Torrijos, with Martínez as his deputy (Ropp 1982, 39). Torrijos had close ties to U.S. intelligence and was deemed to be staunchly anticommunist and willing to defend U.S. interests, as he had done during the 1964 flag riots. He had graduated from the Salvadoran Military Academy, where U.S. influence was solid, and had then pursued advanced military training on U.S. military bases in the Canal Zone. Martínez, on the other hand, had attended Panama's Instituto Nacional and received his military training in Mexico, where U.S. influence was minimal. In March 1969, now-Colonel Boris Martínez promulgated a land reform program and "announced that the Guardia would not halt nationalist anti-Yankee demonstrations" (LaFeber 1989, 126). Torrijos quickly exiled Martínez and moved to take control of the Guardia and the state. The military government, at least for now, would not carry out any revolutionary changes, as officers in Peru had done, and would guarantee U.S. interests.

But some Guardia officers, allied with the oligarchy and suspicious of the military government's revolutionary rhetoric, moved against Torrijos in December 1969, while he was in Mexico City. Torrijos, with the help of Major Manuel Antonio Noriega, another officer with close ties to the CIA, returned to Panama and quickly reestablished his supremacy. On December 15, 1969, the two military leaders of the provisional government, Colonels

José Pinilla and Bolívar Urrutia, resigned. From then on, the Guardia was solidly behind Omar Torrijos, as its commander, and Manuel Noriega, as its chief of intelligence. Military officers with links to the U.S. DOD and CIA were in control of the country, despite fears that Panama was experiencing a Peruvian-style, military-led revolution. The military regime was ideal for preserving U.S. interests since it represented neither the oligarchy nor the far left but had a monopoly over the means of coercion necessary for imposing order. To help lend some legitimacy to the government, the Guardia's General Staff appointed Demetrio Lakas as president, a civilian engineer and friend of Torrijos. The regime was, however, clearly an anticommunist military dictatorship since all political parties were banned, the press was all but closed down, antigovernment groups were repressed, and key leftist leaders were jailed, exiled, or even killed.[2] The Guardia ruled as an institution, but one man was clearly in charge, Omar Torrijos. The new strongman led a government consistent with Washington's Mann Doctrine, which promoted anticommunist authoritarian regimes over weak democracies that could succumb to revolutionary forces.

With the Guardia in charge, the Three-in-One Treaty reached by the U.S. government and Panama in 1967 was summarily put aside. For the new Nixon administration, shelving the accords meant not having to deal with a controversial issue at a time of national unrest over Vietnam and civil rights. For the military regime in Panama, setting aside the agreements delayed a difficult national decision and gave Torrijos the opportunity to reach a new treaty personally. The treaty-generated crisis in Panama was therefore resolved—or, more precisely, delayed—by a military government that eventually received Washington's blessing and support. At first Washington refused to recognize the Provisional Junta, probably because the golpe against Arias was not engineered by U.S. policy makers. But within weeks, Washington embraced the military regime and, once Torrijos and Noriega were firmly in command, let U.S. military and economic aid flow.

The Torrijos military dictatorship was far from popular and thus used repression to stay in power. Students, teachers, citizen groups, and political parties all denounced the Guardia's golpe against Arias. Opposition parties formed the Popular Front, and pamphlets denouncing the regime soon appeared. Leftist parties, including the communist People's Party, and the Arnulfistas organized armed insurrections. The Panameñista Party organized the most serious rebellion in the province of Chiriquí. Guardia officer Manuel Antonio Noriega led the fight against this insurgency, using brutal tactics that involved torture (Kempe 1990, 64–65). The Torrijos regime was able to repress the opposition and defeat these armed movements quite easily, killing some of its principal leaders. The regime also killed a popular Catholic priest, Héctor Gallegos, in the province of Veraguas. Father Gallegos, by competing for the hearts and minds of the peasants in the town of Santa Fe, became an enemy of the military state. Gallegos also represented the potential threat of liberation theology, perceived as a mix of Catholicism and communism. The Guardia's successful campaign against its political opponents and the armed insurgents was of course facilitated by U.S. military training and assistance, both overt and covert. After 1968, there would be no political contestation or participation unless approved by the Guardia-controlled state. And the United States, the region's preponderant power and the leading democracy in the world, supported with alacrity the anti-polyarchic, military regime in order to defend its interests on the isthmus and in the region.

The Torrijos Military Dictatorship

The Torrijos regime can be characterized best as a modernizing, reformist, statist, military dictatorship. As such, the regime was mildly anti-oligarchic but at the same time staunchly anticommunist and pro-U.S. While wreaking havoc on the democratic principle of contestation, the regime nevertheless promoted state-organized popular participation by heretofore marginalized groups and took steps to strengthen the Panamanian state. For these reasons, some American liberals embraced and lauded the Torrijos government, as they had done with the Castro Revolution and Peru's Revolutionary Military Government. Torrijos also led a military regime that promoted nationalism and national sovereignty, even if principally to lend legitimacy to the Guardia's dominant political position. For some, a liberal democracy controlled by an oligarchy was worse than a "progressive" military government that would destroy traditional structures that militated against the development of popular democracy. One way to defend the people from the oligarchy was to enhance the power of a state devoted to serving the people.

Not surprisingly, an essential part of enhancing state power was the rapid strengthening of the Guardia itself. In 1967, the Guardia's manpower had reached a level of 3,855. By 1970, however, the Guardia's personnel numbered about 6,000, an increase of over 30 percent in just three years (Harding 2001, 39). The Guardia also received pay increases and added benefits and became involved in economic enterprises, both legal and illegal, as had been the case under Remón. Additionally, Torrijos reorganized the Guardia along the lines of a professional military, adding an air force and a marine corps and founding a military academy at the Río Hato air base. Although the Guardia was a relatively small military, Panama's military personnel represented a large percentage of enrollees in U.S. military training courses on bases adjacent to the Canal Zone. In addition to training, Washington provided increased economic and military aid to the isthmus (see Wilkie and Contreras 1989, tables 3504–26). The consequence of this massive strengthening of the Guardia was that Panama's armed forces became hyperinstitutionalized vis-à-vis the isthmian civilian institutions, which had lost legitimacy and power. One of the most important barriers to democratization, the armed forces, was now extremely powerful and in full command of the Panamanian state.

To gain some legitimacy, the military government carried out a number of reforms designed to appeal to the less fortunate majority. Ironically, Torrijos adopted the land reform program that Boris Martínez had announced in 1969. The program called for the distribution of land to families in rural areas and the creation of collective farms. The government pledged to provide credit, training, and technical assistance so that agricultural development would result from the progressive agrarian reform. The land reform generated some conflict with the Chiriqui Land Company, a subsidiary of the U.S. company United Brands that had acquired the infamous United Fruit Company, but a compromise was soon reached that satisfied U.S. economic interests and at least some of Panama's interests (LaFeber 1989, 135–36). Land reform was much easier to implement in Panama than in other Latin American countries because a strong, traditional landed elite had never existed on the isthmus. And the land reform was accomplished in a way that fully protected U.S. economic interests, unlike the land reform program of the Arbenz government in Guatemala.

Torrijos also made important changes to Panama's labor laws. As a political force, organized labor had been marginalized and weak for most of the republic's history. Much of this weakness can be attributed to the natural conflict between the interests of labor and the interests of the oligarchy, as well as to U.S. interests in keeping labor suppressed so that the canal construction and operation could be as cost-effective as possible and U.S. businesses could prosper. Racism also played a role, since unskilled labor tended to be nonwhite, thus nonrabiblanco and non-Anglo. In 1972, the Torrijos government approved a new labor code that finally brought labor fully into the political game. The basic elements of the new code were "job stability after two years of employment; collective bargaining at the request of the union; union dues collected of all workers covered by a collective agreement; a bonus after 10 years of employment; and the right to strike" (Phillipps Collazos 1991, 12). The only labor confederation in Panama since 1956 was the AFL-CIO affiliated Labor Confederation of the Republic of Panama, or the

CTRP. The military government, however, established the Consejo Nacional de Trabajadores (National Council of Workers), or CONATO, bringing together practically all labor organizations in a corporatist arrangement. As a result, workers became less marginalized in the political system and acquired some important material benefits. In 1960, 19 unions existed in Panama, with 17,247 members. By 1970, the number had grown to 67 unions with 21,614 members. And in 1975, the number of unions had mushroomed to 217, with 80,550 card-carrying members (Phillipps Collazos 1991, 62). Ironically, while polyarchy suffered, workers, peasants, and nonwhites in general seemed to be making both material and political progress.

The Authoritarian 1972 Constitution

After ruling by decree for four year, Torrijos and his hand-picked president moved to institutionalize *el proceso revolucionario* (the revolutionary process). Part of this ambiguous "process" was to codify the substantial political power held by Torrijos and the Guardia. The regime created a new legislative assembly called the Asamblea de Representantes de Corregimientos (Assembly of Municipal Representatives) with a total of 505 seats. These representatives were elected directly, overrepresented rural areas, were loyal to the revolutionary process, and consequently served as a rubber stamp for Torrijos's initiatives. The new Assembly promulgated a new constitution on October 11, 1972, and, bowing to Torrijos, elected Demetrio Lakas as president for a six-year term. Concurrently, the constitution made Omar Torrijos "Maximum Leader," giving him substantial political power. As Ropp points out, the new constitution gave Torrijos "the power to appoint government ministers, members of the Electoral Tribunal, National Guard officers, and members of the Supreme Court (among others). He was also charged with coordinating all government activities" (1982, 41).

Despite the constitutional and civilian veneer, Torrijos led autocratically a government whose dominant political institution was the Guardia. The regime could also be classified as bureaucratic-authoritarian since civilian government officials fully cooperated with the Torrijos-Guardia–led government. In addition to the new Assembly, the 1972 constitution established the General Council of State and the National Legislative Council, both of which were dominated by the executive branch, which was in turn dominated by Torrijos's coterie and the Guardia. In fact, the Legislative Council was given principal responsibility to write legislation, while the new Assembly served simply as a vehicle for approving or rejecting proposed legislation. As a result, contestation was not one of the regime's chief characteristics, neither from political parties nor even from within the state itself. While participation was encouraged, it was mobilized, guided, and directed by the Torrijos-Guardia–run state, as in a communist or fascist regime.

The 1972 constitution, however, was not a complete departure from previous Magna Cartas. The new law of the land continued the expansion of the state as did the 1946 constitution. The new constitution promoted social rights, state intervention in the economy, centralized national education, and the expansion of civil service careers. Article 241, for example, stated: "The State will plan economic and social development, through specialized organizations or departments whose organization and functioning will determine the law." Consequently, the Panamanian state took on a leading role in the nation's social and economic development, and its actions would by caveat create law. Nevertheless, the regime established by this new constitution was neither communist nor socialist since the new charter was still an economically liberal constitution that protected private property and enterprise (Fábrega P. 1991, 225–26). Essentially, the 1972 constitution established a regime that, although authoritarian, raised the power of the state and limited the power of the commercial elite or oligarchy. Ropp observed that Panama's military regime "continued and even accelerated" the "expansion of the Panamanian State," virtually doubling state employment from 1971 to 1980, from 60,000 to 107,000 (1992, 217).

A major departure from previous constitutions, however, was that the Guardia was given a "deliberative" and powerful role within the state, and the president was unable to exercise control over that institution. The fact that Torrijos had powers similar to those of the president and could control key appointments raised the political prominence of the Guardia. The new charter granted the Guardia chief responsibility for national defense as well as for maintaining social order, as was now common in other institutional military regimes in the region. The Guardia, however, not only acquired more power but also underwent an important ideological transformation that would affect fundamentally Panama's relations with the United States. In a period of just four years, the Guardia came to be led by officers who looked less toward the United States for answers to social and political problems. By the time the 1972 constitution had been promulgated, most high-ranking officers in the Guardia were graduates from military academies in Colombia, Mexico, Peru, and Venezuela (see Ropp 1982, 46–47). These officers had come to believe strongly in the viability and effectiveness of the "national security state" as well as in the need for social change in order to ameliorate social turmoil. Strong nationalism was also a characteristic of the attitudes imbued in these Latin American military institutions, to an extent that the United States came to be seen as a selfish hegemonic power, part of the problem rather than the source of national salvation. Peru represented the most important example of this anticommunist and anti-U.S. nationalism on the part of the armed forces. Mexico as well had for decades exhibited an "independent" foreign policy, meaning that it did not always support U.S. foreign policy, and education at its military institutions reflected this attitude. So, while Washington had initially been happy to have CIA "assets" Torrijos and Noriega in the driver's seat in Panama, over time the Guardia leadership became increasingly nationalistic and antigringo. This change in attitude, while perhaps partly explained by where these officers received their military training, no doubt also resulted from increasing frustration with U.S. hegemony and arrogance, principally since Washington was in no hurry to restructure the U.S.-Panamanian relationship as it had promised at the heels of the 1964 crisis.

Under Omar Torrijos's 1972 constitution, then, Panama did not emulate America, since polyarchy was trampled upon and the state became increasingly involved in guiding and even controlling the economic arena. And, although Panama would continue to preserve vital U.S. economic and strategic interests, both on the isthmus and in the region, the Guardia's increasing nationalism would eventually compel Torrijos to demand that the United States abrogate the infamous 1903 accord and negotiate a new relationship with the isthmus.

The Torrijos-Lakas Administration

The stage was thus set for a more powerful Panamanian state to promote some limited socioeconomic modernization and also assert a more autonomous foreign policy. During the Torrijos-Lakas administration, the latter being the junior partner, Panama's military-constitutional government launched an ambitious, multifaceted program for national development, by promoting industrialization, rural development, education, health, economic growth, mixed and state economic ventures, and construction of national infrastructure. Past governments had attempted to do the same but had relied principally on the economic elite, with the state serving only as facilitator and cheerleader. This new regime, however, would put the responsibility for national development squarely on the shoulders of the state and the Guardia. The rapid growth of state agencies meant that heretofore marginalized professionals and skilled workers were incorporated into the country's politico-military-bureaucratic class. As a result, nonrabiblancos, or people of color, now filled more prominent government positions (Harding 2001, 92). Panama's "revolutionary process" thus introduced a racial and class component, providing another reason for some scholars to applaud the so-called Torrijos Revolution.

The Panamanian state took on a plethora of tasks and grew in size with the creation of several new government agencies. For example, in the economic realm, the Torrijos-Lakas government built three sugar refineries, a copper mining company, expanded the Colón Free Trade Zone, established a state-run cement company, and passed a series of tax laws that turned Panama into a "banker's paradise" (LaFeber 1989, 137), eventually luring over one hundred international banks to the isthmus. In order to increase social services, the government created the Ministry of Health and the Ministry of Housing and established a state-run telephone company. To foment national economic development, the government established several state financial institutions, such as the Banco de Desarrollo Agropecuario (Agro-livestock Development Bank), the Corporación Financiera Nacional (National Financial Corporation), or COFINA, and the Banco Hipotecario Nacional (National Mortgage Bank). These are just a few examples of the hundreds of state-led activities and state-run organizations that the Torrijos-Lakas government inaugurated, all of which strengthened the state and helped to lend legitimacy to the regime.

The Torrijos-dominated regime could never have taken on such a comprehensive set of economic and state initiatives without extensive financial support. Previous governments had been limited in what they could accomplish both because they kept the state out of the economic arena and because they lacked the necessary investment capital. The United States and various international financial institutions, or IFIs, treated Torrijos's regime with financial largesse. Washington loaned large sums of money to Panama via the Inter-American Development Bank and the Agency for International Development. In addition, the World Bank and the International Monetary Fund supported many of Panama's new projects. For decision makers in Washington, who had significant influence over IFIs, it was very important that the Torrijos-led government succeed in maintaining order on the isthmus. Thus, the U.S. government tolerated and bankrolled a repressive military dictator who promoted substantial state involvement in the national economy. The U.S. government supported Torrijos's dictatorship and similar regimes in the region since these authoritarian governments, despite deviating from the democratic and laissez-faire U.S. model, served as bulwarks against communism or democratic socialism. In fact, during the 1960s and 1970s, steeply rising U.S. military assistance is closely associated with democratic breakdown throughout Latin America (Sánchez 2003a). Additionally, although deviating from the U.S. model, the Torrijos regime was quite friendly to U.S. economic interests, passing laws that benefited U.S. banks and multinational corporations (Ropp 1992, 219).

Would-be hegemonic states, therefore, seem to place less value on emulation by subordinate states when they believe that even a small threat to their preponderance of power exists. Policy makers in Washington provided military assistance to the region's countries and supported military regimes because they feared that America's preponderance of power in the hemisphere was at risk. Although a hemisphere replete with capitalist democracies led by the United States constituted Washington's ideal future, during the cold war the primal goal was maintaining U.S. preponderance of power by preventing an extrahemispheric power (the USSR) and ideology (communism) from influencing the region.

Canal Treaty Negotiations Redux

Despite the continuing partnership with Washington, in the early 1970s, General Torrijos began a campaign to restructure Panama's relationship with the United States, calling for the abrogation of the 1903 Hay–Bunau-Varilla Treaty. In 1970, Panama's foreign ministry stated that the 1967 Three-in-One Treaty could not serve even as an initial starting point for negotiating a new relationship with the United States. The new constitution had changed the 1946 constitution whereby Panama, instead of adhering to existing international treaties, would adhere only to those international legal norms that would not "harm the national interest." This constitutional article, purposefully included in the 1972 charter, opened the door for the regime to reject the legitimacy of the 1903 Treaty. From a quid pro quo perspective, Torrijos had helped Washington by preventing social turmoil in Panama and by temporarily setting aside the accords negotiated in 1967. The Maximum Leader believed it was now Washington's turn to return the favor. The Nixon administration, however, was in cold-war mode, besieged by serious domestic political problems and in no rush to "give away" the Panama Canal. Washington rebuked Torrijos's initial diplomatic efforts, so Torrijos and his civilian advisers decided to formulate a domestic and international campaign designed to put pressure on Washington. The military regime's honeymoon with America would soon be over.

The Maximum Leader scored a major victory when he was able to convince the United Nations Security Council to hold a special session in Panama City in March 1973, despite Washington's stiff resistance. During the historic Security Council meetings in Panama, the Torrijos regime was able to make its case against U.S. neocolonialism and was able to convince the Council to vote on a resolution that obliquely criticized the U.S. presence on the isthmus. Although Washington vetoed this watered-down resolution, all other Security Council members voted in favor of it, while the United Kingdom abstained. General Torrijos also highlighted Panama's cause within the Non-Aligned Movement and began to make friends with governments that he knew would rally behind Panama's grievances against the United States, including such United States foes as Cuba and Libya. Washington sent diplomatic signals to Torrijos that he had gone too far, yet only two months after the Security Council's special session on the isthmus, President Nixon informed the U.S. Congress that it was "time for both parties . . . to develop a new relationship" (quoted in Jorden 1984, 199). The Nixon administration deplored Torrijos's tactics and actions, particularly his heightened anti-U.S. nationalism and coziness with leftist regimes. However, the general's actions also worried Washington at a time when the United States seemed to be losing its influence in Latin America, as well as in the world in general. Washington, in fact, had decided to start a dialogue with the Soviet Union and China in an attempt to ameliorate cold war tensions and improve U.S. stature globally. A serious crisis in Panama, especially if it led to the inauguration of an anti-U.S. regime, was something that U.S. policy makers felt they could not afford. Consequently, Washington's chief foreign policy makers relented and began to work with the Torrijos regime on a new U.S.-Panamanian relationship. Weak Panama, by asserting itself during a brief moment of American weakness, was able to get the Great Power's attention.

Negotiations started soon after the Security Council meeting, resulting in a joint U.S.-Panamanian declaration, which was ironed out by U.S. secretary of state Henry Kissinger and Panama's foreign minister Juan Antonio Tack. The so-called Eight Points Declaration, signed in February 1974, called for a new treaty that would abrogate the 1903 accord, eliminate perpetuity, end U.S. jurisdiction over Panama's territory, increase economic compensation to Panama, transfer the canal to Panama, provide for joint canal defense, and promote canal modernization (Pedreschi 1974, 5–6). Washington had finally accepted the notion of abrogating the 1903 Treaty and turning the Canal Zone and the canal back to Panama. It appeared to many observers that Panama had finally bested the region's preponderant power.

But while high-level U.S. foreign policy makers, especially within the State Department, had become convinced that a new treaty with Panama was in the U.S. national interest, intense resistance to "giving away" the canal still persisted within the U.S. government, the U.S. Congress, and the American public. Within the Department of Defense—the institution most opposed to a new treaty—opinions eventually changed as to the value of keeping the Canal Zone. For example, one DOD publication asserted: "At the present, our ability to protect our interests [the canal] through the exercise of this extensive grant of jurisdictional authority is in serious doubt" (U.S. Department of Defense 1976, 6). In essence, the DOD finally came to the realization that isthmian stability and canal defense could be achieved best by turning the U.S. Zone over to the Panamanians. Chief U.S. negotiator Ellsworth Bunker made significant headway when he acquired Pentagon acceptance for a new treaty, but with the proviso that a new accord await the November 1976 U.S. presidential elections (Conniff 1992, 132). Thus, a new treaty with Panama would eventually become the responsibility of President Jimmy Carter.

Washington's new stance was also influenced by the fact that the canal was no longer the economic asset it once was. While an engineering marvel and a godsend for U.S. maritime trade in the early 1900s, the canal now seemed to be obsolete, was becoming more costly to maintain and operate, and was virtually indefensible against missile or terrorist attacks (U.S. Department of Defense 1976; Falcoff 1998, 50–55). U.S. experts knew that by 1999 the canal would have outlived its usefulness, and a new waterway or major modifications to the existing canal would be needed. So, by U.S. election year 1976, veteran policy makers and analysts of the realpolitik and liberal schools alike concurred that the famous canal had lost its vital military and economic importance and that stability in Panama required a treaty that would end the semicolonial relationship established by the infamous 1903 accord.

The 1977 Torrijos-Carter Treaties

When President Jimmy Carter took office in January 1977, a new accord with Panama was at the top of his foreign policy agenda (Pastor 1995). While "justice" for Panama was important to Carter's foreign policy focus on human rights, a new treaty was now clearly in the strategic interest of the United States of America, as noted above. Treaty talks moved at a fast pace since both countries put a premium on fashioning a new bilateral relationship. On September 7, 1977, after only six months of negotiations, President Carter and Maximum Leader Torrijos signed two accords that restructured fundamentally the U.S.-Panamanian relationship (for the full text of the treaties, see LaFeber 1989, 230–48).[3] One accord, the Panama Canal Treaty, finally abrogated the infamous 1903 Hay–Bunau-Varilla Treaty. The Panama Canal Treaty scheduled the elimination of the U.S. Canal Zone in October 1979, provided for the transfer of the canal to Panama at noon on December 31,

1999, and gave the isthmus a much larger financial portion of canal profits. The other agreement, the Treaty Concerning the Permanent Neutrality and Operation of the Panama Canal, or Neutrality Treaty, focused on canal security, committing both nations to preserving canal neutrality, and providing for the defense of the canal for as long as it was in operation. This second treaty was very controversial in Panama for two important reasons: first, it granted the U.S. government security responsibilities virtually in perpetuity; and, second, it legalized the extensive complex of U.S. military bases and operations already in Panama (see Gurdián Guerra 1998, 105). Nevertheless, the Neutrality Treaty provided for an end to the long-standing U.S. military presence on the isthmus, stating:

> After the termination of the Panama Canal Treaty [December 31, 1999], only the Republic of Panama shall operate the Canal and maintain military forces, defense sites and military installations within its national territory. (LaFeber 1989, 242)

So, although Washington maintained its rights to defend the canal indefinitely and kept control of the waterway for another twenty years, Panama would finally take control of the Canal Zone in 1979; and, at the end of 1999, Panama would take over the canal and Washington would close down its military bases and send its soldiers packing. The new treaties thus eliminated most of the irritants of the 1903 accord and opened a new, more amicable chapter in U.S.-Panamanian relations, as well as in U.S.–Latin American relations. This new chapter, however, would be a short one, as we will see below. For the moment, each government now faced the difficult task of selling the new treaties to its respective domestic constituencies.

Ironically, the Carter administration would get the treaties ratified in a less democratic manner than would Torrijos's regime. President Carter only needed the U.S. Senate to ratify the two accords by a two-thirds majority. The general, on the other hand, had to put the treaty before the rubber-stamp Assembly of Representatives as well as before the public via a national referendum. Torrijos, of course, had the advantage of leading a dictatorship that could achieve approval through the exercise of power and outright fraud. The new treaties were very controversial in Panama. Since Torrijos controlled the new Assembly, this body approved the accords rapidly. The general then scheduled a national referendum to be held quickly. The Torrijos regime also dominated the national news media and was thus able to limit debate on the issue. Although the regime mounted a massive pro-treaty campaign, strong opposition to the accords came from students and professionals, and even from some economic elite. The official result of the

October 23, 1977, plebiscite was 506,805 votes in favor and 245,117 votes against the treaties, or 65 percent for and 35 percent against (Pizzurno Gelós and Araúz 1996, 575). It is quite possible, however, that the treaties either lost in the referendum or won by a much narrower margin than the military government suggested (Velásquez 1993, 41–44). Despite the nationalism of the Torrijos regime and its ability to get Washington to dramatically alter the U.S.-Panamanian relationship, many Panamanians rejected the military dictatorship as well as the accords the regime had reached with the United States—for the reasons stated above.

In contrast, although procedurally more simple, the Carter administration had before it a Herculean task in getting the treaties ratified since influential members of the Senate from both the Republican and Democratic parties opposed the new relationship with Panama. Public opinion ran solidly against the treaties and only reached a level of mild acceptance in early 1978 (Hogan 1986, 201). Nevertheless, the Carter administration spent a lot of political, and actual, capital and was able eventually to convince enough members of the Senate to vote against public opinion (Skidmore 1993, 477–97). Hugh Sidey wrote that Carter spent "millions of dollars for a few votes, just like an oldtime pol" (quoted in Hogan 1986, 91).

Carter's need to compromise with key senators to ensure Senate ratification led to a diplomatic crisis. To get the necessary votes in the Senate, President Carter was forced to accept substantial Senate amendments to the agreements that he had already signed with General Torrijos. Senators Sam Nunn and Dennis DeConcini added provisos or clarifications in exchange for their support. First, in the event that canal operations were threatened, the United States reserved the "right to take such steps as [it] deems necessary . . . including the use of military force in the Republic of Panama, to reopen the Canal or restore the operations of the Canal, as the case may be" (LaFeber 1989, 244). This amendment to the accord evoked the 1903 Treaty and the Platt Amendment. In an effort to reassure Panamanians, the U.S. Senate also included a clarification that stated: "This does not mean, nor shall it be interpreted as, a right of intervention of the United States in the internal affairs of Panama. Any United States action will be directed at insuring that the Canal will remain open, secure, and accessible, and *it shall never be directed against the territorial integrity or political independence of Panama*" (LaFeber 1989, 244; my emphasis). Despite this assurance, the United States invaded Panama twelve years later, changed the country's political system, and arrested, tried, and jailed its de facto leader, General Manuel Antonio Noriega. The second important change to the accords addressed the U.S. military presence on the isthmus. The U.S. Senate included a clarification that opened the door for a possible U.S. military presence after the year 1999. Some senators did not want to terminate the U.S. military presence on the isthmus and would not have supported the treaties had the U.S. government not made sure to allow for that option. The Senate included the following words in the instruments of ratification, which carry the same legal weight as the treaties themselves: "Nothing in the treaty shall preclude the Republic of Panama and the United States of America from making . . . agreements or arrangements for the stationing of any United States military forces or the maintenance of defense sites . . . in the Republic of Panama . . . that the Republic of Panama and the United States of America may deem necessary or appropriate" (LaFeber 1989, 244–45). Proponents of a continued U.S. military presence in Panama would years later use this last-minute change to assert that the Panama Canal Treaties *authorized* America to keep U.S. military installations in Panama beyond 1999. Those who made these claims conveniently forgot that the maintenance of U.S. bases after 1999 required Panama's full consent. These two important alterations to the treaties generated deep resentment on the part of the Torrijos regime and the Panamanian public.

The Carter administration achieved Senate ratification of the Panama Canal Treaties only after a costly and concerted pro-treaty campaign directed at the public and the U.S. Senate. On March 16, 1978, after heated debate, the Senate approved the Neutrality Treaty by a razor-thin vote of 68 to 32 (a two-thirds majority is required for treaty ratification). Two days later, the Senate ratified the Panama Canal Treaty by the same narrow margin. The fight for the canal had been intense, but President Carter, armed with a relatively solid high-level consensus over the need for a new accord and using extensive political capital, government largesse, and deal making, succeeded in transforming the U.S.-Panamanian relationship. Despite the intense nationalistic squabbling, opponents and supporters of the Canal Treaties in the United States never lost sight of America's security and economic interests in Panama and in Latin America. To be sure, Washington finally agreed to give up control of the Canal Zone in 1979 and the Panama Canal at the end of 1999. But the United States no longer viewed the canal as a vital economic possession; was able to shake its image as a neocolonial power; legitimated and retained its military bases on the isthmus; defused its poor relations with Torrijos; and still retained its "right" to defend the canal. In sum, from a long-term realpolitik perspective, the United States enhanced or preserved its economic, strategic, and political interests in the region without really losing much.

In Panama, Torrijos and all isthmians had to swallow the alterations to the treaties imposed by Senators Nunn and DeConcini. Despite the fact that they are characterized as a unique example of success in U.S.-Panamanian relations, the 1977 treaty process also represented one of the most dangerous periods in U.S.-Panamanian relations. Angry at the two amendments passed in the Senate and angry at the prospects that the Senate would not ratify the treaties, Torrijos admitted that he considered sabotaging the canal during this tense period, an action that would have generated a regional crisis and compelled the United States to intervene militarily. Torrijos had already developed a secret plan to sabotage the canal if the U.S. Congress did not ratify the treaties. Operation Huele Quemado (Smells Burning) called for two thousand Guardia personnel to carry out small-scale attacks in literally hundreds of locations along the waterway (Ku Sánchez 1998). This extensive sabotage operation would have been impossible to stop and relatively easy for the Guardia to carry out. We can only assume that the Carter administration was aware that this operation was in the works, and that key U.S. decision makers and members of Congress were kept informed. The danger to U.S. interests was clear and present, and keeping the Zone and the outdated canal was not worth the potential risk. In hindsight, the Canal Treaties preserved U.S. interests and only barely defused a potentially serious crisis with Panama.

Despite the optimism generated by treaty implementation on October 1, 1979, U.S.-Panamanian relations continued to suffer, owing to the U.S. House of Representatives' influence in formulating the treaty implementation legislation. The Panama Canal Zone ceased to exist, resulting in great joy among Panamanians of all races and classes.[4] Panama received large parcels of property, thousands of buildings, and a substantially larger share of revenues from canal operations. The Panama Canal Commission, or PCC, took over the operation of the waterway, with a governing board of five U.S. and four Panamanian officials. Nevertheless, the United States retained control of the canal operating area as well as its extensive military facilities. In effect, Washington still "owned" about 60 percent of the territory it had previously controlled. Additionally, the U.S. Congress' implementation legislation, the Panama Canal Act of 1979, put the Department of the Army in control of the Panama Canal Commission. Panamanians as well as U.S. supporters of the treaties had assumed that the PCC would be an autonomous, civilian-led U.S agency, like the old Panama Canal Company (see Furlong and Scranton 1984, 172–204). And, while the unequal salary schedule that had caused so much animosity in Panama was eliminated, employees of the PCC who were U.S. citizens received higher wages and benefits than did their Panamanian counterparts, via a special bonus for service in a tropical environment. The treaty honeymoon ended almost as soon as it had started.

Panama could do nothing to stop this maneuvering by U.S. nationalists in the Senate and House of Representatives. Again, the United States quickly moved to preserve its interests and control the relationship with Panama.

The Troubled Post-treaty Democratic Transition

An unwritten aspect of the treaty negotiations involved Panama's return to democracy. The Carter administration, some senators, and high-level U.S. policy makers were concerned that the U.S. government had finally succeeded in restructuring the U.S.-Panamanian relationship but with a repressive military regime rather than with a democratic government.[5] During the treaty negotiating process, General Torrijos promised the Carter administration that he would democratize Panama soon after treaty implementation by holding elections, legalizing political parties, and restoring the National Assembly. The Maximum Leader knew that his popularity would increase both at home and abroad if he presided over a democratizing process after his treaty "victory." He therefore bowed to U.S. pressure knowing that he could run for president and have an excellent chance of becoming Panama's elected president. In 1978, the Assembly of Municipal Representatives selected Dr. Arístides Royo Sánchez as president, while Ricardo de la Espriella became vice president. The new Assembly had offered the presidency to Torrijos, but the general had ceremoniously declined. Torrijos also left his position as head of state but retained his charge as commander in chief of the Guardia, which still left him with enormous power. More fundamental changes would follow. In October 1978, the government legalized political parties and scheduled an election for 1980 that would restore the National Assembly. And, most important, the regime scheduled national elections for 1984 to elect a president, vice presidents, and national legislators. The transition to democracy that many Panamanians and President Carter desired was finally put in motion.

The September 1980 elections, one year after the elimination of the Canal Zone, was somewhat of a democratic disappointment since key political parties, Liberal and Panameñista, did not participate in protest of the de facto political system. Only six political parties participated: Partido Demócrata Cristiano (Christian Democrat), or PDC; Partido Liberación Nacional (National Liberation Party), or PLN; Partido Frente Amplio Popular (Broad Popular Front Party), or FRAPO; Partido Socialista de los Trabajadores (Worker's Socialist Party), or PST; Partido Revolucionario de los Trabajadores (Worker's Revolutionary Party), or PRT; and the newly forged Partido Revolucionario Democrático (Revolutionary Democratic Party), or

PRD. The PRD had been founded in early 1979 as a party that would pre-serve Torrijos's *proceso revolucionario*. Torrijismo now joined Arnulfismo (panameñismo) in Panamanian politics. PRD leaders hoped that the party would establish itself as a dominant party in a multiparty political system along the lines of the PRI in Mexico. As a result, the 1980 national legislative election did not alter significantly the concentration of political power in the hands of Torrijos, the Guardia, and their civilian collaborators. Additionally, the election added only sixteen elected members to the Torrijos-dominated National Council on Legislation. So far, redemocratization was restricted and controlled.

Events continued to take a turn for the worse even though many observ-ers assumed that the Treaties and the democratic transition would improve the domestic situation in Panama as well as U.S.-Panamanian ties. In July 1981, General Omar Torrijos died in an airplane accident while visiting a rural location as was his trademark. The Maximum Leader's untimely death instantly created a power vacuum as well as a programmatic struggle at a very delicate period of political transition. The regime at this time was in trouble, besieged by protests and saddled with enormous debt, and it now lacked the unifying force provided by the Maximum Leader. When Tor-rijos died, Colonel Florencio Flores ascended to command the Guardia but was "retired" by his ambitious peers since Flores wanted to depoliticize the Guardia (Velásquez 1993, 86). The new Guardia *comandante*, Rubén D. Pare-des, then forced President Royo to resign in July 1982. The fallen president sardonically offered a "sore throat" as the reason for his resignation. Two important factors helped contribute to Royo's ouster: the rising opposition to the regime coming from labor, students, and political parties; and the president's nationalist-Torrijista position that antagonized the United States (Martínez H. 1990, 62–65). Vice President Ricardo de la Espriella took over the presidency from Royo. In addition to removing the president, Paredes cleaned house by removing high-level cabinet members and government officials and stifled criticisms of the regime by closing down opposition newspapers. The stage was thus set for the Guardia to retain control of the isthmus's political system, despite the scheduled elections. And General Paredes was poised to become the PRD's presidential candidate for the May 1984 electoral contest. Instead of the Mexican model of civilian, one-party dominance, Panama now seemed poised to follow the Guatemalan model, where a dominant military ensured that its generals were elected president. Panama's democratization had quickly and unexpectedly become derailed.

Events outside of Panama also conspired to hamper Panama's return to democracy. The Soviet invasion of Afghanistan and the Nicaraguan revolution, both occurring in 1979, intensified U.S. security interests globally and in Latin America. Policy makers in Washington, and particularly the White House, interpreted these two events as a push by the Soviet Union to enhance its global position. Those in Washington who saw Panama as an important strategic chess piece could now marshal a stronger argument for preserving and enhancing the U.S. military presence in the isthmus. These events, along with the Iran hostage crisis, helped to bring a more conservative administration into the White House, led by Ronald Reagan, who had been one of the chief opponents of the Canal Treaty negotiations. The paramount goal in the region for the Reagan administration was to prevent communist penetration. To achieve this goal, Washington supported the counterrevolutionaries in Nicaragua, known as the Contras, who were trying to undermine the leftist Sandinista regime in Nicaragua, and shored up the undemocratic, pro-U.S. regimes in El Salvador and Guatemala that were fighting leftist insurgencies. The regional politico-military environment had changed dramatically in just a few years. In the late 1970s, the principal U.S. concern had been to restore good relations with Panama and with the region. By the early 1980s, however, Washington saw communist influence as its paramount regional concern, since such "expansion" could potentially translate into a corresponding decline in U.S. economic, military, and political influence. U.S. government officials were convinced that U.S. preponderance of power was once again being challenged by an extrahemispheric power (the USSR) that employed its regional surrogate (Cuba) to penetrate the region more effectively. Consequently, as with the Mann Doctrine of the 1960s, Washington began to prefer once more anticommunist, pro-U.S. regimes over weak democratic regimes. The one important difference was that in the 1980s Washington desired the authoritarian regimes to hold elections. The cold war struggle of the 1960s and 1970s had demonstrated that conservative civilian regimes were more effective at combating insurgents and attaining domestic legitimacy than military regimes.

By July 1983, two years after Torrijos's death, the political scene had taken another unexpected turn. General Manuel Antonio Noriega conspired to take control of Panama's Guardia, renaming it the Panamanian Defense Forces (PDF), and had firmly established himself as the isthmus's de facto ruler. Noriega achieved his position of power in classic Machiavellian fashion, by double-crossing other top officers, including Paredes and Colonel Roberto Díaz Herrera, a cousin of Torrijos and reputed to be the officer closest to the deceased general (Martínez H. 1990, 58). In March 1982, Noriega and several fellow officers signed the "Secret Plan Torrijos," designed to ensure Guardia control of the presidency by putting forth General Paredes as the "official" PRD presidential candidate for the 1984 elections. The other signatories to the secret plan agreed to take turns as commander of the PDF. However, when Paredes retired to become the PRD's presidential candidate, Noriega failed to provide his former comrade the Guardia's support for his presidential bid (Koster and Sánchez 1990, 256–57). Noriega then convinced the PRD to back the candidacy of banker Nicolás Ardito Barletta, a pro-U.S. protégé of Secretary of State George Schultz and former vice president of the World Bank. The rise to power of General Noriega and Colonel Díaz Herrera to top PDF positions strengthened the Torrijista line that called for the defense of national sovereignty (Steinsleger 1986, 25–26). Paredes, in contrast, was perceived as more supportive of the United States and its regional goals. What most observers did not know at the time, however, was that Noriega had been working very closely with the U.S. Central Intelligence Agency (CIA) since the 1950s, when he was a cadet at Peru's military academy (Kempe 1990, 26). In hindsight, a political paradox seemed to exist in Panama: Torrijistas were in solid command of the PDF, but Washington's favorite, Barletta, became the PRD's presidential candidate, and the DOD was able to use the isthmus, almost carte blanche, to further its strategic goals. Political paradoxes aside, General Noriega, with support from Washington, essentially undermined the "democratization" process that Torrijos had initiated. Great Power politics, rather than communism, penetrated Panama, resulting in the preeminence of strategic imperatives over the restoration of competitive politics.

Three months before the 1984 elections, another political shake-up occurred: President Ricardo de la Espriella abruptly resigned. Another chief executive had felt the political sting of the PDF and its key officers. In late 1983, de la Espriella had toyed with the idea of being the "official" presidential candidate, and PDF officers feared that he would promote free and fair elections (de la Espriella 1998; Velásquez 1993, 98). Dr. Jorge E. Illueca, the staunchly nationalist vice president who had firmly supported the revolutionary process, assumed the presidency. Despite the political upheaval, the democratic facade was nevertheless moving "forward." Political contestation had returned to Panama with fourteen parties and seven presidential candidates registered to compete in the May 1984 elections. Two presidential candidates dominated the political landscape, however: Nicolás Ardito Barletta represented the Union Nacional Democrática alliance (National Democratic Union), or UNADE, and was the "official" candidate, backed by Noriega, the PRD, the PDF, and Washington; and Arnulfo Arias and his Panameñista Party rallied the diverse opposition under the Alianza de Oposición (Opposition Alliance), or ADO, which also included the Christian Democrats, the newly created Movimiento Liberal Republicano Nacional (National Liberal Republican Movement), or MOLIRENA, bringing together much of the economic elite and the Partido Liberal Auténtico (Authentic Liberal Party). Former PDF commander Rubén D. Paredes, despite his Noriega-engineered fall from grace, ran under the banner of the Partido Nacionalista Popular (Nationalist Popular Party), or PNP. After electoral violence that left four dead and delays in the vote tally, the Electoral Tribunal announced Barletta as the winner with the minuscule margin of 1,713 votes (Arias Peña and Quintero 1994, 19–20). Convincing evidence demonstrated that Barletta did not win the election but rather that he owed his presidency to vote fraud and manipulation by the PDF (see Arias de Para 1984). Although aware of the fraud, Washington and the U.S. embassy in Panama did not criticize the stolen election. Washington favored Barletta and still feared an unpredictable Arias presidency. As in the past, the U.S. government wanted a compliant, pro-U.S. regime that would cooperate with U.S. strategic goals in the hemisphere and efficiently implement the 1977 Canal Treaties. And now the new government could also boast that it was "elected."

The Barletta-Noriega-Washington Triumvirate

The 1984 transition was clearly a farce, since Noriega, the PDF, and Washington retained political power on the isthmus and the new president had won via PDF-orchestrated fraud. Very quickly the new regime came under intense criticism at home and abroad. General Noriega became a lightning rod, owing to the repressive nature of the PDF, his involvement in the drug trade, and his sometimes "anti-U.S." activities. At the same time, President Barletta came under fire at home for implementing austerity measures that negatively affected many Panamanians. Like his mentor Torrijos, Noriega was a complex man. At the same time that he was kowtowing to Washington in matters of U.S. national security, he was pursuing some independent, "nationalist" policies. The general had cooperated fully with Washington by forcing Torrijos's political party, the PRD, to nominate Barletta as its presidential candidate. This nomination was an affront to the PRD's ideology and leadership. The party, after all, had been created to ensure the survival of the revolutionary process. Second, Noriega assisted Washington with its many strategic operations in Latin America, particularly with activities designed to bring down the Sandinista regime in Nicaragua. U.S. defense, antidrug, and intelligence agencies used the complex of U.S. military bases in Panama extensively to carry out operations that had little to do with canal defense. The CIA monitored Soviet and Cuban activities. The National Security Agency operated listening posts and flew thousands of surveillance missions, using numerous specially designed aircraft. The PDF, DOD, and CIA cooperated to provide training to the Contras at various U.S. military facilities in Panama (Spence 1989, 40). And the DOD trained thousands of military personnel from Latin America in numerous U.S. military training facilities on the isthmus, the most visible and controversial being the School of the Americas (SOA). In 1981, the SOA provided 5,000 student-weeks of training for Latin American military personnel. By 1984, the number had increased to 29,000 student-weeks (Steinsleger 1986, 34). The United States of America, therefore, was using the Republic of Panama as a strategic outpost, carrying out activities that not only violated isthmian sovereignty but the sovereignty of other countries in the region. In sum, despite his Torrijista credentials, General Noriega soon behaved as a U.S. lackey, allowing Washington to do as it wished in Central America by using Panama as a strategic platform for U.S. military and intelligence operations (Dinges 1990, 147–64).

At the same time this extensive cooperation was taking place, Noriega, like Torrijos, was also involved in activities that angered some U.S. policy makers and elected officials. In 1983, Noriega spearheaded the foundation of the Contadora Group, formed by Panama, Venezuela, Mexico, and Colombia. These countries agreed to promote a peaceful solution to the internal conflicts raging in the Central American nations of Nicaragua, El Salvador, and Guatemala. Washington viewed this diplomatic approach with skepticism, preferring a unilateral strategy of providing military and economic assistance to the pro–U.S. Salvadoran and Guatemalan regimes and to the Nicaraguan Contras.[6] In 1984, the facilities and land that comprised Fort Gulick, one of the many U.S. military bases on the isthmus, was to be reverted to Panama, as stipulated by the Canal Treaties. Washington had a strong interest in keeping the SOA, housed at Fort Gulick, open and in Panama, to continue its training of Latin American military personnel who often went on to support U.S. strategic goals in the region. After some rocky negotiations, Noriega decided to take over Fort Gulick and force the United States to relocate the school, much to the displeasure of the Reagan administration (*Latin America Regional Reports: Mexico and Central America*, August 17, 1984, 4). The U.S. Department of Defense had to quickly move the school to Fort Benning, Georgia. General Noriega was also involved in numerous illegal activities that should have concerned Washington greatly from the start. Although he had become involved in the drug trade at least by the early 1970s, Noriega was now a major player in cocaine trafficking. Noriega also ignored the U.S. trade embargo against Cuba and sold Western goods and intelligence to the Castro government. Cuba's economic presence was increasing on the isthmus, and Castro's intelligence operations used Cuban business ventures in Panama to monitor the extensive U.S. presence. At the same time that he helped the U.S. government sustain El Salvador's beleaguered regime, Noriega supplied the Salvadoran leftist rebels with weapons as well. And, much to the intelligence community's shock, back in 1974 he had infiltrated U.S. National Security Agency intelligence operations in Panama, something no other country had been able to accomplish (Buckley 1991, 147). While all of this was taking place, Washington conferred upon the general glowing commendations that celebrated his assistance with U.S. antidrug operations (for details concerning Noriega's activities and his regime, see Guevara Mann 1994; Gandásegui 1993; Ropp 1992; Scranton 1991; Dinges 1990; Kempe 1990; and Koster and Sánchez 1990). As long as he cooperated with what Reagan officials considered the key strategic issues, General Noriega was allowed extensive leeway, especially since the general argued that his "other" activities were necessary to maintain his "cover." Needless to say, Noriega probably convinced himself that the money he made from these activities was the price Washington had to pay for his cooperation.

U.S. agencies most likely accepted and even promoted Noriega's seemingly anti-U.S. activities because it gave the general a nationalist veneer, as well as making him a more valuable intelligence asset. These considerations meant that Washington would tolerate a great deal from Noriega, even his extensive involvement in the drug trade and his destructive tampering with Panama's return to democracy. Nevertheless, Washington expected that Noriega, although being involved in some unsavory activities, including undermining isthmian democracy, would always serve as a champion of U.S. interests. At a time when vital U.S. interests seemed to be at stake, Washington's principal concern was preserving those interests rather than encouraging Panama to emulate America's political and economic model, even if it required saddling Panama and working closely with a "thug," as President George Bush would eventually label Noriega.

President Barletta, on the other hand, was a U.S. protégé who carried out economic changes in Panama that he believed were necessary to move the country away from debt and economic stagnation. Barletta supported the "Washington consensus" that called for the lowering of trade barriers, privatization, and reduced government spending. These policies, carried out by a government put in place by fraudulent elections and supported by General Noriega and the PDF, quickly led to a serious legitimacy crisis for the Barletta administration. The president promised to eliminate the economic crisis by infusing new life in the nation's productive sectors, including agriculture, fishing, industry, banking, tourism, and services (Pizzurno Gelós and Araúz 1996, 608–9). Barletta's rhetoric was evocative of the promises of many previous governments, all of which failed to deliver economic salvation and national unity. Less than one month after his inauguration, in November 1984, President Barletta, in a televised speech to the nation, announced a series of economic austerity measures, promoted by Washington, the IMF, and the World Bank. The economic measures would be approved by the National Legislative Council in its last set of actions before turning legislative power over to the newly elected National Assembly. Opponents of the Barletta government immediately established the National Civil Coordinating Committee, or COCINA, bringing together students, teachers, doctors, and professionals to oppose both the austerity measures and new taxes announced by Barletta. By the end of November, both CONATO, the labor peak organization established by the military regime, and COCINA had organized and held demonstrations against the government's economic policies, prompting Barletta to quickly revoke the new taxes but not the austerity measures. The social mobilization and strong civil society that quickly reemerged attacked both the Barletta government and the PDF, calling for the military budget to be made public (Martínez H. 1990, 75).

In the following year, the regime crisis reached a crescendo. CONATO and COCINA continued to put pressure on the government to revoke the externally imposed austerity measures. Consequently, in this period of social and political turmoil, the PDF used repressive measures, employing a special antiriot battalion called the Dobermans. Rather than deterring further public opposition, the repression resulted in increased tensions in the country. In July 1985, the PDF entered the University of Panama, violating that institution's constitutional autonomy and violently putting down student support for a general strike organized by CONATO.[7] In August 1985, the leader of COCINA, Mauro Zúñiga, was kidnapped and beaten by PDF intelligence personnel, auguring a sinister period in PDF repression. It was clear that Panamanians were expecting more democracy than the Barletta government could deliver. The Panamanian people, despite the presence of a repressive regime, consistently took to the streets, demonstrating that they valued and demanded participation despite the cost to their personal safety (see Janson Pérez 1993). Although some scholars have argued that Latin Americans lack democratic values, the people of Panama had shown for many decades that they valued highly political participation and civic engagement.

The Murder of Hugo Spadafora and "MAN's" Fall from Grace

One man, the popular doctor Hugo Spadafora, came to represent the most ominous threat to Noriega and the PDF. Spadafora had served as vice minister of health under Torrijos and had been the leader of an armed Panamanian contingent that supported the Sandinista rebellion. A relatively young, handsome, and bold man, Hugo Spadafora accused Noriega and the PDF of being involved in the trafficking of illicit drugs and weapons (something that was street knowledge on the isthmus). Noriega was informed that Spadafora, who was out of the country, planned to return to Panama to publicly denounce him. On September 14, 1985, Dr. Spadafora's decapitated and mutilated body was found stuffed in a U.S. government mailbag in Costa Rica, near the Panama border. This horrific act sparked the downfall of President Barletta and the eventual demise of Noriega and the PDF. Panamanians were stunned but provoked into action, particularly Spadafora's family, which naturally (and correctly) blamed Noriega himself. The U.S. government knew about Noriega's involvement in the crime, since the National Security Agency had monitored communications that placed the order to kill Spadafora squarely on Noriega (Dinges 1990, 239).[8] While Colonel Díaz Herrera tried to offer up a bogus civilian suspect, President Barletta, in New York City at the time, announced that he would investigate the matter fully. Noriega demanded that Barletta return to Panama immediately. Once back on the isthmus, Barletta made the mistake of going to see General Noriega at his *comandancia* in Fort Amador, a combined U.S.-Panamanian facility. Noriega then forced the president to sign a letter of resignation at the point of a gun and after threatening his family. Barletta's "resignation" brought Vice President Eric Delvalle to the presidency. The change of presidents, of course, did nothing to ameliorate the economic and political crisis, since Noriega and his PDF were still in charge.

In Washington and at the U.S. embassy in Panama, someone must have been cursing. The Frankenstein that U.S. policy makers had created and supported had simply gone too far by removing Washington's handpicked president. But despite Noriega's blunt move, it would be months before Washington would officially turn on Noriega and begin to withdraw economic and military support for the "thug." From this point, Panama fell into a downward spiral. The government was unable to implement policies effectively. The PDF could barely maintain order. And the U.S. government began to distance itself from Noriega and to urge him to step aside, realizing that the general was a danger to canal treaty implementation and to political stability on the isthmus. Washington had helped to create the Guardia for the purpose of maintaining stability and preserving U.S. interests on the isthmus, but now the PDF was one of the key sources of instability, and its officers and commander were exhibiting signs of anti-U.S. nationalism. Once the U.S. government began to vilify the general, the opposition in Panama became more and more emboldened, augmenting the already serious regime crisis.

General Manuel Antonio Noriega—whom U.S. officials mockingly (and sometimes affectionately) referred to as *MAN* or *Manny*—perhaps straddled the line between cooperation with Washington and nationalism once too often. The U.S. government's decision to distance itself from Noriega, while encouraged by Barletta's removal from power, was the result principally of the general's inability and unwillingness to cooperate with U.S. goals and maintain order on the isthmus. As noted above, Noriega had been involved in activities that had angered U.S. lawmakers and policy makers, but "Manny's" cooperation with U.S. efforts to bring down the Sandinista government in Nicaragua and with other U.S. strategic operations in the hemisphere had guaranteed U.S. economic and military support. By 1986, however, the situation had changed significantly. The general had ordered the assassination of a popular opposition figure and had removed Washington's man from the presidency. Noriega had also refused to cooperate with U.S. efforts to start negotiations on the permanence of U.S. bases past the year 1999. As early as 1983, Washington had tried to start talks with the PDF, but the general was not prepared to negotiate.[9] And, as noted above, Noriega forced the DOD to close down the School of the Americas, which policy makers viewed as a strategically vital U.S. training facility. Noriega's PDF, while cooperating on some important fronts, maintained close links with the PRD, a political party that still insisted that all U.S. soldiers should leave the isthmus at the end of 1999. In fact, the PDF's weekly television program would always end with U.S. troops marching away from the camera as the commentator proudly pronounced that Panama would finally achieve full sovereignty once all U.S. troops withdrew from the isthmus at noon on December 31, 1999.

More generally Washington was increasingly concerned about the proper disposition of the 1977 Canal Treaties. Noriega appeared to be setting up the PDF as the institution principally responsible for treaty implementation. As the leading political institution, the PDF was acquiring all reverted properties and had been reorganized and strengthened in order to take over prime responsibility for canal defense after the year 1999. The PDF was parceling out the reverted properties as perks to its officers and hangers-on. The U.S. government had expected the PDF to professionalize in order to take over the task of canal defense; in fact, combined U.S.-Panamanian defense exercises were increased and intensified for this purpose (Leis 1985, 95). However, Washington did not expect the PDF to have prime responsibility for the entire treaty implementation process, especially since the Canal Treaties committed the U.S. government to help prepare the government of Panama for taking over canal operations in the year 2000. Nor was the PDF supposed to retain control of all civilian institutions that needed to be strengthened in order to effectively take over canal operations after the year 2000. Finally, Washington had been embarrassed by having to renegotiate its relationship with Panama with a military dictator; it would be doubly embarrassing to turn over the canal and all its military facilities at the end of 1999 to another military-dominated regime, particularly one that was increasingly nationalistic and while the rest of the region was returning to democracy.

The last nail sealed Noriega's coffin when the Iran-Contra affair hit the press and then came under congressional investigation in late 1986. The hearings exposed the Reagan administration's military assistance to the Contras, despite a congressional ban, as well as "Manny's" involvement in the affair and his many other illicit and anti-U.S. activities. The scandal led to the removal from office of National Security Advisor John Poindexter, CIA director William Casey, and Under Secretary of State for Inter-American Affairs Elliot Abrams. These three men were Noriega's most ardent supporters in Washington. Once the Contra war was taken off the strategic agenda, Washington only saw Noriega's many faults, and the general appeared to be of no real value for preserving U.S. interests. Almost immediately, "Manny" became a pariah, and the Reagan administration leaked damning information about him to the U.S. Congress and to the U.S. press (see Hersh 1986). Washington then began to take systematic steps to force the general from power (see Kempe 1990; Koster and Sánchez 1990; and Scranton 1991). Although some bureaucratic wrangling certainly took place, U.S. policy was aggressive, logical, and clearly focused on removing Noriega from power, especially once the general reacted negatively and forcefully to the various U.S. efforts to topple him.

Meanwhile President Delvalle was attempting to keep the economy afloat. To deal with the country's enormous debt, which drained 37 percent of government spending in 1985 (Harding 2001, 168), Delvalle negotiated with the IMF and agreed to certain conditions, such as privatization and reduced government spending, in order to acquire some debt relief. These actions naturally eroded the regime's already limited support, and antigovernment protests continued.

In June 1987, another serious crisis erupted when Noriega forced Colonel Roberto Díaz Herrera to retire. Colonel Díaz Herrera then had an immediate bout of remorse and confessed his and the general's sins. He accused Noriega of Spadafora's murder, election fraud in 1984, and drug trafficking and admitted that he himself had bought an expensive home with the money he had illicitly earned by selling visas to Cubans who hoped to enter the United States via Panama. Díaz Herrera became the opposition's (and America's) darling overnight and holed himself up in his house, creating a stand-off with General Noriega. His declarations mobilized the opposition, which quickly created the Cruzada Civilista Nacional (National Civil Crusade), composed of professionals, business groups, students and labor organizations (De Arias 1991; Janson Pérez 1993). On July 10, the Dobermans brutally repressed massive demonstrations that called for Noriega's resignation. The day earned the name *Black Friday*, with about six hundred people arrested and about six hundred injured (Pizzurno Gelós and Araúz 1996, 622). Washington could now conveniently use Díaz Herrera's confessions as reasons for removing support from Noriega.[10] The crisis escalated rapidly. By February 1988, the Reagan administration had withdrawn economic and military assistance, suspended the isthmus's sugar quota, imposed economic sanctions, and allowed the Justice Department to indict the general on charges of drug trafficking. Washington also coaxed President Delvalle into attempting to remove Noriega from power. Instead, the general replaced Delvalle with Secretary of Education Manuel Solís Palma. Washington cleverly used the dispute to recognize Delvalle as Panama's chief of state and helped the president-in-limbo to organize opposition to Noriega from exile in the United States.

Earlier, in January 1988, Washington had made a last-ditch effort to negotiate with General Noriega. Two high-level U.S. emissaries went to Panama with offers of money and legal immunity in return for Noriega's retirement and departure from Panama. "Manny," however, was increasingly defiant. Washington then turned up the heat, imposing severe economic sanctions (using the International Emergency Economic Powers Act), carrying out military exercises and clandestine actions, funding would-be insurgents, encouraging opposition in Panama and in exile, and fomenting discord within the PDF in hopes of producing a golpe against Noriega.[11] In March 1988, Colonel Leonidas Macías attempted a golpe against Noriega that failed miserably. Several analysts have argued that Washington's policies toward the Noriega regime were chaotic, but there is no doubt that, while different agencies urged varying tactics, the U.S. government applied ever-increasing pressure on the Noriega regime once it became convinced that the general was a liability rather than an asset (Sánchez 2002). Washington was determined to oust the general and would take all necessary steps to do so.

On May 7, 1989, Noriega retaliated by holding elections as scheduled. His handpicked candidate, friend and business partner Carlos Duque, led the pro-regime Coalición de Liberación Nacional (National Liberation Coalition), or COLINA, backed by the PRD, and most of the parties and leaders that had backed Barletta in the 1984 elections. The opposition had lost its key leader, since "el Hombre," Arnulfo Arias, had died in August 1988. Guillermo

Endara, who paled in comparison to Arias, led the Alianza Democrática de Oposición Cívica (Civic Opposition Democratic Alliance), or ADOC, comprised of the Partido Panameñista Auténtico (Authentic Panameñista Party), or PP; the Partido Liberal Auténtico (Authentic Liberal Party), or PL; the Christian Democratic Party, and MOLIRENA. Arias's Panameñista Party had experienced some turmoil, and the government ruled that Arias's followers could not use the Panameñista Party symbols. Thus Endara, a true Arnulfista, ran for president under the Authentic Liberal party. The opposition, despite these maneuvers and vote fraud, nevertheless won an overwhelming victory, showing that even Noriega's supposed supporters had betrayed the general. Since international observers were present, including former U.S. president Jimmy Carter, Noriega denounced the "foreign interference" and annulled the electoral outcome. When Endara and his first and second vice presidents, Christian Democrat Ricardo Arias Calderón and MOLIRENA's Guillermo "Billy" Ford, participated in a rally against the fraudulent ruling, pro-Noriega operatives dressed in civilian clothes physically attacked the three defenseless political leaders. This horrific show of regime brutality was filmed and televised to the world. The U.S. government pointed out that Cuba had helped Noriega organize "goon squads."

On October 3, 1989, disgruntled PDF officers once again attempted to oust the general. This well-planned effort, led by Major Moisés Giroldi, also failed and resulted in the summary execution of the intrepid major and several of his followers. In a chain of events resembling a suspense novel, Giroldi's men captured Noriega as he entered PDF general staff headquarters. Strangely, Major Giroldi engaged Noriega in a long discussion while the latter's loyal troops rallied to his rescue. U.S. troops in Panama did not seal off road access to the headquarters, even though Giroldi had previously urged SOUTHCOM to do so. Although Giroldi could have removed Noriega from power and thus eliminated the principal rationale for a U.S. invasion, the major was a Torrijista, and Washington feared that the PDF would continue its nationalist stance sans Noriega. Troops loyal to Noriega eventually arrived, and Giroldi released the general. At this point, it must have been clear to U.S. strategists that Noriega would not be removed by someone who was sympathetic toward Washington. For the U.S. government, time was running out since on January 1, 1990, a Panamanian would for the first time lead the Panama Canal Commission's board of directors, in accordance with the Canal Treaties. Noriega had already nominated Altamirano Duque, but the U.S. government was sure to reject the general's nominee, which would then lead to a crisis concerning the operation of the famous canal and the implementation of the 1977 Treaties. Policy makers in Washington knew that the options were now quite limited and that they would need to take drastic action. Even though the cold war was practically over, Washington would not accept a scenario where the leader of a small country in the Western Hemisphere would challenge U.S. power and get away with it, particularly since control of the canal and the fate of U.S. military bases were at stake.

From this point on, Panama and Washington were on a collision course that would prompt the U.S. government to become directly involved in Panama's domestic affairs, in violation of the 1977 Treaties and both the UN and OAS Charters. U.S. officials would later argue that U.S. direct involvement in the Giroldi-led golpe would have represented U.S. meddling in Panama's affairs, yet months later President George Bush ordered the DOD to invade the country to remove General Noriega from power and reshape its political system. A couple of months after Giroldi's failed coup, on December 15, 1989, Noriega restored the Torrijos-era Assembly of Municipal Representatives and declared that Panama was in a "state of war" with the United States. But the events used by Washington to sell the invasion to the American public came one day later. On December 16, a PDF soldier shot a U.S. Army intelligence officer, Lieutenant Roberto Paz, as he ran a roadblock close to the PDF comandancia. Why Lt. Paz would be in such close proximity to such a sensitive location at such a delicate time generated much discussion and speculation. In another part of Panama City, the PDF detained and allegedly mistreated a naval officer and his wife. President George Bush highlighted these two events when justifying the invasion of Panama on December 20, 1989. The U.S. president gave four reasons for the military invasion: to protect U.S. citizens, to bring democracy back to Panama, to stop the illegal flow of drugs through Panama, and to defend the Panama Canal (Weeks and Gunson 1991, 12). Little had changed in over one hundred years: the United States, as it had done since before Panama's independence, directly intervened in Panama's domestic politics, even after it had dramatically restructured the U.S.-Panama relationship.

Institutional Military Rule and U.S. Hegemony

The 1968 military golpe put a dramatic end to Panama's limited and brittle democracy. The increased contestation and participation of the period beginning in 1930 came to a quick halt. The Torrijos-dominated military regime that emerged concentrated political power in Panama as never before. The Guardia took power in Panama and put an end to civilian rule principally to prevent a social revolution on the isthmus, à la Cuba. Panama's oligarchs and Washington supported the Guardia's move because a revolution in Panama would also threaten their interests. Despite the breakdown of democracy, however, the Guardia strengthened the Panamanian state and brought previously marginalized sectors into the political game. While some observers have viewed this as a positive step, Torrijos at the same time used repression, excluded other sectors from politics, and put the Guardia in total control. Whatever positive steps he may have taken were more than overshadowed by his many antidemocratic and repressive actions. Although Torrijos and the Guardia served U.S. interests well by preventing a second Cuba from emerging in Panama, eventually the Maximum Leader asked Washington to pay the price for his willingness and ability to maintain stability and preserve U.S. interests. General Torrijos initiated a crusade both nationally and internationally to restructure the U.S.-Panamanian relationship. Although Washington resisted initially, the general had achieved too much autonomy to be ignored and applied enough pressure to force the U.S. government to bargain. The outcome, the 1977 Canal Treaties, however, was more the result of a changed international context and the decreasing importance of the famous canal than of Torrijos's power vis-à-vis the United States. Despite the restructured relationship, Washington invaded the isthmus after the new PDF, led by Manuel Noriega, resisted the maintenance of U.S. military bases on the isthmus, and appeared to be derailing treaty implementation, soiling America's image, and challenging U.S. leadership. No doubt, after the U.S. invasion Panama was poised to experiment with democracy once again. But the military regime of 1968–89 was the product of U.S. tampering as much as the product of any inherent Panamanian militarism.

In terms of our theoretical framework, the most important transformations during this period of military rule include the complete elimination of liberal democracy and the development of a more autonomous state. As for U.S. hegemony, emulation was forsaken for the advancement of U.S. strategic interests, that is, the preservation of U.S. preponderance of power. Although the Noriega regime attempted to assert its power, Washington made it quite clear who was in charge by invading Panama despite assurances in 1977 that America would not intervene in the isthmus's domestic politics. The 1989 U.S. invasion demonstrates that when a subordinate state charts out its own independent policy, the preponderant power will react quickly and decisively.

From the U.S. Occupation to the End of the U.S. Military Presence and Beyond

Democracy Restored and Sovereignty Attained?

The U.S. invasion of Panama was a blitzkrieg—executed rapidly and with overwhelming force. This invasion and the resulting occupation allowed Washington to achieve its key goals on the isthmus—remove General Noriega from power, eliminate the PDF as a political force on the isthmus, and install a pro-U.S. government. The U.S. military occupied Panama for a relatively short time since the government elected in May 1989 was on the sidelines waiting to assume power. Despite Washington's heavy hand, the postinvasion period saw the flowering of democracy and the enhancement of Panama's sovereignty. Since 1989, Panama has held three free and fair national elections, as well as three national referenda. On three occasions, an opposition party has won the presidency, resulting in the alternation of power. On December 31, 1999, the U.S. government transferred operation of the Panama Canal to the Republic of Panama and closed down all military bases on the isthmus. After a long struggle, Panama finally acquired sovereignty over its entire territory.

Operation "Just Cause" and the "Puppet" Endara Government

Policy makers in Washington termed the U.S. invasion of Panama "Operation Just Cause." Zonians mockingly referred to the U.S. military blitzkrieg as "just cuz." Neither appellation captured the reality of this U.S. attack against the Noriega regime and the PDF. The U.S. government cited important reasons for invading Panama, but the reasons had more to do with U.S. power and interests on the isthmus and in Latin America than with the official reasons provided by President George Bush. Yes, Washington was concerned about the canal, but principally because it wanted to ensure that the increasingly anti-U.S. Noriega regime did not control the important waterway. Beyond canal defense, the U.S. government was concerned about its presence on the isthmus and in Latin America beyond December 31, 1999. Other reasons certainly played a role, such as the war against drugs, matters of pride, etc., but Washington's principal concerns in 1989 had to do with regional strategy and the preservation of hegemony. Despite the canal's decreasing economic importance, Washington would never turn over such an important, symbolic waterway to a nationalist dictatorship.

By February 1990, Washington pulled out its invasion forces, although some ten thousand U.S. troops still remained on the isthmus. The U.S. military, while successful in defeating the PDF, failed in maintaining order as an occupying force. Extensive looting occurred, further damaging Panama's businesses and suggesting that once U.S. interests were restored, stability on the isthmus was not a major concern for Washington. While the Bush administration promised economic relief, the U.S. Congress appropriated only a fraction of the $1 billion in economic assistance proposed by the executive. Washington was also responsible for many civilian deaths in Panama, leading some observers to conclude that the DOD had used excessive force and not enough care in its military operations. Much of the controversy centered on the assault against the PDF's comandancia in the poor neighborhood of Chorrillo, where much of the housing was wooden, dating back to the days of the French canal effort. Raging fires resulted in the deaths of at least hundreds of civilians, and some estimates suggest perhaps thousands died (Barry et al. 1995, 147–48). Some Panamanians demanded restitution, but the U.S. government argued that it was not liable for casualties and property damages resulting from war. Panama's government, of course, was too weak and dependent on U.S. assistance to demand reparations. Consequently, Washington was able to assert its influence over the Endara government on several important issues.

Panama's postinvasion government was devoid of legitimacy and inherited a ruined economy. Despite the fact that President Endara had clearly won the May 1989 election, the new government was able to take the reigns of power only because of the U.S. military invasion. Highlighting U.S. preeminence, Endara and his two vice presidents were sworn into office on a U.S. military base just prior to the U.S. invasion. U.S. economic sanctions leveled against the Noriega regime and the extensive looting in the immediate postinvasion period had left the Panamanian economy in shambles. To a large extent, the Endara administration became simply a caretaker government that paved the way for the postinvasion period's first truly democratic elections in 1994 (Scranton 1995). The Endara administration was also in such desperate need of U.S. economic assistance that many isthmians viewed government officials simply as "implementers of US policy" (Harding 2001, 181).

One of the first acts of the Endara government was to eliminate the PDF. No doubt, many Panamanians detested the institution that had grown increasingly political, corrupt, and repressive. But Panamanians also understood that the isthmus needed some sort of security force in order to abide by the defense commitments outlined in the 1977 Treaties. Washington, however, had decided that the PDF had to be eliminated since its officer corps was steeped in nationalism and anti-U.S. sentiment. Despite the need for a national debate and owing to U.S. pressure, the Endara government decreed the abolishment of the PDF on February 12, 1990. The government then established the Fuerzas Públicas de Panamá (Public Forces of Panama), or FPP, a new national police force, financed principally by the U.S. government. Only PDF officers considered "professional" or not affiliated with Noriega were allowed to lead the new institution. But finding an experienced officer to command the new FPP who was not "tainted" by old PDF attitudes was almost impossible. In December 1990, Colonel Eduardo Herrera Hassan, who briefly served as police commander, was freed from jail by his supporters in a brief putsch against the Endara government. The U.S. military stepped in quickly and put down the rebellion, highlighting Washington's continued dominance. The government finally appointed a civilian police chief and purged the FPP of "all remaining PDF loyalists" (Harding 2001, 183). By 1993, the FPP would grow to 11,650 personnel, 6,000 of whom were from the former PDF (Sieder and Dunkerley 1994, 26).

In order to bring legitimacy to the Panamanian government's decision to eliminate the armed forces, the Endara administration had wanted to hold a national plebiscite as early as 1990. The National Assembly, however, led by Vice President Arias Calderón and his PDC, began to add other constitutional reforms to the referendum, delaying the process. Eventually, 113 articles were up for amendment. In March 1991, Endara submitted a proposal that modified only 11 articles, all dealing with the PDF. Endara then removed PDC members from his administration, prompting Arias Calderón to resign and withdraw the PDC from the government coalition. This left the Endara government with a legislative minority and the PRD as the key opposition party. When the dust settled, the national referendum included changes to 58 articles of the 1972 constitution (Scranton 1993, 75–77). In August 1992, the Frente Nacional Por el NO a las Reformas Constitucional (National Front for No to the Constitutional Reforms), or FRENO, was founded to rally the population to reject the proposed constitutional changes. FRENO and its supporters were against reforming the 1972 Torrijos constitution because they wanted a constitutional convention to write a new Magna Carta. The most widely publicized and discussed amendments, however, concerned the important decision to abolish the armed forces. On November 15, 1992, the "no" vote won by a substantial 2–1 margin. To a large extent "this result reflected the genuine unpopularity of the Endara regime" (Sieder and Dunkerley 1994, 22). Others viewed the vote as a repudiation of the U.S. invasion and as a national desire to retain a military. In 1994, however, the National Assembly, responding to U.S. pressure, went against the popular will and eliminated Panama's armed forces anyway.

In the shadow of invasion, the Endara administration had difficulty charting out independent policy. Other nations in the region remained aloof toward the isthmus, owing to the manner in which Endara attained power. Practically every government in the region had condemned the U.S. invasion and viewed Endara as a willing accomplice. While some effort was made to integrate Panama into the Central American community, such integration was limited and not economic in scope (Furlong 2000, 34–42). To make matters worse, Washington urged Endara to begin negotiations over a continued U.S. military presence on the isthmus past the year 1999. On this issue, President Endara resisted U.S. pressure since his popularity was very low and his political party, the Arnulfistas, had long promoted eliminating the U.S. military presence in the country. Although he resisted on the issue of bases, the president and his administration were beholden to the United States for assuming power and for Panama's economic recovery. In 1990, the Panamanian economy was practically on its knees (Millet 1990, 7). Consequently, with the exception of the issue of U.S. military bases, the Endara government cooperated fully with Washington in economic and other matters. Financial aid became a foreign policy imperative, thus minimizing the government's ability to chart out an independent foreign policy. In fact, U.S. economic assistance was tied to Panama adopting new legislation that would limit bank secrecy, something that Washington desired for its ever-expanding war on drugs (*Latin America Weekly Report*, November 20, 1990, 7).

The Endara government, nevertheless, took a number of steps that helped to restore some of Panama's position in the international arena. One accomplishment was the reincorporation of Panama into the Río Group, which had grown out of the Contadora Group and included other influential nations in the region. The Contadora nations had expelled Panama late in the Noriega crisis. The Endara government also established the Autoridad Regional Interoceánica (Inter-Oceanic Regional Authority), or ARI. ARI was designed to oversee the disposition of the lands and facilities that Panama would receive pursuant to the 1977 Canal Treaties. The vast majority of these properties were still held by the United States since Washington wanted to keep its military bases as long as possible and the Noriega crisis had significantly slowed down the reversion process. Many Panamanians wanted to ensure that the isthmus would accrue the benefits that had eluded them in the past, so one of Panama's most pressing issues in the early 1990s concerned the efficient use of the properties that had been and were to be reverted by 1999, as well as the assumption of the canal.

On December 31, 1999, Panama would become responsible for operating and defending the canal. The Canal Treaties charged the Panama Canal Commission (PCC), created in 1979, with ensuring that the canal operation would gradually involve increasing numbers of Panamanians so that by 1999 the canal transfer would be seamless. The Noriega regime had thrown a monkey wrench into this plan since, from roughly mid-1987 to the end of 1989, the U.S.-Panamanian conflict precluded cooperation on treaty matters. Now that Noriega and the PDF were gone, Washington was once again working to make the canal transition completely successful (Bocanegra 1998). Another important issue, however, was the reversion to Panama of large U.S.-controlled areas and an enormous number of facilities. While some of the areas and facilities to be reverted were part of the Canal Operating Area, U.S. military defense sites constituted most of the properties to be reverted. The Panamanian Association of Business Executives, realizing the vast economic potential of these properties, formed an investigative committee that produced a report in 1992 recommending that the Panamanian government formulate a master plan for the use of all properties that were to be reverted to Panama by 1999. While the report made some recommendations as to the potential use of some properties, it excluded several key U.S. military bases, like Howard AFB and Rodman Naval Station, since the committee knew that the U.S. government was very interested in keeping these facilities (Comisión Para Asunto del Canal 1992, 59–68). Soon after the promulgation of this report, in February 1993, the Endara government established ARI and charged the organization with developing a master plan for managing all the reverted properties. In 1993, the vast majority of these properties were still held by the United States since Washington wanted to keep its military bases as long as possible. The Central American civil wars were finally winding down, but the DOD was still extensively involved in counternarcotics operations, military-to-military ties in the region, espionage operations, and regional strategic goals, all of which were administered from U.S. military bases on the isthmus (U.S. Southern Command 1997a, 1997d, 1997e).

To address the 1999 transfer of canal operations to Panama, President

Endara created a presidential commission. In January 1994, the commission published a preliminary report. One of the most important recommendations made was that the Panamanian state should establish a Panamanian agency that would replace the U.S.-controlled PCC on December 31, 1999. The report recommended that such an agency, to be called the Autoridad del Canal de Panamá (Panama Canal Authority), or ACP, should be an autonomous, private institution, free from political influence (Presidential Commission for Canal Affairs 1994, ii, x). President Endara pushed through the legislation necessary to give this organization a legal basis. Many observers, Washington, and canal users believed that the Panamanian government should be as distant as possible from the operation of the ACP as a way to prevent political meddling. Canal users had expressed concern over the possibility of increased tolls after Panama took control of the canal. The U.S. government worried that the use of canal revenues for political purposes would undermine canal efficiency. Consequently, the establishment of the ACP as an autonomous, semiprivate agency soothed these concerns. On the other hand, Panamanians were concerned that, even after attaining full sovereignty and control of the canal, their country would still fail to benefit from its strategic geographic position. They feared that ACP and ARI would respond to international business and U.S. interests rather than Panamanian interests. Hypocritically, even though Washington had created the PCC as a government agency under the DOD, it insisted that Panama create a semiprivate organization to operate the canal.

Perhaps Endara's greatest achievement was his ability to stay in office for a full term and to help prepare for Panama's first truly free and fair election. Although voters rejected the referendum on constitutional amendments in 1992, the Endara government put through some important electoral changes that enhanced Panama's democracy. First, in May 1990, Endara appointed three new magistrates to lead the Electoral Tribunal, lending that institution much-needed legitimacy. The new magistrates worked assiduously to regain the Tribunal's independence and professionalism. Then, in 1993, Panama's electoral code was revised in preparation for the upcoming elections. An important reform put the FPP under Tribunal command six days prior to the elections and until official results were promulgated (Scranton 2000, 106–12). Endara's government also refrained from using state resources to assist the "official" candidate, as had been common practice for many years (Scranton 1995, 71). In addition to the government's efforts, the United Nations Development Program office in Panama, known as PNUD for its Spanish acronym, organized two meetings, in August 1993 and April 1994, designed to begin a political dialogue among leading political actors. The August meeting, held at the Hotel Bambito in the province of Chiriquí, brought together all political parties, the business community, labor groups, university students, and the Catholic Church in an effort to bring more confidence to the electoral process and establish a national agenda that could be used by the yet-to-be-elected government. Five presidential candidates attended the April meeting held in Panama City. Although two key candidates—Mireya Moscoso of the Arnulfista Party and Ruben Blades of the newly created Papa Egoró Party—did not attend, the process started at Bambito was continued in a spirit of cooperation and national unity. The Catholic Church also formed a Justice and Peace Commission in 1993 that convinced the political parties to sign an Ethical and Moral Accord concerning the upcoming elections (Solórzano Martínez 1997, 27–34). While the two meetings organized by PNUD do not meet all of the requirements of an elite pact, as in Colombia and Venezuela in 1958, they certainly created an atmosphere of dialogue and national cooperation. As a result, the stage was set for free and fair elections in May and a peaceful presidential transition in October 1994.

Return of the PRD: The Pérez Balladares Government

The elections were unusual not only in their honesty and relative amity but also in that the focus was on political parties and key individuals rather than on two competing multiparty coalitions. In total, six presidential candidates and sixteen political parties contested political power, but only four presidential candidates captured most of the national attention. Ernesto Pérez Balladares was the PRD candidate and headed the Pueblo Unido coalition. Pérez Balladares, a banker, had been a longtime PRD leader and had lost the party's nomination in 1984 to Barletta only because of Noriega's involvement in the process. Mireya Moscoso de Gruber represented the Arnulfista party and led the Alianza Democrática. Moscoso was Arnulfo Arias's widow, had been his personal secretary, and had risen to leadership status in the old caudillo's party. A new political party also entered the scene—Papa Egoró. Ruben Blades founded and led this party, with the help of scholars, socialists, and nationalists who were disappointed with the country's political turn away from the revolution and the "people." Blades, an internationally known composer, singer, and movie actor, had very high name recognition. Finally, Rubén Carles, leader of MOLIRENA and former second vice president, led the Cambio 94 coalition (Priestly 1994, 11–14). The voters would have plenty of choices at the polls.

The 1994 electoral results played a dirty, perhaps justified, trick on Washington. Even though Noriega's military regime had been pulled out by the roots, Pérez Balladares and the PRD still won a plurality of the vote. The vote ran heavily against the more visibly pro-U.S. parties since the vast majority of the voters cast their lot with the PRD (33 percent); the Arnulfistas (29 percent); and the left-of-center Papa Egoró (18 percent). It is difficult to determine whether such a backlash against the "opposition" parties of the 1980s was in fact a strong rejection of the U.S. invasion, simply a rejection of the Endara government, or a widespread desire to return to a populist/nationalist past á la Arias or Torrijos. Nevertheless, the election left U.S. officials with the difficult task of attempting to negotiate a continued U.S. military presence with the party and protégés of Omar Torrijos, a classic case of historic irony.

From the outset, the Pérez Balladares administration applied a two-pronged strategy in its relations with the United States. First, the country cooperated fully with the neoliberal economic policies Washington had been promoting throughout Latin America. President Pérez Balladares accelerated the privatization program the Endara government started, even though in the past the PRD had promoted policies that strengthened the state and protected domestic industry. Cable and Wireless, a British telecommunications firm, purchased state-owned INTEL, the nation's telephone company. Also up for sale were Panama's social security, sewage, and utilities systems. Panama privatized its ports and began selling to investors the former Canal Zone properties it had been slowly acquiring from the U.S. government. Consistent with neoliberal reforms, the Pérez Balladares administration slashed tariffs, allowing the country to join the World Trade Organization in 1997. These policies pleased Washington greatly since they were similar to the policies Barletta had tried to implement a decade earlier. The PRD had made an economic right turn and now favored neoliberal, over statist, economic policies.

In conjunction with privatization, however, Pérez Balladares began to diversify Panama's economic and political ties. The Hong Kong–based firm Hutchinson-Wampoa led a consortium that won concessions to develop Panama's two principal ports, Balboa on the Pacific side and Cristóbal on the Atlantic. From the U.S. perspective, for the first time ever, a "foreign" company would be operating a major economic operation adjacent to the canal. Most troubling to some key players in Washington was that this particular company was home-based in the People's Republic of China, since Britain had turned over Hong Kong to China in July 1997. While the economic strategy was to open the economy to investment from all over the world in order to grow the national economy, Panama concurrently sought to minimize

Washington's economic influence through diversification. President Pérez Balladares also attempted to link Panama economically with as many nations as possible by becoming involved in the Central American Common Market, joining the Andean group, seeking bilateral trade agreements with Chile and Mexico, and promoting the nation's banking center in Panama City and the Duty Free Zone near Colón on the Atlantic side. So, while it was implementing the economic policies the Washington consensus promoted, the Pérez Balladares administration at the same time attempted to minimize U.S. control of Panama's economy through political and economic diversification.

Panama's most important resources—its geographic location and the canal—provided the greatest potential for allowing the isthmus to become more independent and economically vibrant. Since Panama was but years away from assuming control of the canal, the Panamanian government did what it could to convince the global community that Panama would be able to operate efficiently and defend effectively the vital waterway. In September 1997, Panama held a global conference called the Universal Congress on the Panama Canal. At the Congress, the Pérez Balladares administration tried to highlight Panama's economic potential and assure canal users that the isthmus was ready and able to effectively assume canal operations at the end of 1999 (Raven and Manfredo 1997). Unfortunately for Panama, the Pérez Balladares administration decided to invite Taiwan to the Congress, angering China and creating a delicate problem for the international community. As a result of Taiwan's inclusion, only three heads of state attended the Congress, and the United Nations was forced to withdraw funding (*Latin America Weekly Report*, September 9, 1997, 432). Nevertheless, the Canal Congress, still a major event, went a long way to convince canal users that Panama was taking major steps toward taking over canal operations from the United States in a professional manner.

To assure the international community and Washington that Panama was prepared to operate the canal responsibly, the Pérez Balladares administration also formally established the Autoridad del Canal de Panamá (ACP) that the Endara presidential commission had promoted. The legislation creating the ACP, passed under the Endara government as stated above, stipulated that the organization would be an autonomous, national agency, in an effort to guarantee that the canal would be depoliticized.[1] When President Pérez Balladares appointed the ACP's governing board, however, criticism rapidly ensued, since several appointees were relatives or cronies of the president. Pérez Balladares's attempts to assure the world that Panama could run the canal, therefore, were undermined somewhat by his own choices. But the biggest challenge for Pérez Balladares was the changing relationship with the United States.

The Centro Multinacional Antidrogas: No CMA!

No issue was as important and controversial as the negotiations over a continued U.S. military presence on the isthmus. For some Panamanians, the end of the U.S. presence would signal Panama's final attainment of sovereignty. For others, the departure of U.S. soldiers meant that Panama would lose an important source of revenue. Early into the Pérez Balladares administration, Washington made it clear that it wanted to begin negotiating a continued U.S. military presence on the isthmus after 1999. At first, the Pérez Balladares administration appeared to be amenable to reaching an accord that would allow a few U.S. bases to remain on the isthmus. He appointed Gabriel Lewis Galindo, a man who was positively inclined toward the United States, as his foreign minister. But almost as soon as exploratory talks began in February 1995, they came to a halt because the United States insisted that it would not pay rent on any future bases in Panama. President Pérez Balladares countered by stating, "No payment. No bases" (Pérez Balladares 1999)(my translation). At the end of 1996, however, Pérez Balladares proposed the creation of a Centro Multinacional Antidrogas (Multinational Anti-Drug Center), or CMA, to be composed of several nations, with civilian leadership, and a small, mostly U.S., military component. This proposal represented a good political compromise for both sides. It allowed Washington to hold firm on not paying for bases yet retain a military presence on the isthmus, while the Panamanian government could say that it had stood firm on the issue of U.S. bases after 1999. On a visit to Washington, D.C., President Pérez Balladares discussed the creation of a CMA with President Clinton, giving the proposal the necessary impetus to renew negotiations.

Bilateral talks on a CMA began in earnest in mid-July 1997. But mistrust developed almost immediately. Washington chose as its chief negotiator Ambassador John Negroponte, a veteran U.S. diplomat who was intimately involved in the Reagan administration's Central American containment policy and who had acquired the nickname *Mr. Death Squad*. Negroponte was not well-received or liked by the Panamanian negotiators, who were forced to choose a new negotiating team in June 1996, owing to Lewis Galindo's death. Ricardo Alberto Arias became the new foreign minister. Jorge Ritter became the new chief negotiator for the CMA. Ritter was a well-known Torrijista who had supported Noriega's regime up to the last moment, as foreign minister and then as ambassador to the United Nations, where he had directed caustic language at the United States. Washington classified him as "ultranationalistic" and "anti-U.S." Second in command in the negotiations was Adolfo Ahumada, another Torrijista, who had played a role in the 1977 Canal Treaty negotiations and who had been classified a "radical" and "Marxist" by U.S. negotiators during those years (Jorden 1984, 270–71). Negroponte appealed to the conservatives in Washington who wanted to ensure that the United States did not "give in" to Panama, as they believed had happened with the 1977 Canal Treaties. Ritter appealed to the powerful Torrijista element within the ruling PRD, with one party official saying, "We knew if Ritter was negotiating the deal, we wouldn't have to worry that the Americans would trick us somehow" (*Miami Herald*, September 30, 1997). But since each chief negotiator appealed to nationalists in each country, the potential for harmonious negotiations was diminished greatly.

The playing field had certainly changed for Washington, since these new "nationalist" Panamanian negotiators had serious questions and reservations about Negroponte and about a continued U.S. military presence. By September 1997, Negroponte left his position as chief U.S. negotiator, citing retirement as the reason for departure. Just prior to his "retirement," *Miami Herald* reporter Glenn Garvin wrote: "The talks between Negroponte and Ritter grew so tense that the two men decided to recess for four days before meeting again in Washington" (August 18, 1997). Although both sides minimized the importance of Negroponte's departure, it was clear that in order for a CMA agreement to be reached, the cold war warrior had to exit the scene.[2] The United States replaced Negroponte with Thomas E. McNamara, assistant secretary of state for political and military affairs and a career diplomat without an incriminating past. It seemed that Jorge Ritter and Panama had won. Ritter had been successful at removing the unacceptable Negroponte from the negotiating table. Ritter quickly paid a price, however. Less than two weeks after Negroponte's retirement and after Panama refused to remove Ritter from the negotiating process, *El Nuevo Herald*, Miami's Spanish-language newspaper, published a story charging that Ritter, while ambassador to Colombia, had become involved in illegal financial activities with at least one known drug trafficker. Later that month, the *Miami Herald* followed up on the story (or, more precisely, leak), reporting that Ritter may have also been involved in money laundering (September 30, 1997). Officials in Panama, if they had forgotten the Noriega affair, were reminded that U.S. intelligence agencies had volumes of information on Panamanian politicos that Washington could use at will to put them in jeopardy. Nevertheless, despite this U.S. pressure, the Pérez Balladares administration insisted on keeping Ritter on as chief negotiator, and the talks resumed at a faster pace since both sides felt that time was running out.

From September to December 1997, a half-dozen rounds of talks took place. Both sides had argued that an agreement needed to be finalized by December, since each country had lengthy constitutional or fiscal processes that needed to be accomplished prior to the time that U.S. troops were scheduled to depart Panama. According to Panamanian law, the national legislature in two consecutive sessions had to approve the agreement, which then had to be accepted by a public referendum within three months. On the U.S. side, the accord would be considered an executive agreement and thus would not require Senate ratification. But the U.S. DOD argued it needed some lead time in order to arrange for the departure of U.S. troops if no agreement was reached. Additionally, in November 1998 a national election would take place in the United States, and Panama would hold a referendum on a constitutional amendment allowing for a second, consecutive presidential term. Negotiators on both sides were eager to take as much domestic politics as possible out of the CMA talks. Finally, on December 23, the two negotiating teams triumphantly announced that they had reached an agreement, adding that only rudimentary legal details and translations were required before the two sides would sign an accord establishing the CMA.

But the initial euphoria quickly subsided when President Pérez Balladares announced that some important "issues" remained to be worked out. Then, on January 12, 1998, Pérez Balladares stated that he could not sign the agreement as currently written. Panama's about-face generated great concern and disappointment in Washington and raised the ire of the U.S. Congress, especially Senator Jesse Helms, a longtime opponent of the Canal Treaties and a proponent of retaining U.S. military bases in Panama. A new and catastrophic round of negotiations resulted from what had been assumed to be a fait accompli. The process was further complicated when vice foreign ministers from Brazil, Colombia, and Mexico who were in Panama to consider their participation in the CMA demanded that the center concern itself with both the production and *consumption* of illegal drugs, a clear allusion to the U.S. responsibility in the illegal narcotics traffic. Panama then suggested that more nations be brought into the negotiating process prior to reaching a final agreement. In that same week, a broad grassroots coalition emerged in Panama for the purpose of defeating the CMA in the upcoming national referendum. The group, called MONADESCO (National Movement in Defense of Sovereignty), comprised fifty labor, human rights, and academic organizations. McNamara left Panama without a signed agreement, infuriated, and with a very difficult diplomatic challenge ahead of him.

The controversy climaxed on January 27, when the Mexican newspaper *Excélsior* published the text of the accord reached in late December, with a critical assessment of the agreement by high-level Mexican officials (Becerra Acosta 1998). Although Panamanian officials had leaked some bits and pieces of the potential agreement, until then the Panamanian public knew very little about the CMA negotiations, criticized by many as "secretive" and "nondemocratic." All that had been revealed was that the CMA would be a civilian, multinational antidrug center, with a small military component. The Pérez Balladares administration continuously refuted critics who charged that the center would constitute "disguised" U.S. bases (*bases disfrazadas*). Once *Excélsior* made the accord public, though, it became clear that the CMA was much more than had been advertised, particularly since the U.S. military would retain many of the same rights and privileges it had enjoyed during the entire century. Many Panamanians saw the CMA as a ruse for the perpetuation of the American military presence on the isthmus. First, the accord did not stipulate how many U.S. troops, or troops from any other country, would be stationed at the center. Second, Panama put several key facilities at the service of the CMA, including Howard AFB, Fort Kobbe, Rodman Naval Base, and Galeta Island, among others. Third, the agreement included existing U.S. military bombing ranges, meaning that Panama would have to maintain these ranges and that the U.S. government would be able to depart Panama without cleaning them up, as stipulated by the 1977 Canal Treaties (Lindsay-Poland 2003). Fourth, and most important, the agreement would allow the United States to carry out "other missions," in addition to the counternarcotics operations for which the CMA was designed. The clarification of what these other missions would be became a key point of contention between the two sides. The agreement that emerged, despite being negotiated by some of Panama's leading "nationalists," nevertheless allowed the United States to maintain a sizeable military presence on the isthmus with considerable autonomy and without much oversight from the Panamanian state. To ensure that Washington would not be constrained by international organizations, the agreement also forced Panama to forgo appealing to any international body, such as the United Nations or the Organization of American States, if a disagreement over the CMA arose. While neither President Pérez Balladares nor Minister Jorge Ritter would admit that they or the PRD had leaked the CMA agreement to *Excélsior*, Panama's political elite knew very well that the demise of the 1926 Kellogg-Alfaro accord had been precipitated by a leak to the Cuban and Costa Rican press.

The talks deteriorated very quickly and never recovered momentum. By April 1998, President Pérez Balladares was stating publicly that the CMA

negotiations and the draft accord had turned into a "*mamotreto*," essentially
an unwieldy ream of papers. He added that the United States had insisted
on having jurisdiction over its military personnel and on performing "other
missions" and that Panama could not accept those two privileges (*El Panamá América*, April 2, 1998). Adding fuel to the fire, President Pérez Balladares stated bluntly that he had made a "mistake" because from the outset the
U.S. government had tried to obtain military bases in disguise. U.S. secretary
of defense William Cohen then announced a plan to accelerate the closure
of U.S. military bases in Panama, perhaps still convinced that Panama really wanted U.S. bases to remain and would accept those bases only under
threat of their removal.[3] In mid-April, McNamara issued a statement saying that a CMA agreement could guarantee the continuation of the "special
relationship" between the United States and Panama, but that the United
States would have to begin to implement alternative plans very soon. "Once
these alternate plans are implemented the opportunity for an anti-narcotics
center in Panama will be lost," he warned (U.S. Information Service 1998).
The unwritten message, of course, was that the "special relationship" could
be undermined by the failure of the CMA. For many Panamanians, however,
that relationship may have been "special" but not necessarily beneficial for
the isthmus.

On August 20, 1998, the referendum on presidential reelection was held.
Those who voted "no" to presidential reelection outnumbered, by 2 to 1,
those who supported Pérez Balladares's bid for another presidential term.
With President Pérez Balladares a lame duck and general elections scheduled for May 1999, the CMA talks collapsed completely, although some
members of Congress continued to call for a continuation of negotiations.
Finally, in the following month, negotiators formally announced that the
talks had reached their end. The U.S. government would have to close down
all military installations and remove all U.S. military personnel from the
isthmus by noon, December 31, 1999. The end to the U.S. military presence
in Panama was finally approaching. Panamanians did not celebrate, but neither did they seem to regret the end to the negotiations. It appeared that
small, weak Panama had bested the American eagle (Falcoff 1998). According to one U.S. government official, at U.S. embassy functions soon after the
failure to establish a CMA, U.S. diplomats joked about who would take the
fall for "losing Panama."

An important part of this diplomatic struggle and debate over the CMA
centered on the economic value of the U.S. bases to the Republic of Panama.
On one hand, the DOD argued that Panama stood to lose about $370 million
if U.S. forces left the isthmus. Detailed studies by two economists, how-

ever, put the loss at between $130 and $200 million (Fernández B. and Galán Ponce 1997; Galán Ponce 1995). For many years, very few Panamanians had focused on the potential benefits of the vast areas and numerous properties that would revert to Panama under the provisions of the Canal Treaties. As time passed and as Panama became more democratic, an increasing number of Panamanians began to think about and discuss the financial benefits that could potentially accrue to the nation if these properties were used for economic rather than military purposes. Nicolás Barletta, as director of ARI, argued that Panama could stand to gain about $1.5 billion from the use of the reverted properties (*Latin America Weekly Report*, June 15, 1995, 263). Architect Ricardo Bermúdez also pointed out that Panama City's urban development had been severely hampered by the linear growth forced upon the city by the plethora of U.S. defense sites that lined the canal. He argued that civilian use of the bases would allow the city to grow in a much more rational, concentric pattern (Bermúdez 1998). It is clear that over the years Washington had tended to overestimate the financial value of the military bases because its estimates ignored the potential financial rewards of using those territories and facilities for commercial purposes. It was almost taken for granted that Panamanians would be incapable of using these properties wisely and thus would not be able to capitalize on the properties and their attendant economic potential. Panama, for example, as a maritime crossroads, had never been able to build a port for cruise ships, owing to the monopoly held by U.S. military bases on land adjacent to the Caribbean and Pacific approaches to the canal. Panama had also never been able to provide much-needed services to transiting ships. Clearly, the closure of U.S. bases would allow Panama to more fully exploit its strategic location. In fact, as we have seen in previous chapters, throughout the 1900s Panama's leaders had quarreled with Washington over economic opportunities and benefits that the former believed the isthmus should be able to derive from the canal. One important unknown benefited Washington greatly—What would happen to Panama politically and economically once the U.S. bases were gone? This troubling unknown convinced many Panamanians that they should support bilateral negotiations with the United States on the establishment of a CMA.

In addition to the economic dimension was the concern for canal security. Washington argued that Panama, now conveniently devoid of a military, would be ill-equipped to defend the canal effectively. Panama, on the other hand, agreeing with a long line of domestic scholars and political leaders, insisted that neutrality assured the best canal defense (Franco V. 1997). Concerns about canal security intensified during negotiations over the CMA, when allegedly several incursions by paramilitary forces and Colombian guerrillas occurred in Panama's Darién region, adjacent to Colombia. Adding more fuel to the controversy, in April 1998, the Defense Intelligence Agency leaked a report concluding that armed rebels controlled about 40 percent of Colombia's territory (*Latin America Weekly Report,* April 21, 1998, 175). The border incidents, along with leaked information, convinced many Panamanians and even some outside observers that Washington was directing a covert campaign to make the situation in Panama seem at near-crisis level, necessitating a continued U.S. military presence (*Latin America Weekly Report,* December 2, 1997, 573).[4] Nevertheless, President Pérez Balladares and his key advisors remained confident that neutrality rather than U.S. military bases would better protect the canal. As a precautionary measure, however, the president initiated Operation Peace and Sovereignty, sending over one thousand police to the Darién frontier. The upcoming national elections would be of paramount importance since the new president would preside over canal reversion and the final withdrawal of U.S. troops and would be responsible for Panama's security and prosperity without a substantial U.S. presence.

Those who remembered vividly the PRD's long association with the PDF feared that the party of Torrijos would not give up political power via the ballot box. The opposition viewed the referendum on presidential reelection as the PRD's attempt, albeit unsuccessful, to stay in power by keeping Pérez Balladares in the Palacio de las Garzas. Some observers were also worried that the PRD at some point would resurrect the PDF, thus raising the ugly head of militarism once more. But positive signs were also visible. New legislation forced Panama's political parties to democratize internally, as U.S. political parties had done in the 1970s, by selecting presidential candidates via primary elections. Rather than being chosen by the party leadership only, the presidential candidates would be vetted by all party members. The primaries were a result of an electoral reform law passed by the National Assembly in July 1997 that also strengthened the Electoral Tribunal, regulated political advertising, and mandated that parties nominate a certain percentage of women to run for political office (Scranton 2000, 116–17). The Electoral Tribunal also pushed for legislation that would provide state funds to political parties "to strengthen party organization and provide election-related training for members," and instituted digitized voter-registration cards (Scranton 2000, 114, 120). Clearly, Panama's democratic political system was becoming more institutionalized, competitive, and participatory.

In addition to these positive changes, the national dialogue, initiated at the Bambito meetings prior to the 1994 elections, continued during the Pérez

Balladares presidency. Bambito III took place in December 1994 but did not yield any sort of agreement or pact among the participants. Nevertheless, the process continued, resulting in a series of meetings at the Hotel Coronado in 1996. The dialogue began in May at the Encuentro Panamá 2000, where once again all political parties, civil society, and the government participated. Now that the electoral process was not of paramount concern, the national dialogue focused on the reversion of the Panama Canal. On May 28, the participants signed a document titled *Visión Nacional Panamá 2000* (National Vision Panama 2000). Even though the Arnulfistas did not participate in this dialogue, they eventually accepted the process and the National Vision document. The signatories committed themselves to equitable national development, demilitarization, and democratic deepening. But the brief document mostly addressed the canal, its vitality to national development, and the need for an effective, apolitical Panama Canal Authority. The participants also agreed to continue the national dialogue for the purpose of further discussing the reversion of the canal and all associated properties, including the U.S. military bases (See Solórzano Martínez 1997, 123–30). At a third meeting at Coronado, on September 24, 1996, the participants signed another "declaration" concerning the national plan for the use of reverted properties as proposed by ARI. The accord, reached by consensus, articulated a desire to ensure that all Panamanians derived benefits from the canal and the reverted properties. The Bambito and Coronado meetings represented a first-ever effort at national dialogue among the key political forces. These encounters helped to foment trust and engender consensus over the democratic process as well as on what to do with Panama's most important asset—the canal. The famous waterway, more than anything else, represented a national galvanizing force. While perhaps not representing a formal elite settlement on the democratic process (Burton and Higley 1987), certainly these meetings taking place over several years and attended by the key political forces on the isthmus manifest a major step toward elite unity and national consensus. Panama now had stronger civilian institutions, no military, relatively institutionalized political parties, and a modicum of national and elite unity.

Return of the Arnulfistas: The Moscoso Government

Despite some concerns, then, the climate for a free and fair electoral process continued to improve. Eventually, three presidential candidates led coalitions formed by thirteen political parties. Martín Torrijos, son of the famous Maximum Leader, headed the Nueva Nación (New Nation) coalition, composed of the PRD; the Partido Solidaridad (Solidarity Party); the Partido Liberal Nacional (National Liberal Party); and Papa Egoró. Mireya Moscoso represented the Union por Panamá (Union for Panama), constituted by the Arnulfistas; the Partido Liberal (Liberal Party); MOLIRENA; the Movimiento Renovación Nacional (National Renovation Movement), or MORENA; and Cambio Democrático (Democratic Change). The third coalition, Acción Opositora (Opposition Action), was led by the PDC, and included Partido Renovación Civilista (Civil Renewal Party); the Partido Nacionalista Popular (Nationalist Popular Party); and the Partido Liberal Auténtico (Authentic Liberal party). Alberto Vallarino, an Arnulfista who had lost control of the party in the primary to Arias's widow, Mireya Moscoso, led this third coalition and was the PDC candidate. Martín Torrijos and Mireya Moscoso, heirs to Panamanian nationalism and populism, however, were the main contenders. Regardless of who won the contest, Panama would enter the third millennium, acquire the canal, and witness the final exit of U.S. troops, with a historic if not heroic figure at the helm. Mireya Moscoso emerged victorious in the May 1999 elections, becoming Panama's first woman president. The elections were also enormously important since an opposition party won and took office without incident. The electoral results also demonstrated once more the popular appeal of the two traditionally nationalist and populist parties. Moscoso received 44.8 percent of the vote, and Torrijos won 37.8 percent, while Vallarino received 17.4 percent (Pérez 2000a, 140; De Janón 1999).

Mireya Moscoso de Gruber continued the two-pronged strategy of the previous administration. Although the Arnulfistas were vocal and longtime critics of the PRD, both parties were forged in populist doctrine that pointed to Panama's exploitation by the "gringos." Consequently, Moscoso stood firm on forcing the U.S. government to close down all military bases and also continued the policy of diversifying Panama's economic and political relations so that the isthmus would be more independent and less susceptible to U.S. influence. At the same time, however, Moscoso, as the PRD had done, cooperated with the neoliberal economic policies promoted by Washington.

Despite Arnulfista populist rhetoric, Panama continued its move toward privatization, free trade, and promoting foreign investment—policies normally viewed as detrimental to the masses by populist leaders. Although these policies were consistent with Washington's neoliberal mantra, they nevertheless gave Panama the opportunity to move toward diminishing the isthmus's economic dependence on the United States, by encouraging investment by nations other than America. Thus Panama began talks with the United States on a free trade agreement but at the same time became engaged in negotiating free trade agreements with its neighbors in Central America, the Dominican Republic, and Taiwan. ARI continued its plan to allow many nations and investors to partake in the reverted Canal Zone property bonanza. In addition to the modernization of Panama's two key ports by Hong Kong–based Hutchinson-Wampoa, the Taiwanese firm Evergreen acquired rights to operate a container facility at the Atlantic side of the Canal, near the city of Colón. Several Taiwanese companies also established manufacturing plants in an industrial park located in the former Fort Davis U.S. military base. Other projects included a cruise-ship port and shopping facility on the Pacific entrance of the canal, an ecotourism facility in the town of Gamboa, a "City of Knowledge" at the former site of Fort Clayton, and a multimodal transportation hub at what used to be Howard Air Force Base.

In the political arena, the Moscoso administration continued to diversify and strengthen Panama's diplomatic ties. In November 2000, Panama hosted the Tenth Iberoamerican Conference, bringing together the leaders of Spain, Portugal, the Spanish-speaking countries of Latin America, and Brazil. The United States is notably excluded from the annual Iberoamerican conferences, while Cuba is welcome. Additionally, Panama continued to be active in the Central American Parliament and other multilateral international bodies. In fact, Panama has offered former Canal Zone facilities to many international and regional groups at substantial savings to enhance its international standing and make use of reverted properties. And Panama signed the Rome Accord, which established the International Criminal Court despite strong U.S. misgivings about the new international tribunal. The efficient and safe operation of the canal in its first year under Panamanian management enhanced Panama's international status. Before 1999, analysts and canal users wondered whether the small nation would be able to effectively assume the operation of the waterway (Falcoff 1998, 49–73). In the year 2000, however, the number of accidents was the lowest in the canal's history; the number of ships that passed through the canal was at an average high of forty-two per day; canal transit time declined from 33 to 29.7 hours; and Panama's revenues from canal operations amounted to $166.8 million (*Latin America Weekly Report*, January 16, 2001, 3). Those who argued that Panama was not prepared to operate or defend the canal for the most part remained silent.

Panama, however, still needed to convince critics that the canal was secure, despite problems along the Colombian border. Consequently, the Moscoso administration embarked on a project to develop a Strategic Plan for National Security. While not receiving complete national support, the Strategic Plan put forth long-held Panamanian beliefs about the isthmus's role in the world. The plan was developed principally through the initiative of the Arnulfista party, but with the assistance of the Christian Democratic Party and even the PRD. An underlying principle of the plan is the notion of neutrality as the underpinning for canal defense and Panamanian national security. Consequently, the plan prohibits the stationing of any foreign troops or the establishment of any foreign military facilities on Panamanian territory, of course alluding to the United States. Additionally, the plan promotes the principle of multilateral, rather than unilateral, security, once more indirectly maligning the U.S. "right" under the Neutrality Treaty of 1977 to unilaterally assure the defense of the canal in perpetuity. In fact, the plan states that Panama's greatest threat to its national security lies in the erroneous notion that assessing canal security can be done unilaterally (by the United States) (*Plan Estratégico de Seguridad Nacional* 1999). Panama stood firm then on its position that once the canal became a national asset the waterway's security would be achieved through neutrality and multilaterally and *not* by Washington alone as had been the case since 1914.

To assure that the United States would not become convinced that the canal was in danger, President Moscoso continued to address the conflict in Colombia. U.S. policy makers worried that the high levels of violence in Colombia resulting from guerrilla warfare, the illegal narcotics trade, and paramilitary forces would "spill over" into Panama, Ecuador, and Venezuela, threatening the canal and the isthmus's stability. The Moscoso government took several actions: doubling the number of police in the Darién region; calling for the United Nations to be involved in solving the problem; meeting with Colombian president Andrés Pastrana; and promoting an agreement that arranged for the security chiefs of Colombia's five contiguous neighbors to meet regularly to discuss border and security concerns. These multilateral efforts were designed to deal with the serious Colombian conflict but also to ensure that the United States would not, under its Plan Colombia,[5] act unilaterally or completely monopolize the situation.

Despite some cooperation with Washington on security concerns, President Moscoso, like her predecessor, stood firm on not allowing Washington to retain troops or military bases on the isthmus. Before taking office, Moscoso stated, "As long as I'm president there will be no foreign military bases in Panama" (quoted in *Latin America Weekly Report*, July 13, 1999, 321). Nevertheless, in November 1999, newspapers reported that Moscoso was working on a "secret deal" with Washington that would allow U.S. troops to remain on isthmian soil. Although the Moscoso administration attempted to dispel those rumors, negotiations were indeed taking place on some sort of maritime intelligence agreement and on a "status of forces" agreement to clarify the status of any U.S. troops that might be operating in Panama in the future. The U.S. government was certainly not giving up on firming up some sort of security agreement with Panama prior to the transfer of the canal. But, in the end, the Moscoso administration flatly rejected a formal "status of forces" accord with Washington. The administration did, however, agree to an antidrug arrangement whereby the FPP would get economic aid and training while U.S. agencies would be able work with the FPP to combat the illicit drug traffic. In an effort to diminish the U.S. "presence" and keep the canal neutral, Panama's government asked that the United Nations take a role in the Darién border problem with Colombia. Clearly, Panama's goal was to continue to cooperate with Washington while at the same time limit U.S. influence on the isthmus and stand firm on not allowing U.S. troops to be stationed or carry out operations on the isthmus.

President Moscoso's most singular moment as president occurred on December 31, 1999, when Panama took control of the canal and the U.S. military presence on the isthmus officially ended. Only four months after taking office, President Mireya Moscoso enjoyed the privilege of presiding over the transfer of the famous canal from the United States to the Republic of Panama. While PRD supporters thought it fitting that Martín Torrijos, son of the late General Torrijos and losing presidential candidate, should have had the honor of receiving the canal, Mireya Moscoso, as the widow of Arnulfo Arias and presidential candidate of the Arnulfista party, also merited the honor. Arias and Torrijos above all others had personified Panamanian nationalism and populism, if not democratic ideals. This great moment in Panamanian, and indeed world, history was bittersweet, however. The Clinton administration decided to minimize the importance of the event, lest Democratic presidential candidate Al Gore be seen as the inheritor of President Carter's policy of "giving away" the canal. As a result, the official U.S. representative was the U.S. secretary of transportation, a clear dismissal of this important event. Nevertheless, former president Jimmy Carter fittingly attended the historic event. Many Panamanians, while not necessarily surprised, were certainly deeply disappointed. At noon, on December 31, 1999, a giant digital clock that had been erected outside the U.S.-built, Romanesque Panama Canal Commission building dramatically counted down to zero. Thousands of red, white, and blue balloons, the colors of the U.S.-inspired Panamanian flag, were released, and the thousands of people who surrounded the administration building cheered and embraced, in a unique expression of national unity and catharsis. For most of the people present,

Panama had finally achieved its elusive sovereignty—paradise regained. For others, who had been accustomed to the extensive U.S. presence and tutelage, the fear of uncertainty spoiled the moment. And, for those Zonians who had already lost much in 1979, the turnover was the death knell of their own American paradise in the tropics. That evening, at midnight, as the year 2000 was born, an observer in the Bay of Panama could see fireworks light up Panama City and as far as the eye could see, but it was impossible to tell whether people were celebrating the New Year or exhibiting renewed national pride.

Mireya Moscoso's celebrations were short-lived. Although as an Arnulfista she promoted social justice and an end to poverty, Panama's poor benefited little during her tenure in the Palacio de las Garzas. Moreover, her administration came under intense criticism for alleged corruption and frivolous spending, causing her popularity to plummet. Soon after taking office, Moscoso presented all seventy-one members of the Legislative Assembly with a Cartier watch worth about $2,000. In September 2003, labor unions, students, and civic groups demonstrated against the Moscoso government, precipitated by a financial and leadership crisis in the nation's social security system. To be fair, corruption charges also tainted the PRD, since several legislators from that party came under investigation for taking bribes. Corruption in Panama became so prominent an issue that a nongovernmental organization, the Movimiento Ciudadano Anticorrupción (Anticorruption Citizen's Movement) was formed. The democratic system, nevertheless, weathered financial troubles, persistent poverty, high unemployment, protests, and government corruption, paving the way for the third set of free and fair national elections since the U.S. invasion.

The PRD Strikes Back: The Martín Torrijos Government and More of the Same

On May 2, 2004, Panamanians elected Martin Torrijos as their new president, resulting in alternation in power for the third consecutive time. Torrijos's Patria Nueva (New Nation) coalition, composed of the PRD and the Partido Popular (Popular Party, formerly the Christian Democrats), received 47.44 percent of the vote. Former president Guillermo Endara, supported by the Solidarity Party, attained 30.86 percent of the vote. Owing to the unpopularity of the Moscoso administration, José Miguel Alemán, who led the coalition Vision de País (Country's Vision), composed of the Arnulfistas, MOLIRENA, and the PLN, received only 16.39 percent. Finally, Ricardo

Martinelli's Democratic Change Party won a mere 5.31 percent (Jackson 2004). In addition to winning the presidency handily, the PRD managed to win an absolute majority in the new seventy-eight-seat National Assembly, with forty-two seats. Its majority was even larger considering that its electoral ally, the PP, won one seat. The Arnulfistas managed to win the second-largest bloc, with a total of seventeen seats, while the rest of the seats went to Solidarity, MOLIRENA, Democratic Change, and the PLN (*Latin American Weekly Report*, May 18, 2004). Although it took a beating in the presidential vote, the Arnulfistas were still the second most popular political party in the legislative branch, continuing the trend toward a two-party system. Panama's smaller political parties tend to be much less popular vehicles for individuals to attain political clout that "only appear during electoral contests" (Leis 1984)(my translation).

Martín Torrijos's election once again emphasized the popularity of presidents and political parties that appeared to represent nationalism and social justice. In his victory speech, Torrijos said boldly, "Today I call for a new social pact, to end poverty, corruption and hopelessness" (quoted in Jackson 2004). Martín Torrijos, however, would follow the broad parameters of his predecessors' policies: promoting democracy and neoliberalism at home, while concurrently attempting to diversify international economic and political ties. The new president, although the son of the Maximum Leader, was educated in the United States, attending St. John's Military Academy in Wisconsin (a boarding school) and studying political science and economics at Texas A&M University. Also, the young Torrijos worked at McDonald's Corporation Headquarters in Chicago before returning to the isthmus in 1992 (*Latin American Weekly Report*, May 4, 2004). Once back in Panama, Omar's son quickly rose to the top of the PRD hierarchy. Torrijos, therefore, was not unlike many Latin American leaders in the post–cold war period: nationalistic and anti-imperialist but succumbing to America's appeal, particularly after the fall of the communist bloc. By the 1990s, nationalists and even most leftists in Latin America had abandoned their efforts at finding an independent path to development for their nations and instead accepted the U.S. model of liberal democracy and neoliberal economic policy. In Panama, the Torrijos government, although using populist rhetoric at times, followed this trend by continuing to promote procedural, liberal democracy and free trade agreements. His administration has proposed to reform the judicial system, to prosecute cases of government corruption, including corruption under the Moscoso administration, and to amend the Torrijos constitution, in an effort to eliminate its most authoritarian laws, such as "gag" laws directed against the popular press.

Hegemony Achieved and Democracy Regained

The United States of America achieved hegemony in Panama by the 1990s, as it did in the rest of Latin America. In the 1980s, two important transformations took place in the region: the move toward U.S.-inspired neoliberal economic policies and redemocratization. The debt crisis in the 1980s allowed the IFIs to press the countries of the region to reduce government spending, reduce tariffs, privatize state enterprises, and promote foreign investment. These neoliberal policies essentially dismantled the statist policies that most countries in the region had implemented, often under institutional military rule. In Panama, under General Omar Torrijos, the Panamanian state had become increasingly involved in the economy and in promoting redistributive policies. Once General Noriega took power, his handpicked president, Ardito Barletta, pushed through unpopular neoliberal policies. By the 1990s, most of the countries in the region had succumbed to the Washington consensus, in effect accepting U.S. economic leadership and emulating U.S. economic policies. The economic crisis of the late 1970s and 1980s generated regime crises all through the region. Since most governments at the time were authoritarian, the effect was a return to democracy. Reductions in U.S. military assistance and the end of the cold war also aided the regional shift toward democracy (Sánchez 2003a). As military regimes became less useful for Washington's region goals and statist models—communist or fascist— lost their legitimacy, the countries of the region came to fully embrace democracy and neoliberalism as the new road toward utopia (Castañeda 1993). Washington had finally achieved preponderance of power and emulation by the subordinate states—hegemony—in Latin America.

Interestingly enough, democracy emerged later in Panama, where the United States had the longest and strongest presence, than in most countries in the region,. As we have seen, Panama had been blessed with better-than-average preconditions for democratic development. A traditional landed elite never existed on the isthmus. Instead, Panama's commercial, urban elite supported liberalism even before the nation achieved independence. During the twentieth century, the isthmus slowly achieved greater national unity and socioeconomic development, resulting in a politically viable middle and working class. At the same time, however, Panama's elite and Washington feared social mobilization, prompting the formation of the Guardia Nacional for the purpose of repressing calls for more contestation and participation. Slowly, the Panamanian state grew in size and strength, but it was not until the inauguration of institutional military rule that the state grew to its maximum strength, reaching an unprecedented level of autonomy (Ropp

1992). Once the United States removed General Noriega and the PDF from power, however, all the pieces were in place for democratization: a liberal elite, national unity, a relatively strong state, sufficient socioeconomic level, elimination of the armed forces, and strong support for democracy, from both elites and the citizenry. But Panama, as with most developing nations, still suffers from some racial and ethnic tensions, a state that has difficulty providing basic collective goods, and significant levels of inequality. Compounding these problems, Panama's policy options are seriously constrained since Washington and IFIs for the most part determine what the isthmus can and cannot do in the economic realm. Panama now controls the canal and the Zone, and the military has been tamed, but paradise on the isthmus still remains a distant dream.

Conclusions and Implications

Panama's Democracy and U.S. Hegemony in a Globalized World

Attempts at simplifying history and explaining political stability and change are always difficult and open to criticism. Nevertheless, if we are to understand the most salient forces that propel political change, some amount of generalization and simplification is necessary. I have examined U.S.-Panamanian relations and isthmian political development with an eye toward social science theories that focus on power distribution in order to explain international interactions and the advent and consolidation of democracy. While Panama's documented history is replete with detail and lacunae, this relatively brief review of the isthmus's history in the past 150 years still reveals much about U.S. hegemony and Panamanian democracy.

Hegemony and Its Effects

There is no doubt that the United States had established itself as a nation-state with a clear preponderance of power in the Western Hemisphere by the early 1900s. While the United States was not a major player at the time of the 1823 Monroe Doctrine, by the end of the nineteenth century Washington was a principal actor in the hemisphere and exhibited global ambitions. Although this study cannot establish why the United States was able to attain such great power, I can nevertheless assert that Washington's policy toward Panama since the mid-1800s has been logical and directed toward the goal of preserving and augmenting U.S. power. Not until the end of World War II, however, did the nations of Latin America willingly emulate the United States' political and economic system. That hegemonic moment was brief in that the cold war and, more important, the Cuban Revolution introduced a competing model into the hemisphere. Although scholars suggest that the so-called communist threat was minimal, U.S. policy makers defended U.S. economic and security interests quickly and decisively lest socialism and single-party rule become the preferred models in the hemisphere. With the demise of the USSR in 1991, the return of democracy, and the adoption of

Washington-supported neoliberal policies in the 1980s, however, America can now be said to be truly the hegemonic power in Latin America. At no other point in history has U.S. power been as preponderant and have so many countries in the region emulated willingly the U.S. economic and political models.

Panama, as we have seen, played an important role in America's rise to hegemony in Latin America. From the building of the transcontinental railroad in the 1850s, to the construction of the Panama Canal during 1904–14, to the establishment of a large complex of U.S. military facilities in the 1900s, the isthmus served Washington's economic, political, and strategic interests in Latin America and even globally. A myriad of U.S. officials, businesspersons, scholars, as well as private individuals over the years worked assiduously to preserve and expand U.S. interests in Panama as elsewhere. Although they often had different priorities, these Americans more likely than not took steps to increase U.S. power and influence, whether by helping U.S. businesses, advancing U.S. military goals, supporting U.S. theories about political development, or simply promoting the image and culture of the American colossus. It is impossible to *prove* the hypothesis that an invisible hand created hegemony. The history of U.S.-Panamanian relations, however, suggests that Washington was relentless in its drive toward hegemony and that probably thousands of U.S. citizens, public and private, contributed to the amassing of U.S. power over the decades. The invisible hand is probably the best possible explanation of how a democracy can continue to accumulate power in the international arena despite the apparent conflict in U.S. foreign-policy decision making. Certainly, scholars who employ the bureaucratic politics paradigm, instead of realism, and look at competing interests in U.S. policy making provide a very important part of foreign policy analysis (see Furlong and Scranton 1984). I would suggest, however, that bureaucratic politics is akin to understanding different types of trees in a forest, whereas realism attempts to explain how forests are born, survive, and die. In other words, realism focuses on broad power changes, while bureaucratic politics examines policy difference in narrower historical moments. To understand foreign policy making and the international system, we need both approaches. A key area of theory building would seek to find a way to combine both approaches—realism and bureaucratic politics—to explain international interactions.

An important contribution of this study is that power accumulation at the international level has important repercussions for the domestic politics of subordinate states. Scholars who study democratization have increasingly focused on domestic politics, in effect discarding theories suggesting that international variables play a role in domestic political development (see, for example, Diamond et al. 1999, 57). This study posits that the concentration of power that the United States attained in the Western Hemisphere had tremendous influence on the distribution of power at the state level in Panama. Since Washington viewed Panama as a prized possession, the U.S. government over the years had a vested interest in maintaining the pro-U.S. status quo on the isthmus. At first this meant support for Colombia's rule over the isthmus, which stifled isthmian self-determination and nationalism. Then it translated into supporting oligarchic rule, which limited contestation and participation on the isthmus. Then it meant assisting the development of a strong National Guard that would become a dominant political actor and would trample democratic institutions. Then it meant backing a military regime devoid of any democratic characteristics. Not until after 1989 did Washington take steps to promote the establishment of a democratic regime on the isthmus, and that occurred only after Panama's military had become anti-American and a barrier to the proper disposition of the Panama Canal Treaties of 1977. In the 1990s, the United States achieved hegemony over Panama and the Western Hemisphere since almost every country in the region adopted American democracy and U.S. economic policies, in hopes that emulating the hegemon would yield political stability and economic prosperity. But the historical record suggests that, for most of the twentieth century, power concentration at the international level militated against a plural distribution of power at the state level in Panama. Rather than viewing Panama as an authoritarian, militaristic, underdeveloped nation with scant support for democratic politics, as many analysts have done, we need to understand that power concentration at the international level, principally U.S. power, was a major influence in slowing movement toward democratization on the isthmus.

Despite an international context nonconductive for democratization, however, many Panamanians struggled for political empowerment as early as the 1800s. These struggles for inclusion climaxed in the 1920s and 1960s and culminated in the inauguration of democracy in the early 1990s. Panama's democratic development, as with all other countries, is a history of both advances and setbacks, both at the domestic and international levels of analysis. Now that we have examined Panama's long road toward democracy, can we say that the isthmus has achieved all the preconditions for the establishment and consolidation of democracy?

Democracy's Preconditions

Panama's democratic development suffered intially from a lack of national unity. While racial and cultural diversity is something to celebrate, a weak nation-state like Panama will find it more difficult to establish national unity in a diverse environment, particularly when the state is unable to meet the needs of the citizenry. External forces also played an important role in precluding the forging of national unity on the isthmus, since the U.S. government introduced foreign workers when it constructed a railroad in the mid-1880s and dug the Panama Canal in the early 1900s. Additionally, U.S. interests at times heightened differences between Hispanic Panamanians and antillanos and indigenous peoples on the isthmus, as happened with the 1925 Kuna rebellion, for example. Thus, an important explanation for Panama's political instability, and its inability to inaugurate a democracy, has been the lack of national unity and the lack of a viable, relatively autonomous nation-state capable of forging such unity. This is not to say, however, that Panamanians were nondemocratic—"subjects" or "parochials"—in their political orientations. Since the 1800s, Panamanians, both elite and nonelite, have demonstrated the high degree of political participation and affinity toward liberalism that is necessary for the development of democracy. In fact, from the 1920s, many Panamanians demanded inclusion into the political system while oligarchs and U.S. policy makers conspired to limit their political participation. The average Panamanian, in fact, seemed to have internalized democratic values sooner than did the isthmian elite or elites in Washington, D.C.[1]

Nevertheless, elites in Panama supported republican government and liberalism as early as the 1800s. Unlike other countries in the region, Panama's elite were liberal, urban, and principally involved in commerce. But Panamanian liberals, like liberals elsewhere in the 1800s and early 1900s, did not support full contestation and popular political participation. In the early 1900s, Panama's oligarchy feared liberalization and thus appealed to the U.S. government for assistance in preserving its control over the political system. Washington willingly obliged in holding back liberalization since the inclusion of new sectors into the political system appeared to threaten U.S. interests. Beginning in the 1930s, Panamanian elites and would-be power contenders looked to political models other than democracy, even if briefly and superficially. In the 1930s, Arnulfo Arias looked to Germany and Italy's reliance on a strong state and appeal to the fatherland as a way to achieve Panamanian development. After the 1959 Cuban Revolution, increasing numbers of Panamanian nationalists wondered if the Cuban model would

Table 8.1. GDP Per Capita for Countries in Central America (1995 US$)

	1982	1992	2002
Costa Rica	2,647	3,123	3,938
El Salvador	1,313	1,477	1,787
Guatemala	1,475	1,401	1,552
Honduras	696	702	712
Nicaragua	656	422	496
Panama	2,984	2,875	3,419

Source: World Bank (2004).

not be the most effective way to achieve sovereignty and self-determination. In the late 1960s, the oligarchy and armed forces embraced militarism as the most effective way to preserve social order and promote national progress. By the 1980s, however, most Panamanians rejected socialism, statism, and militarism and longed for liberal democracy. After the 1989 U.S. invasion, universal agreement existed on the isthmus that democracy was the best political system for Panama. Panama's elites had finally realized that liberal democracy did not jeopardize their key interests. By then, Washington too had come to accept the notion that democracy in Panama would not harm U.S. power and interests in the long run, particularly since U.S. economic and security interests appeared safeguarded.

If only socioeconomic development and class structure determined democratization, we might very well have expected Panama to develop a polyarchy well before most other countries in Latin America. First, compared to other countries in Central America, Panama has achieved a relatively high level of development. Many democratization studies have concluded that one of the best predictors of democratic development is economic development or level of gross domestic product (GDP) per capita. Table 8.1 shows the GDP per capita (in constant 1995 US$) for the countries in Central America, including Panama, in three different years: 1982, two years before the 1984 elections; 1992, soon after the second recent inauguration of democracy; and 2002.

As we can see, Panama is the only country in the region that has kept pace with the GDP per capital of Costa Rica, a country that has had a stable democratic government since 1948 (see Peeler 2004). Guatemala and El Salvador are the only two countries that are relatively close to the higher GDP per capita levels for Costa Rica and Panama, but these two countries have suffered from a legacy of powerful, traditional landed elites (see Paige 1997). Thus, by the mid-1980s, Panama had reached whatever threshold scholars deemed necessary for democratic development.

Table 8.2. Percentage of Economy Derived from Industry, Services, and Agriculture for Selected Countries in Central America

	Panama		Costa Rica		Guatemala	
	1990	2002	1990	2002	1990	2002
Agriculture	9	6	18	8	26	22
Industry	15	14	29	29	20	19
Services	76	80	53	62	54	58

Source: World Bank (2004).

More important, Panama's class structure has been more conducive to democratic development than most countries in Latin America. Students of Panamanian politics have pointed out repeatedly that commercial, urban elites dominated the political system for most of the country's history (Conniff 1992; LaFeber 1989; Soler 1989). Panama never suffered from a strong, traditional landed oligarchy that has made democratic development difficult in many countries of the region (Paige 1997; Rueschemeyer, Huber Stephens, and Stephens 1992). This economic, structural factor, more than any other measure of socioeconomic development, can best predict the likelihood of democratic development. Table 8.2 shows the GDP contributions by economic sector for Panama, Costa Rica, and Guatemala in 1990 and 2002. We can see that Panama's economy relies least on the agricultural sector. And the industrial and service sectors overwhelmingly overshadow agriculture, which is still not the case for Guatemala.

The social mobilization of the 1920s led by professionals, students, and workers that culminated in the 1930 revolution is testimony to the relatively early socioeconomic development in the isthmus. In fact, since Panama's socioeconomic development compares most closely with Costa Rica's, we must wonder why it was that the isthmus had such a delayed democratic development.

On the negative side, the democratic potential of Panama's relative success with socioeconomic development was undermined by the high level of inequality on the isthmus. In 1980, inequality in Panama, measured by the Gini coefficient, surpassed all countries in Central America, except for El Salvador (Zimbalist and Weeks 1991, 123). While inequality alone may not prevent the inauguration of democratic government, it will certainly hinder the consolidation of a liberal democratic regime since participation in the political process may be stymied, national divisions may arise, and populism may appeal to many citizens.

Early in its history as a republic, Panama eliminated its armed forces, albeit owing to foreign pressure. Unfortunately, during the 1930s and 1940s, as social mobilization increased and nationalist forces demanded inclusion into the political system, Panama revived militarism by strengthening and eventually "professionalizing" its national police. This militarization, as pointed out in previous chapters, was encouraged and financed by the U.S. government. The result was the Guardia Nacional, a pseudomilitary organization that became a major political actor and eventually took over the reins of power. As the oligarchy lost the little legitimacy it had, the armed forces grew stronger, yielding an uncharacteristic isthmian praetorianism. The anticommunist crusade led by Washington, which called for the armed forces to become engaged in the maintenance of internal order, contributed significantly to the Guardia's involvement in politics. Only after the U.S. government invaded Panama in 1989 to rid itself of Noriega and the PDF did democracy return to the isthmus. Although Panama's liberal oligarchs were eager to strengthen the National Police in order to preserve their interests, the notorious Guardia would probably not have become as powerful as it did without the blessing and support of Washington. Panama's antidemocratic militarism, therefore, may be as much a foreign export as it is a homegrown product (see Harding 2001; and Pearcy 1998). It is clear, however, that strong military institutions that become engaged in maintaining internal order are perhaps one of the most important barriers to democratic development (Lowenthal and Fitch 1986).

Although we can argue that now a strong national consensus over the democratic rules of the game exists on the isthmus, Panama still lacks strong, comprehensive national unity. This national fragmentation is to a large extent the product of ethnic and racial divisions. Despite the Panamanian state's efforts at creating one national identity, the isthmus continues to be a collage of identities. Ethnic and racial divisions, however, are not necessarily a barrier to democratic inauguration or consolidation. They constitute a roadblock only if those differences prevent the emergence of national unity or consensus. Panama's elites no longer have a problem with the political inclusion of antillanos or indigenous peoples into the political system. Nevertheless, there is still too high a level of mistrust among Panamanians of different backgrounds. The Hispanics (the idealized Panamanian), the antillanos, the Kuna, as well as other indigenous peoples, do not trust each other sufficiently. Compounding this problem is the fact that the benefits of society, both political and economic, are not equally distributed; and, despite the existence of full contestation and participation, antillanos and indígenas are not adequately represented. We cannot forget, however, that this is a problem that many other democratic societies share, including the United States. The difference is that Panama's state is not strong enough to forge greater national unity via public education, that is, socialization. Democratic theorists, therefore, should heed Epstein's suggestion that more focus be given to the role of education in democratic consolidation (2005).

The overpowering influence of the United States constitutes one of Panama's principal problems with democratic development. Panama's decision makers had little leeway in their domestic and foreign policy during the years that Washington had an overwhelming presence on the isthmus, and particularly when U.S. decision makers felt that American interests were being threatened. Panama's self-determination and sovereignty took a back seat to U.S. interests, and there was nothing Panamanians could do about their subordinate condition. Panamanians at times did challenge the United States—rejecting the 1926 Kellogg-Alfaro Treaty and 1947 base rights agreement, for example. We have seen, however, that these were usually pyrrhic victories, never constituting a real challenge to U.S. power and interests. Over the years, the U.S. government took numerous steps that limited Panama's democratic development, self-determination, and sovereignty: introducing large numbers of non-Panamanians into the isthmus, militating against the forging of a strong national identity; physically bisecting the country, preventing natural economic and urban development; taking advantage of Panama's strategic location at a key period of global trade expansion; maintaining an extensive complex of military facilities on the isthmus for pursuing both regional and global strategic goals; intervening repeatedly in Panama's political and economic affairs; keeping the Panamanian state weak, making national development more difficult; helping to create and strengthen the Guardia, an institution that trampled upon democracy. These are just the most glaring examples. This is not to say that the U.S. government is solely responsible for Panama's troubles with democratic development. My purpose is to demonstrate that Washington often did not assist and often militated against democratic development on the isthmus, either inadvertently or consciously. Democracy, therefore, as some scholars would suggest, does not necessarily flow from industrialized democracies to the less-developed nation-states. On the contrary, at times certain groups in developing nations are pushing for polyarchy while industrialized democracies take actions that either directly or indirectly subvert those efforts. As Rudolph convincingly shows, the Panamanian people are civic-minded and more than willing to participate politically, even against great odds (1999).

Panama's Prospects for Democratic Consolidation

The 1990s presented Panama with perhaps the best context in its history for democracy's inauguration and consolidation. As pointed out above, the isthmus had attained some degree of elite and national unity, and democracy was perceived as the best political game; socioeconomic development and the class structure were conducive for liberalization; and the armed forces had been eliminated. Additionally, the regional hegemon—the United States—stopped supporting a repressive, military-dominated political system and eventually eliminated the corrupt and politicized armed forces it had created. Despite persistent inequality and racial and ethnic divisions, Panama now enjoys most of the prerequisites for democratic development. Since the 1989 U.S. invasion, Panama has held three free and fair national elections (meeting Peeler's rule of three electoral cycles) and two national referenda on constitutional reforms. In each of the national elections, alternation in power occurred, meaning that the incumbent party lost to an opposition party and turned over power in a constitutional manner (Singer 2005).

In addition, the nation's political institutions are becoming increasingly institutionalized and vibrant. Two relatively strong political parties have emerged in Panama's political system—the Arnulfistas (PA) and the Peredistas (PRD). Even though several other parties exist, most voters identify with these two political parties (CID-Gallup Latin America 1999).[2] The PA and PRD are likely to remain dominant since they have a relatively long history and are viewed by the citizenry as representative of Panamanian nationalism. Even though in the 2004 election the Arnulfista presidential candidate came in third in the vote tally, the PA managed to achieve the second-largest bloc in the Legislative Assembly. The small political parties that represent the remnants of oligarchic political forces will certainly continue their, to date, unsuccessful efforts at forming a significant political force. If they fail, they will most likely find a home in the PRD or the Arnulfista Party, however unlikely that may seem at this moment. If they succeed, then Panama could very well have three strong political parties in the not-too-distant future, a prospect that should not harm the nation's drive toward democratic consolidation. The isthmus's political history demonstrates that Panamanians are more than willing to become engaged politically, and over the years many civic organizations have emerged demanding inclusion and policy changes. The people of Panama have been political participants for many decades, à la Almond and Verba (1963), on numerous historical occasions willing to pay with their lives to attain freedom and self-determination. During the so-called Noriega crisis, Panamanians took to the streets without regard for their safety to protest against the PDF repressive regime, knowing quite well that their lives could be in danger (Janson Pérez 1993).

Panama, however, has to overcome some important challenges to democratic consolidation. While progress has been made, the isthmus still is far from institutionalizing a truly independent judiciary, national legislature, and electoral tribunal, although the latter may be said to have achieved true autonomy and effectiveness. Panama must also ensure that economic prosperity does not benefit only the upper and middle classes. In order for inequality in Panama to decline, the gap in wealth between the city and the rural areas must become less stark. If Panama continues to be a divided nation in terms of wealth, race, and ethnicity, then it will most likely go down the path of populism, instability, and renewed authoritarianism.

Another serious and seldom-mentioned problem for Panama is the continuing power of the United States. While elections are held on the isthmus now on a regular basis, Panama's political elite are severely constrained in their policy options because of pressure from Washington and other international forces. The "Washington consensus," promoting neoliberal economic policies, has now been adopted by the Arnulfistas and the PRD, even though these parties have historically promoted a nationalist and populist political agenda. In effect, Panama's political elite cannot determine the basic outlines of their country's economic policies. Now that the United States is the only Great Power with influence in Latin America, U.S. hegemony has been fully achieved and the options for Panama and other countries in the region are dramatically limited. As long as Panama's citizens and elites support democracy and neoliberalism, democracy will continue to flourish. But if democracy and neoliberalism do not yield at least minimum benefits for the masses, then populism will become more appealing and democracy will be skating on thin ice. Scholars must also consider whether a country can be considered to be a functioning democracy if its economic policy is being determined externally. When power is concentrated in the international arena, democracy at the domestic level may be a mirage.

This general assessment of Panama's prospects for democratic consolidation may seem overly, or even naively, positive. There has been a tendency recently to paint the Panamanian future as bleak and potentially chaotic, especially in terms of economic stability and democratic development. This negative tendency can be found among analysts both in the United States and in Panama. From the U.S. perspective, Panamanian stability and prosperity is assumed to derive from the U.S. presence. Now that the U.S. presence has been dramatically reduced, these analysts predict a troubled future for the isthmus. This perspective is curious considering the fact that an extensive and prolonged U.S. presence did not save Panama from the problems endemic in Latin America, and it in fact may have prolonged and intensified those problems. From the Panamanian position, the advent of democratic politics has unleashed an enormous volume of political criticism that, although representing a positive step, has tended to magnify the country's failures with democratic development. This criticism is positive in that exaggerating the nation's weaknesses may prevent the development of major flaws that could seriously harm democracy's prospects. However, nonpartisan analysts should be able to see beyond the rhetoric and confusion of today and take a longer, more analytical look at Panama's current progress with democracy. Panama may not be paradise, but it now belongs mainly to the Panamanians, who have wanted and deserved democracy for a very long time.

Lessons for U.S. Foreign Policy: Can U.S. Hegemony Be Maintained?

While this book focuses principally on Panamanian political development and how the power structure in the international system has affected that development, U.S. policy toward Panama and U.S. hegemony have also necessarily been foci of this book. In reviewing the history of U.S.-Panamanian relations, several interesting aspects or weaknesses of U.S. foreign policy behavior stand out. At a time when the United States has achieved hegemony in Latin American and seems ready and willing to attain global hegemony, the "lessons" from Panama become even more relevant.

1. The U.S.-Panamanian relationship demonstrates a U.S. obsession with "hard" rather than with "soft" power. In effect, Washington appeared to be more interested in short-term realpolitik than in long-term American influence. Usually Washington responded to Panama's quest for democracy and self-determination with military aid or with direct military intervention. This tendency to be concerned with the immediate power game rather than the long-term ideological game may simply be a manifestation of the fact that the United States felt threatened by extrahemispheric powers for much of the U.S.-Panamanian relationship that we have examined: first, Washington was concerned with the British and French, then with Germany, then with the Soviet Union. Now that it has no challengers in the region—since global terrorism of the Islamist variety finds no roots or support in the region—the United States should focus more on soft power, which is so necessary for the establishment

of hegemony. Unless a preponderant power is able to achieve, and master the use of, soft power, subordinate states will not want to emulate the hegemon. An increased emphasis on soft power would require that the United States be more careful in how it uses its economic and military power. The more Washington uses coercion, the more likely it will be that the subordinate states of the region will resist U.S. leadership. The so-called Global War on Terrorism upon which the United States has embarked has the potential of alienating the countries of Latin America even more since Washington, as in the past, is ignoring the region's socioeconomic concerns for the sake of narrow U.S. strategic and security interests. Likewise, Washington's obsession with neoliberalism can undermine Latin America's support for the U.S. model if these economic policies do not produce a better life for the average person in the region. Already a number of countries in Latin America—Argentina, Bolivia, Brazil, Chile, and Venezuela—have elected left-leaning presidents who are increasingly critical of the Washington consensus. Hegemony works only when the subordinate states become convinced that the hegemon is willing to sacrifice some of its interests to attain both its own and collective interests. Once subordinate nations lose faith in the hegemon's self-serving "altruism" and ideology, then hegemony may soon be lost. As with scientific paradigms, however, it is unlikely that the region's countries will abandon democracy and neoliberalism unless new and seemingly better economic and political models appear on the horizon. In such a situation, the United States will retain a preponderance of power but will lose any hopes of maintaining its hegemony in the region.

2. The U.S.-Panamanian relationship also demonstrates a U.S. affinity to form alliances with nefarious characters and antidemocratic forces. Once again, these unsavory links may reflect a lack of power, in that to attain a preponderance of power the hegemon must first use Machiavellian tactics. Once hegemony is achieved, however, the hegemon must become a legitimate leader, meaning that associations with corrupt, repressive, and power-hungry individuals would need to be eliminated or at least minimized. Torrijos and Noriega were useful for Washington since they helped to prevent a second Cuba in Panama and assisted with U.S. regional goals. In the future, however, Washington must ensure that it forms relationships with truly democratic leaders, accepting their decisions even if they appear contrary to U.S. interests in the short term. If Wash-

ington undermines democratic leaders or associates itself with unsavory, undemocratic characters, as it did in the past, then responsible leaders in the region will stop looking toward the United States as a model worthy of emulation. Now that it seems to have adopted an agenda of promoting democracy, Washington must focus on defending polyarchy globally and not just when democracies are sympathetic to U.S. interests. Such a policy, however, should not be characterized as altruistic but rather as an effort to promote long-term hegemonic interests.

3. Finally, the U.S.-Panamanian relationship has taught us that Washington has tended to be indifferent toward its policies that have indirectly undermined democracy. U.S. policy makers did not seem concerned that supporting oligarchic or military leaders would undermine democratic development. Once again, such a callous disregard for antidemocratic actions may be a reflection of the fact that for most of the U.S.-Panamanian relationship that we have observed, Washington was first and foremost concerned with establishing a U.S. preponderance of power in the hemisphere. Democratic development in Panama from the 1930s to the 1970s appeared to be a threat to U.S. economic and military power in the region, so Washington ignored democracy while it focused on enhancing its hard power. Now that U.S. hegemony seems relatively solid in the hemisphere, Washington must resist taking actions that may indirectly undermine democratic consolidation, such as supporting the further institutionalization and domestic involvement of the armed forces in the region. If Washington undermines democracy in the region, it may still retain a preponderance of power, but it will lose its hegemony since once emulation falls by the wayside, a decline in soft power will soon follow.

To sum up, Panama is poised as never before for democratic consolidation. Panama, in fact, was in a better position than most countries in the region to establish a democracy early in its history, owing to its liberal ideology and lack of a landed oligarchy. Panama had problems inaugurating democracy early, like Costa Rica, principally because for decades the oligarchy, with U.S. help, resisted allowing for contestation and popular participation. Once the United States achieved regional hegemony, Panama inaugurated a democracy that stands a good chance of being consolidated. But Panama's democracy is weakened by the fact that its policy options are severely limited, owing to the existence of hegemony at the international level. While power is now less concentrated on the isthmus, it is still highly concentrated at the international level. Democracy may be able to survive in such an asymmetrical international context, but if at some point this power differential prevents the average Panamanian from improving his or her life, then calls for populism, anti-imperialism, and even an end to democracy will rise once again, and paradise will continue to be an elusive goal both for Panama and for the United States.

Notes

Chapter 1. Hegemony and Democracy

1. I use "Iberoamerica" (the Spanish-speaking countries in the region and Brazil) because it is in these countries that the United States has established itself as a hegemon. The English-speaking Caribbean-basin nations, for example, still retain strong economic and political ties to Great Britain.

2. This racist element in democratic development is similar to what happened in the American South with the civil rights laws of the 1960s. Southern elites were extremely hesitant to accept changes. However, once they realized that greater participation by blacks would not result in revolutionary changes, southern elites lost their fear of civil rights laws.

Chapter 2. From the Emergence of U.S. Dominance to the "Taking of the Isthmus"

1. The term *communication* was used in the nineteenth and early twentieth centuries when referring to international links via interoceanic contact. Thus, the isthmus was described often as a means of "communication."

2. The term *Hanseatic* originates from medieval Germany, when merchants who carried out trade with foreign lands founded a merchant guild. While the merchants' key goal was free trade, they formed the guild or association for the purpose of protection.

3. Arosemena, as others, nevertheless cautioned against Panama coming under the influence of the United States. In this sense, Panama's intellectuals reflected the sentiments of Cuba's José Martí.

4. The urban, commercial elite of European origin were referred to as the *intramuros* because they lived within the walls of the city. Those of the *arrabal* represented the rest of the population, composed of mestizos, poor whites, blacks, and indígenas, who lived outside the walls.

5. While some people object to the use of the term *America* to refer to the United States, I use the term because it is used by people in the region not only to refer to U.S. citizens (*los Americanos*) but also because it symbolizes Washington's appropriation of the region.

6. Washington did not definitively decide to build the canal in Panama until the early 1900s. Nevertheless, U.S. decision makers knew that Panama's geographic position was vital for global communication and commerce very early on. Even if a canal were not built in Panama, it would be necessary to ensure control of the isthmus lest some other power do so.

7. De Lesseps was not an engineer but simply a promoter. Until the age of forty, he had been a diplomat.

8. In a much-quoted phrase, Teddy Roosevelt announced some years after the events surrounding the Panamanian Revolution, "I took the isthmus and let Congress deliberate."

Chapter 3. From the Building of the Panama Canal to the Great Depression

1. *Entreguismo* refers to individuals who turn over the country or its resources to external interests.

Chapter 4. From the "Good Neighbor" to the End of World War II

1. The term *rabiblanco*, or white-tailed, is used by people in Panama to refer to those who are of European descent and members of the oligarchy. More often than not, the term has a negative connotation.

2. I must point out, however, that the United States built roads, particularly the one to the Río Hato air base and the one linking Panama City and Colón, first and foremost for what Washington defense planners saw as canal defense needs.

Chapter 5. From the Cold War to the End of the "Special Relationship"

1. This historic incident has generated many varying descriptions and interpretations. Some Panamanians blamed the United States for all Panamanian casualties and for inciting the crisis, while some observers in the United States and in the Canal Zone blamed Panamanians for the crisis and for most of the deaths. While no one will ever know the complete story, it is clear that Zone police and Zone vigilantes did in fact fire into the crowds and that U.S. troops or Zone police were not responsible for many of the Panamanian casualties. Regardless of the specific acts during this crisis, the violence that ensued on January 9, 1964, represented to a large extent pent-up hostilities toward the United States on the part of many Panamanians who were tired of American neocolonialism and colonial attitudes.

2. In Latin America, it has been common practice to assign opposition military officers to foreign posts as attachés or diplomats. Although the officers realized that they were being marginalized, most did not balk because these diplomatic postings came with sizeable financial rewards and opportunities.

Chapter 6. From U.S. Support of Dictatorship to the U.S. Invasion

1. At the time of Panama's military takeover, Argentina, Brazil, and Peru had already succumbed to institutional military rule, as the armed forces of the region, supported by Washington, took control to prevent communist groups from assuming power or undermining order.

2. Panama's military regime was not as brutal as some of the notorious military governments of the 1960s and 1970s, like those in Brazil, Argentina, or Chile. However, it is important to note that the Torrijos, and then Noriega, regimes used brutal tactics against opponents and were responsible for mass arrests, beatings, and executions. For a chronicle of the lengthy resistance against the military regimes, see Janson Pérez (1993).

3. Not surprisingly, in the United States, the treaties are known as Carter-Torrijos, while in Panama they are referred to as Torrijos-Carter.

4. Several Panamanians expressed to me the strong feelings and memories that the elimination of the Zone in 1979 evoked in them. The end of the Canal Zone in 1979 represented a joyous moment for most if not all Panamanians, despite their class, race, feelings toward the United States, or political orientation.

5. In fact, the Carter administration spent a great deal of effort to produce propaganda that characterized the Torrijos autocracy as a benevolent dictatorship.

6. Although Guatemala refused U.S. military assistance in 1978, the CIA with the help of the Israeli government continued to support the Guatemalan armed forces, and U.S. military aid was resumed in 1983 after the military regime agreed to hold elections in 1984 (Jonas 2000, 120–21; author's personal experience).

7. I lived close to the University of Panama at the time and, upon returning from work at Howard Air Force Base, witnessed the aftermath of the clash between students and the PDF. The streets were so full of trash and large debris that I had to weave around to drive through. Several cars were overturned and charred from being set on fire. The Panamanian security guard at my apartment building excitedly said to me as I entered the building, "Captain, you should have been here—it was just like Vietnam!" I asked him if he had been in Vietnam (since Panamanians served in the U.S. military), and without missing a beat, he said, "No, but I saw it on TV."

8. At the time of Spadafora's capture, Noriega was in Paris but remained in telephone contact with key PDF officers. The NSA intercept of a conversation with Noriega went as follows: "We have the rabid dog," to which Noriega responded, "You know what to do with a rabid dog."

9. I was sent to Panama by the U.S. Air Force in summer of 1983 to work in the combined U.S.-Panamanian military board established to begin discussing the status of U.S. bases past 1999. Upon arriving in Panama, I was informed that the group could not begin negotiations because Noriega still did not want to discuss the permanence of U.S. bases in Panama.

10. Incredibly enough, U.S. officials often exhibited surprise and shock at Colonel Herrera's accusations even though a number of U.S. government agencies knew the details of Noriega's illegal activities quite well. Most likely, those officials either knew the party line or were basically out of the loop on Noriega's history and thus believed their own faulty rhetoric.

11. I interviewed several individuals in the opposition who were exiled and worked with U.S. officials, most likely CIA, on various plans to overthrow Noriega.

Chapter 7. From the U.S. Occupation to the End of the U.S. Military Presence and Beyond

1. For timely information on the canal operations and plans, see the Panama Canal Authority's Web page at www.pancanal.com/eng/index.html.

2. Interestingly enough, Negroponte's retirement was short-lived. He moved on to very important positions—U.S. ambassador to the United Nations, U.S. ambassador

to Iraq, and director of national intelligence—only a few years after his supposed "retirement" from the State Department in 1997.

3. Since at least as early as 1983, U.S. decision makers worked under the assumption that the Panamanians were using the permanence of U.S. bases on the isthmus as a bargaining chip, but that they actually wanted the bases to stay, principally for the sake of economic benefits and added security. On several occasions, U.S. planners suggested that the U.S. government should close down at least one important military facility to let the Panamanians know that the U.S. was serious (which of course it was not since the military facility would be removed simply as a signal). This cat-and-mouse game continued until the end. What U.S. decision makers never fully understood was that the Panamanians had some very sound reasons for wanting the U.S. military bases gone from the isthmus.

4. During the "crisis" over paramilitary and guerrilla incursions into Panamanian territory, one television channel in Panama broadcast footage of alleged FARC guerrillas openly operating in the Darién region. Oddly enough, the footage showed guerrillas sporting freshly ironed fatigues. Some of the women guerrillas wore what appeared to be designer shirts under their fatigue shirts and makeup, and their nails were long and manicured, even as they carried rifles. The legitimacy of this particular guerrilla incursion was clearly suspect.

5. The Clinton administration unveiled Plan Colombia in 1999 as a renewed U.S. effort to assist the besieged Colombian government with the threat posed by illegal narcotics; however, the plan was most certainly also designed to make up for the loss of antidrug operations in Panama by providing large amounts of military and other aid to Colombia. Most of the nations in the hemisphere have been skeptical of the plan (see, for example, *Latin America Weekly Report*, June 27, 2000, 292).

Chapter 8. Conclusions and Implications

1. Elites in Washington could certainly take actions to undermine democracy in Panama while at the same time believing strongly in democracy in their own country.

2. According to a recent CID Gallup poll of Panamanian voters, 26 percent identify with the Arnulfista Party; 23 percent identify with the PRD; and 40 percent are undecided, leaving very few voters for the remaining parties (see "Encuesta CID Gallup Panamá," *El Panamá América*, September 1, 1999).

Bibliography

Abbot, Willis J. 1922. *The Panama Canal: An Illustrated Historical Narrative*. New York: Syndicate.

Acosta, David. 1999. *Patria y CMA*. Panama City: Impresos Modernos David.

Albert, Steve. 1993. *The Case against the General: Manuel Noriega and the Politics of American Justice*. New York: Charles Scribner's Sons.

Alfaro, Ricardo J. 1959. *Medio siglo de relaciones entre Panamá y los Estados Unidos*. Panama City: Secretaría de Información de la Presidencia de la República.

Allison, Graham T. 1999. *Essence of Decision: Explaining the Cuban Missile Crisis*. 2nd ed. New York: Longman.

Almond, Gabriel, and Sidney Verba. 1963. *The Civic Culture: Political Attitudes and Democracy in Five Nations*. Princeton: Princeton University Press.

Anguizola, Gustave. 1977. *The Panama Canal: Isthmian Political Instability from 1821 to 1977*. Washington, D.C.: University Press of America.

———. 1980. *Philippe Bunau-Varilla: The Man behind the Canal*. Chicago: Nelson-Hall.

Araúz, Celestino Andrés. 1994a. *Panamá y sus relaciones internacionales, estudio introductorio*. Vol. 1. Panama City: Editorial Universitaria.

———. 1994b. *Panamá y sus relaciones internacionales, estudio introductorio, notas y antología*. Vol. 2. Panama City: Editorial Universitaria.

Arce, Enrique J., and Juan B. Sosa. 1971. *Compendio de historia de Panamá*. Panama City: Impresora Litho Panamá.

Arias Calderón, Ricardo. 1987–88. "Panama: Disaster or Democracy." *Foreign Affairs* 66 (Winter): 328–47.

Arias de Para, Raúl. 1984. *Así fue el fraude: Las elecciones presidenciales de Panamá, 1984*. Panama City: Imprenta Edilito, S.A.

Arias, Harmodio. 1970. *The Panama Canal: A Study in International Law and Diplomacy*. New York: Arno.

Arias Peña, Rosario, and Iván Quintero. 1994. *Historia política de Panamá*. Panama City: Comité Ecuménico de Panamá.

Arosemena Alvarado, Rafael. 1997. *En el ojo de la crisis*. Mexico City: Esfera Servicios Editoriales.

Arosemena G., Diógenes A. 1997a. *Historia documental del Canal de Panamá: Época pos-colonial*. Vol. 1. 2nd ed. Panama City: Instituto Nacional de Cultura.

———. 1997b. *Historia documental del Canal de Panamá: La república y el canal*. Vol. 2. 2nd ed. Panama City: Instituto Nacional de Cultura.

———. 1997c. *Historia documental del Canal de Panamá: Los últimos tratados canaleros*. Vol. 3. 2nd ed. Panama City: Instituto Nacional de Cultura.

———. 1998. *Seis ensayos históricos y el chatarrismo canalero.* Panama City: Litho Editorial Chen.

———. 1999. *Brevario histórico sobre el problema canalero.* 2nd ed. Panama City: Instituto de Estudios Políticos e Internacionales.

Arrocha Graell, Catalino. 1975. *Historia de la independencia de Panamá: Sus antecedentes y sus causas, 1821–1903.* Panama City: Academia Panameña de la Historia.

Atlantic Council. 1996a. "Defining a New Relationship: The Issue of U.S. Access to Facilities in Panama." Policy Paper Series. July.

———. 1996b. "Testing a Special Relationship: The Panama Canal Transition." *Bulletin* 7 (April 5): 1–4.

Autoridad de la Región Interoceánica. 1997. "Proyectos y empresas establecidas dentro de las áreas canaleras." Panama City: Autoridad de la Región Interoceánica. July.

Ballesteros, Isiás B. 1965. *El drama de Panamá y América, nuestras relaciones con los Estados Unidos.* Panama City: Imprenta Nacional.

Baranyi, Stephen. 1994. "Panama's Security Dilemmas—Solutions on the Horizon." *Jane's Intelligence Review* 6 (July): 328–31.

Barry, Tom, and John Lindsay-Poland, with Marco Gandásegui and Peter Simonson. 1995. *Inside Panama: The Essential Guide to Its Politics, Economy, Society, and Environment.* Albuquerque: Interhemispheric Resource Center Press.

Bartlett, Randall. 1973. *Economic Foundations of Political Power.* New York: Free Press.

Batista, Juan Luis, Abdiel Zárate, and Herasto Reyes. 1995. "Bases militares: Pulso de la nación." *La Prensa* (insert), May 16.

Baxter, Richard, and Doris Carroll. 1965. *The Panama Canal: Background Papers and Proceedings of the Sixth Hammarskjöld Forum.* Dobbs Ferry, N.Y.: Oceana Publications.

Becerra Acosta, Jeanette. 1998. "Panamá concede "Excesivas Responsabilidades" a Washington en el CMLN 1998." *El Excelsior,* January 27.

Beluche, Olmedo. 1994. *Diez años de luchas políticas y sociales en Panamá, 1980–1990.* Panama City: Impresora Tavial, S.A..

———. 1996. *La verdad sobre la invasión.* 4th ed. Panama City: Editorial Portobelo.

Bendix, Reinhard. 1978. *Kings or People: Power and the Mandate to Rule.* Berkeley and Los Angeles: University of California Press.

Bennett, Ira E. 1915. *History of the Canal: Its Construction and Builders.* Washington, D.C.: Historical Publishing Co.

Berger, Mark. 1995. *Under Northern Eyes: Latin American Studies and U.S. Hegemony in the Americas, 1898–1990.* Bloomington: Indiana University Press.

Bergsten, C. Fred, Robert Keohane, and Joseph Nye. 1975. "International Economics and International Politics: A Framework for Analysis." *International Organization* 29 (Winter): 3–36.

Bermúdez, Ricardo. 1998. "CMA: Propuesta de creación del Centro Multinacional de Lucha Contra el Narcotráfico." Panel, Facultad de Comunicación Social, Universidad de Panamá, March 3.

Bernal, Miguel Antonio. 1985. *Los Tratados Carter-Torrijos: Una traición histórica.* 2nd ed. Panama City: Ediciones Nari.

Bethancourt, Rómulo Escobar. 1981. *Torrijos, ¡Colonia Americana no!* Bogotá: Carlos Valencia.

Biesanz, John. 1952. "Economy of Panama." *Inter-American Economic Affairs* 6 (Summer): 3–28.

Biesanz, John, and Mavis Biesanz. 1955. *The People of Panama.* New York: Columbia University Press.

Binnendijk, Hans, and L. Erik Kjonnerod. 1997. "Panama 2000." *Strategic Forum*, National Defense University, Institute for National Strategic Studies, no. 117, June.

Bishop, Farnham. 1916. *Panama: Past and Present.* New York: Century.

Blasier, Cole. 1985. *The Hovering Giant: U.S. Responses to Revolutionary Change in Latin America, 1910–1985.* Rev. ed. Pittsburgh: University of Pittsburgh Press.

Bocanegra, Jaime. 1998. Interview by author. June 9. Canal Transition Office, Panama Canal Commission, Panama City, Panama.

Bocock, Robert. 1986. *Hegemony.* London: Tavistock.

Boersner, Demetrio. 1996. *Relaciones internacionales de América Latina.* Caracas: Nueva Sociedad.

Bonilla, Leonidas. 1998. Sergeant (retired), Panamanian Defense Forces. Interview by author. February 23. Panama City, Panama.

Bósquez, Everardo, Marco A. Gandásegui, and Luis Navas. 1990. *Invasión, militarismo y democracia.* Panama City: Instituto de Estudios Nacionales.

Buckley, Kevin. 1991. *Panama: The Whole Story.* New York: Simon and Schuster.

Bull, Hedley. 1977. *A Study of Order in World Politics.* 2nd ed. New York: Columbia University Press.

Bunau-Varilla, Philippe. 1913. *Panama: The Creation, Destruction, and Resurrection.* London: Constable.

Burton, Michael G., and John Higley. 1987. "Elite Settlements." *American Sociological Review* 52 (June): 295–307.

Busey, James L. 1974. *Political Aspects of the Panama Canal: The Problem of Location.* Tucson: University of Arizona Press.

Carles, Rubén Darío. 1968. *Reminiscencias de los primeros años de la República de Panamá, 1903–1912.* Panama City: La Estrella de Panamá.

Castañeda, Jorge G. 1993. *Utopia Unarmed: The Latin America Left after the Cold War.* New York: Vintage.

Castillero Pimentel, Ernesto. 1953. *Panamá y los Estados Unidos.* Panama City: Editorial Humanidad.

———. 1961. *Política exterior de Panamá.* Panama City: Impresora Panamá, S.A.

Castillero Reyes, Ernesto J. 1995. *Historia de Panamá.* 11th ed. Panama City: n.p.

———. 1999. *Historia de la comunicación interoceánica y de su influencia en la for-*

mación y en el desarrollo de la Entidad Nacional Panameña. Panama City: Editora Sibauste.

Castrellón, Franklin D. 1998. Director, local media/community relations, Panama Canal Commission. Interview by author. June 11. Panama City, Panama.

Castro, Nils. 1987. "Objetivos estratégicos de Estados Unidos en Panamá." San José, Costa Rica: Comité de Solidaridad con el Pueblo de Panamá.

Centro de Estudios Latinoamericanos. 1993. "Síntesis histórica de los partidos políticos en Panamá." *Coyuntura 94.* Panama City: Centro de Estudios Latinoamericanos.

———. 1997a. "Bases militares." *Tareas,* no. 95.

———. 1997b. "La gesta del 9 de Enero." *Tareas,* no. 97.

Challener, Richard D. 1973. *Admirals, Generals, and American Foreign Policy, 1898–1914.* Princeton: Princeton University Press.

Chen Daley, Mercedes. 1990. "The Watermelon Riot: Cultural Encounters in Panama City, April 15, 1856." *Hispanic American Historical Review* 70: 85–108.

CID-Gallup Latin America. 1999. "Análisis de los partidos políticos." In "Encuesta CID Gallup-Panama," insert. *El Panamá América.* Panama City: El Panamá America. www.epasa.com/cid-gallup/index.html.

Collier, David, ed. 1979. *The New Authoritarianism in Latin America.* Princeton: Princeton University Press.

Collin, Richard H. 1990. *Theodore Roosevelt's Caribbean: The Panama Canal, the Monroe Doctrine, and the Latin American Context.* Baton Rouge: Louisiana State University Press.

Comisión del Canal de Panamá. 1997. *El Canal de Panamá: Una visión para el futuro.* Panama City: Comisión del Canal de Panamá.

Comisión del Tribunal Electoral. 1997. *Código electoral.* Panama City: Departamento de Imprenta.

Comisión Para Asunto del Canal. 1992. "Análisis y recomendaciones para la optima utilización de las áreas y bienes revertidas y por revertir de acuerdo a los tratados de 1977. Panama City: Sistemas Jurídicos, S.A.

Conn, Stetson, and Byron Fairchild. 1960. *The Western Hemisphere: The Framework of Hemisphere Defense.* Washington D.C.: Government Printing Office.

Conniff, Michael L. 1985. *Black Labor on a White Canal: Panama 1904–1981.* Pittsburgh: University of Pittsburgh Press.

———. 1992. *Panama and the United States: The Forced Alliance.* Athens: University of Georgia Press.

Conte-Porras, Jorge, and Eduardo E. Castillero L. 1998. *Historia de Panamá y sus protagonistas.* Panama City: Distribuidora Lewis.

Crowell, Jackson H. 1969. "The United States and a Central American Canal, 1869–1877." *Hispanic American Historical Review* 49 (February): 27–52.

Dahl, Robert A. 1957. "The Concept of Power." *Behavioral Science* 2 (July): 201–15.

———. 1971. *Polyarchy: Participation and Opposition.* New Haven: Yale University Press.

De Arias, Marisín V. 1991. *Sedición: Evolución sociológica de un movimiento*. Panama City: Publicaciones Lewis S.A..

De Janón, Luis. 1999. *Panamá: Elecciones generales, 1999*. Panama City: Editorial Rajatabla.

De la Espriella, Ricardo. 1998. Former Panamanian president. Interview by author. April 16. Panama City, Panama.

Del Moral, Octavio. 1992. *Diagnostico crítico de la democracia en Panamá*. Panama City: Movimiento de Abogados Profesión y Ley.

De St. Malo A., Guillermo, and Godfrey Harris. 1993. *The Panamanian Problem: How the Reagan and Bush Administrations Dealt with the Noriega Regime*. Los Angeles: Americas Group.

Denton, Charles F. 1967. "Interest Groups in Panama and the Central American Common Market." *Inter-American Economic Affairs* 21 (Summer): 49–61.

Diamond, Larry. 1999. *Developing Democracy: Toward Consolidation*. Baltimore: Johns Hopkins University Press.

Diamond, Larry, Jonathan Hartlyn, Juan J. Linz, and Seymour Martin Lipset. 1999. *Democracy in Developing Countries: Latin America*. 2nd ed. Boulder: Lynne Rienner Publishers.

Diaz Espino, Ovidio. 2001. *How Wall Street Created a Nation: J. P. Morgan, Teddy Roosevelt, and the Panama Canal*. New York: Four Walls Eight Windows.

Díaz Herrera, Roberto. 1988. *Panamá: Mucho más que Noriega*. Caracas: Cromotip.

———. 1999. Colonel (retired), Panamanian Defense Forces. Interview by author. June 14. Panama City, Panama.

Diez Castillo, Luis A. 1981. *Los cimarrones y los negros antillanos en Panamá*. Panama City: Rudas.

———. 1990. *El Canal de Panamá y su gente*. Panama City: Litografía Especializada, S.A.

Dimock, Marshall E. 1934. *Government-Operated Enterprises in the Panama Canal Zone*. Chicago: University of Chicago Press.

Dinges, John. 1990. *Our Man in Panama*. New York: Random House.

Donnelly, Thomas, Margaret Roth, and Caleb Baker. 1991. *Operation Just Cause: The Storming of Panama*. New York: Lexington.

Downs, Anthony. 1957. *An Economic Theory of Democracy*. New York: Harper and Row.

Dubois, Jules. 1964. *Danger over Panama*. Indianapolis: Bobbs-Merrill.

Duddy, Patrick. 1998. Director, Public Affairs Office, U.S. embassy. Interview by author. February 7. Panama City, Panama.

Dumbrell, John. 1995. *The Carter Presidency: A Re-evaluation*. New York: Manchester University Press.

DuVal, Miles P., Jr. 1947. *Cadiz to Cathay: The Story of the Long Diplomatic Struggle for the Panama Canal*. Stanford, Calif.: Stanford University Press.

Ealy, Lawrence O. 1951. *The Republic of Panama in World Affairs, 1903–1950*. Philadelphia: University of Pennsylvania Press.

———. 1971. *Yanqui Politics and the Isthmian Canal*. University Park: Pennsylvania State University Press.

Easton, David. 1953. *The Political System*. New York: Knopf.

Elton, Charlotte. 1990. *¿Rivales o aliados? Japón y Estados Unidos en Panamá*. Panama City: Centro de Estudios y Acción Social Panameño.

Epstein, Erwin H. 2005. "Education as a Fault Line in Assessing Democratisation: Ignoring the Globalising Influence of Schools." In *International Handbook on Globalisation, Education and Policy Research: Global Pedagogies and Policies*, edited by Joseph Zajda, 613–30. London: Springer.

Evans, G. Russell. 1997. *Death Knell of the Panama Canal?* Fairfax, Va.: National Security Center.

Evans, Peter, Dietrich Rueschemeyer, and Theda Skocpol, eds. 1985. *Bringing the State Back In*. Cambridge: Cambridge University Press.

Fábrega P., Jorge. 1991. *Ensayos sobre historia constitucional de Panamá*. 2nd. ed. Cali, Colombia: Editora Jurídica Panameña.

———. 1999. *Constitución política de la República de Panamá*. Panama City: Álvarez.

Falcoff, Mark. 1998. *Panama's Canal: What Happens When the United States Gives a Small Country What It Wants*. Washington D.C.: AEI Press.

Farnsworth, David N., and James W. McKenney. 1983. *U.S.-Panama Relations, 1903–1978*. Boulder, Colo.: Westview.

Fernández B., Marco A., and José Galán Ponce. 1997. "Evaluación económica del retiro de las bases militares." In *Panamá 2000: La transición del canal a la soberanía de Panamá*, 159–218. Guatemala: Instituto Centroamericano de Estudios Políticos.

Figueroa Navarro, Alfredo. 1982. *Dominio y sociedad en el Panamá Colombiano, 1821–1903*. Panama City: Editorial Universitaria.

Flanagan, Edward M. 1993. *Battle for Panama: Inside Operation Just Cause*. Washington, D.C.: Brassey's.

Forbes-Lindsay, Charles. 1926. *Panama and the Canal Today*. Rev. ed. Boston: L. C. Page.

Franck, Harry A. 1970. *Zone Policeman 88: A Close Study of the Panama Canal and Its Workers*. New York: Arno.

Franco, Joaquín F. 1958. *La zona libre de Colón o una institución fundamental para la economía panameña*. Colón, Panama City: Imprenta Hernández.

Franco V., Ramón. 1997. *La neutralidad permanente en los tratados del canal*. Panama City: Universidad Santa María la Antigua.

Fukuyama, Francis. 1992. *The End of History and the Last Man*. New York: Free Press.

Furlong, William L. 2000. "Panama, a Nation Apart: Its Foreign Policy and Its Challenges." In *Post-Invasion Panama: The Challenges of Democratization in the New World Order*, edited by Orlando J. Perez, 29–58. Lanham, Md.: Lexington.

Furlong, William L., and Margaret Scranton. 1984. *The Dynamics of Foreign Policymaking: The President, the Congress, and the Panama Canal Treaties*. Boulder, Colo.: Westview.

Fuson, Robert H. 1964. "Land Tenure in Central Panama." *Journal of Geography* 63 (April): 161–64.

Galán Ponce, José. 1995. "Impacto económico del retiro de las bases militares." In *Impacto económico del retiro de las bases y del reintegro del canal y sus áreas adyacentes*, FIEES Seminar Report, Fundación Istmeña de Estudios Económicos y Sociales (Isthmian Foundation for Social and Economic Studies), series FIEES #2, July.

Gandásegui, Marco A. 1974. "Industrialización e inversiones extranjeras en Panamá." *Estudios Sociales Centroamericanos* 7 (January-April): 1–34.

———. 1989. "Panamá: Crisis política y agresión económica." 2nd ed. Panama City: Centro de Estudios Latinoamericanos.

———. 1993. "The Military Regimes of Panama." *Journal of Interamerican Studies and World Affairs* 35 (Fall): 1–17.

———. 1998. *La democracia en Panamá*. Panama City: Centro de Estudios Latinoamericanos.

———. 2003. "Democracia y movimientos sociales en Panamá: En el centenario de la República." *South Eastern Latin Americanist* 47 (Summer/Fall): 35–70.

Gandásegui, Marco A., Andrés Achong, and Iván Quintero. 1980. *Las luchas obreras en Panamá, 1850–1978*. Panama City: Centro de Estudios Latinoamericanos.

Gilboa, Eytan. 1995–96. "The Panama Invasion Revisited: Lessons for the Use of Force in the Post Cold War Era." *Political Science Quarterly* 110 (Winter): 539–62.

Gill, Stephen. 1990. *American Hegemony and the Trilateral Commission*. Cambridge: Cambridge University Press.

Gills, Barry, Joel Rocamora, and Richard Wilson, eds. 1993. *Low Intensity Democracy: Political Power in the New World Order*. Boulder, Colo.: Pluto.

Gilpin, Robert. 1987. *The Political Economy of International Relations*. Princeton: Princeton University Press.

———. 2001. *Global Political Economy: Understanding the International Economic Order*. Princeton: Princeton University Press.

Gjording, Chris N. 1991. *Conditions Not of Their Choosing: The Guaimí Indians and Mining Multinationals in Panama*. Washington, D.C.: Smithsonian Institution Press.

Gleijeses, Pietro. 1991. *Shattered Hope: The Guatemalan Revolution and the United States, 1944–1954*. Princeton: Princeton University Press.

Gólcher, Ileana, ed. 1999. *Este país, un canal: Encuentro de culturas*. Panama City: Editora Sibauste.

Goldrich, Daniel. 1962. *Radical Nationalism: The Political Orientations of Panama-*

nian Law Students. East Lansing, Mich.: Bureau of Social and Political Research, University of Michigan.

————. 1966. *Sons of the Establishment: Elite Youth in Panama and Costa Rica.* Chicago: Rand McNally.

González H., Simeón E. 1977. *Industrialización y producción capitalista en Panamá.* Panama City: Centro de Estudios Latinoamericanos.

————. 1990. "Sociología del 'Torrijismo' (Mito y realidad de un proceso)." Panama City: Imprenta de la Universidad de Panamá.

————. 1994. *Panamá 1970–1990: Ensayos de sociología política.* Panama City: Imprenta de la Universidad de Panamá.

Goodman, Louis W., William LeoGrande, and Johanna Mendelson Forman, eds. 1990. *Political Parties and Democracy in Central America.* Boulder, Colo.: Westview.

Grant, Rebecca. 1991. *Operation Just Cause and the U.S. Policy Process.* Santa Monica: Rand Corporation.

Guevara Mann, Carlos. 1994. *Ilegitimidad y hegemonía: Una interpretación histórica del militarismo Panameño.* Panama City: Editorial La Prensa.

————. 1996. *Panamanian Militarism: A Historical Interpretation.* Athens: Center for International Studies, Ohio University.

Gurdián Guerra, Reymundo. 1997. *Las bases militares y el informe Hathaway: El desarrollo nacional frente a los intereses Norteamericanos en Panamá.* Panama City: Editorial Portobelo.

————. 1998. *La presencia militar de los Estados Unidos en Panamá: Antecedentes, evolución y perspectivas.* Panama City: Imprenta de la Universidad de Panamá.

Gutiérrez Villalobos, Sonia. 1996. "Three Theories for Press Support for the U.S. Administration during the Panama Invasion." *Identidad Centro Americana* 3 (August): 111–31.

Haglund, David G. 1984. *Latin America and the Transformation of U.S. Strategic Thought.* Albuquerque: University of New Mexico Press.

Harding, Robert C. 2001. *Military Foundations of Panamanian Politics.* New Brunswick, N.J.: Transaction.

Harris, David. 2001. *Shooting the Moon: The True Story of an American Manhunt Unlike Any Other, Ever.* Boston: Little, Brown.

Haskin, Frederick J. 1913. *The Panama Canal.* New York: Doubleday, Page.

Healy, David. 1988. *Drive to Hegemony: The United States and the Caribbean, 1898–1917.* Madison: University of Wisconsin Press.

Hebard, R.W. 1955. *The Panama Railroad: The First Transcontinental Railroad, 1855–1955.* New York: Macmillan.

Heckadon Moreno, Stanley. 1993. "Impact of Development on the Panama Canal Environment." *Journal of Interamerican Studies and World Affairs* 35 (Fall): 129–49.

Held, David. 1987. *Models of Democracy.* Stanford, Calif.: Stanford University Press.

Herrera Hassan, Eduardo. 1998. Colonel (retired), Panamanian Defense Forces. Interview by author. May 13. Panama City, Panama.

Herrera J., Ligia. 1994. *Regiones de desarrollo socioeconómico de Panamá, 1980–1990: Transformaciones ocurridas en la década.* Panama City: Centro de Estudios Latinoamericanos.

Hersh, Seymour. 1986. "Panama Strongman Said to Trade in Drugs, Arms and Illicit Money." *New York Times,* June 12.

Higley, John, and Richard Gunther, eds. 1992. *Elites and Democratic Consolidation in Latin America and Southern Europe.* Cambridge: Cambridge University Press.

Hill, Howard C. 1966. *Roosevelt and the Caribbean.* New York: Russell and Russell.

Hobbes, Thomas. 1962. *Leviathan: Or the Matter, Forme and Power of a Commonwealth Ecclesiasticall and Civil.* Edited by Michael Oakeshott. New York: Collier.

Hobson, John M. 2000. *The State and International Relations.* New York: Cambridge University Press.

Hogan, J. Michael. 1986. *The Panama Canal in American Politics: Domestic Advocacy and the Evolution of Policy.* Carbondale: Southern Illinois University Press.

Howarth, David. 1966. *Panama: Four Hundred Years of Dreams and Cruelty.* New York: McGraw Hill.

Howe, James. 1998. *A People Who Would Not Kneel: Panama, the United States, and the San Blas Kuna.* Washington, D.C.: Smithsonian Institution Press.

Hughes, William. 1999. *Pobreza y riqueza en Panamá.* Panama City: Servicio Paz y Justicia en Panamá.

Hughes, William J. 1998. U.S ambassador to Panama. Interview by author. May 21. Panama City, Panama.

Independent Commission of Inquiry on the U.S. Invasion of Panama. 1991. *The U.S. Invasion of Panama: The Truth behind Operation "Just Cause."* Boston: South End Press.

Instituto Centroamericano de Estudios Políticos. 1997. *Panamá 2000: La transición del canal a la soberanía de Panamá.* Guatemala: Instituto Centroamericano de Estudios Políticos.

Instituto de Estudios Nacionales. 1996. "Universitarios frente a las bases militares." Panama City: Imprenta de la Universidad de Panamá.

Instituto del Canal de Panamá y Estudios Internacionales. 1993. "Reflexiones ambientales en el área interoceánica." Panama City: Imprenta de la Universidad de Panamá.

———. 1995. "Comentarios al discurso del embajador estadounidense en Panamá." Panama City: Imprenta de la Universidad de Panamá.

———. 1996. *Las bases militares y el desarrollo nacional.* Vol. 2. Panama City: Imprenta de la Universidad de Panamá.

Inter-American Commission on Human Rights. 1979. *Report on the Situation of Human Rights in Panama.* Washington, D.C.: Organization of American States.

Intercarib, S.A./Nathan Associates, Inc. 1996. "Plan de usos del suelo del area del canal." Vol. 1, Executive Summary, June 26.

International Commission of Jurists. 1964. *Report on the Events in Panama, January 9–12, 1964*. Geneva: ICJ.

Jackson, Eric. 2004. "Record PRD Election Sweep." *Panama News: Panama's English-Language Online Newspaper*, Vol. 10, issue 9, May 9–22, www.thepanamnews.com.

Jaén Suárez, Omar. 1978. *La población del istmo de Panamá del siglo XVI al siglo XX*. Panama City: Impresora de la Nación.

Janson Pérez, Brittmarie. 1993. *En nuestras propias voces: Panamá protesta, 1968–1989*. Panama City: Litho Editorial Chen, S.A.

———. 1997. *Golpes y tratados: Piezas para el rompecabezas de nuestra historia*. Panama City: Litho Editorial Chen, S.A.

Jervis, Robert. 1976. *Perception and Misperception in International Politics*. Princeton: Princeton University Press.

Johnson, Harry. 1976. "Panama as a Regional Financial Center: A Preliminary Analysis of Development Contribution." *Economic Development and Cultural Exchange Survey* 24 (January): 261–86.

Johnson, Willis F. 1906. *Four Centuries of the Panama Canal*. New York: Henry Holt.

Jonas, Susanne. 2000. *Of Centaurs and Doves: Guatemala's Peace Process*. Boulder, Colo.: Westview.

Jones, Kenneth E. 1990. *Tiempos de agonía: Expulsando el dictador de Panamá*. Panama City: Focus.

Jorden, William J. 1984. *Panama Odyssey*. Austin: University of Texas Press.

Kemble, John H. 1943. *The Panama Route, 1848–1869*. Berkeley and Los Angeles: University of California Press.

Kempe, Frederick. 1990. *Divorcing the Dictator: America's Bungled Affair with Noriega*. New York: G. P. Putnam's Sons.

Kempe, Frederick. 1992. "The Panama Debacle." In *Conflict Resolution and Democratization in Panama: Implications for U.S. Policy*, edited by Eva Loser, 1–20. Washington, D.C.: Center for Strategic and International Studies.

Keohane, Robert O. 1980. "The Theory of Hegemonic Stability and Changes in International Economic Regimes, 1967–1977." In *Change in the International System*, edited by Ole R. Holsti, Randolph M. Siverson, and Alexander L. George, 131–62. Boulder, Colo.: Westview.

———. 1984. *After Hegemony*. Princeton: Princeton University Press.

Kindleberger, Charles P. 1981. "Dominance and Leadership in the International Economy: Exploitation, Public Goods, and Free Rides." *International Studies Quarterly* 25, no. 2 (June): 242–54.

Knapp, Herbert, and Mary Knapp. 1984. *Red, White, and Blue Paradise: The American Canal Zone in Panama*. New York: Harcourt Brace Jovanovich.

Koster, Richard M. 1998. Author. Interview by author. June 11. Panama City, Panama.

Koster, R. M., and Guillermo Sánchez B. 1990. *In the Time of the Tyrants: Panama, 1968–1990*. New York: Norton.

Krasner, Stephen D. 1976. "State Power and the Structure of International Trade." *World Politics* 28 (3): 317–47.

———. 1995. "Power Politics, Institutions, and Transnational Relations." In *Bringing Transnational Relations Back In*, edited by Thomas Risse-Kappen, 257–79. Cambridge: Cambridge University Press.

Ku Sánchez, Benjamín. 1998. Lieutenant (retired), Panamanian Defense Forces. Interview by author. May 13. Panama City, Panama.

Lachman Varela, Rubén, Melissa Vallarino Bernat, and Víctor Ramos López. 1997. *¿Sabes tu adonde va la economía de Panamá? Una visión del desarrollo nacional*. Panama City: Poligráfica.

LaFeber, Walter. 1989. *The Panama Canal: The Crisis in Historical Perspective*. Updated ed. New York: Oxford University Press.

Lagos, Medoro. 1988. *Noriega: Legitimas alternativas de la causa de Panamá*. Panama City: Editorial Renovación.

Landes, David S. 1998. *The Wealth and Poverty of Nations: Why Some Are Rich and Some So Poor*. New York: Norton.

Langley, Lester D. 1967. "The World Crisis and the Good Neighbor Policy in Panama, 1936–1941." *Americas* 24 (October): 137–52.

———. 1970. "U.S.-Panamanian Relations since 1941." *Journal of Interamerican Studies* 12 (July): 339–66.

———. 1976. *Struggle for the American Mediterranean: United States–European Rivalry in the Gulf-Caribbean, 1776–1904*. Athens: University of Georgia Press.

Lasswell, Harold D. 1936. *Politics: Who Gets What, When, How*. New York: McGraw-Hill.

Latin American Regional Reports: Mexico and Central America. London: Latin America Newsletters Ltd.

Latin American Weekly Report. London: Latin America Newsletters Ltd.

Leis, Raúl. 1984. "Radiografía de los partidos." Panama City: Centro de Capacitación Social.

———. 1985. *Comando sur: Poder hostil*. 2nd ed. Panama City: Centro de Estudios y Acción Social Panameño.

Leonard, Thomas M. 1973. "The Commissary Issue in United States–Panamanian Relations." *Americas* 30 (July): 83–109.

———. 1981. "The 1977 Panama Canal Treaties in Historical Perspective." *Journal of Caribbean Studies* 2 (Autumn-Winter): 190–209.

———. 1988. "United States Perception of Panamanian Politics, 1944–1949." *Journal of Third World Studies* 5 (Fall): 112–38.

———. 1993. *Panama, the Canal, and the United States: A Guide to Issues and References*. Claremont: Regina Books.

Linares, Julio E. 1995. *Tratado concerniente a la neutralidad permanente y al funcionamiento del Canal del Panamá: De un colonialismo Rooseveltiano a un neo-*

colonialismo senatorial. Panama City: Instituto de Estudios Políticos e Internacionales.

Lindbloom, Charles E. 1977. *Politics and Markets: The World's Political Economic Systems*. New York: Basic.

Lindsay-Poland, John. 2003. *Emperors in the Jungle: The Hidden History of the U.S. in Panama*. Durham, N.C.: Duke University Press.

Linz, Juan J., and Alfred Stepan, eds. 1978. *The Breakdown of Democratic Regimes: Latin America*. Baltimore: Johns Hopkins University Press.

———. 1996. *Problems of Democratic Transition and Consolidation: Southern Europe, South America, and Post-Communist Europe*. Baltimore: Johns Hopkins University Press.

Lipset, Seymour Martin. 1959. "Some Social Requisites of Democracy: Economic Development and Political Legitimacy." *American Political Science Review* 53, no. 1 (March): 69–105.

Liss, Sheldon B. 1967. *The Canal: Aspects of United States Panamanian Relations*. Notre Dame, Ind.: University of Notre Dame Press.

Looney, Robert E. 1976. *The Economic Development of Panama*. New York: Praeger.

López Tirone, Humberto. 1995. *Panamá: Una revolución democrática*. Lisbon: Joan Boldó I Climent.

Loser, Eva, ed. 1992. *Conflict Resolution and Democratization in Panama: Implications for U.S. Policy*. Washington D.C.: Center for Strategic and International Studies.

Loveman, Brian. 1999. *For La Patria: Politics and the Armed Forces in Latin America*. Wilmington, Del.: Scholarly Resources.

Lowenthal, Abraham F., and J. Samuel Fitch, eds. 1986. *Armies and Politics in Latin America*. Rev. ed. New York: Holmes and Meier.

Mack, Gerstle. 1944. *The Land Divided: A History of the Panama Canal and Other Isthmian Projects*. New York: Knopf.

Macridis, Roy C. 1992. *Contemporary Political Ideologies: Movements and Regimes*. 5th ed. New York: HarperCollins.

Maechling, Charles. 1990. "Washington's Illegal Invasion." *Foreign Policy* 79 (Summer): 113–31.

Mainwarring, Scott, and Timothy Scully, eds. 1995. *Building Democratic Institutions: Party Systems in Latin America*. Stanford, Calif.: Stanford University Press.

Major, John. 1980. "Wasting Asset: The U.S. Reassessment of the Panama Canal 1945–1949." *Journal of Strategic Studies* 3 (September): 123–46.

———. 1983. "'Pro mundi beneficio'? The Panama Canal as an International Issue, 1943–1948." *Review of International Studies* 9 (February): 17–34.

———. 1990. "The Panama Canal Zone, 1904–1979." In *Cambridge History of Latin America*, edited by Leslie Bethal, vol. 7. Cambridge: Cambridge University Press.

———. 1993. *Prize Possession: The United States and the Panama Canal, 1903–1979*. Cambridge: Cambridge University Press.

Manfredo, Fernando. 1993. "The Future of the Panama Canal." *Journal of Interamerican Studies and World Affairs* 35 (Fall): 103–28.

Manwaring, Max G. 1993. "The Security of Panama and the Canal: Now and for the Future." *Journal of Interamerican Studies and World Affairs* 35 (Fall): 151–70.

Marques, Jaime G. 1989. *Panamá en la encrucijada: ¿Colonia o nación?* Panama City: Editorial Renovación Comercial, S.A.

Marshall, Logan. 1913. *The Story of the Panama Canal.* n.p.: L. T. Myers.

Martínez H., Milton. 1990. *Panamá, 1978–1990: Una crisis sin fin.* Panama City: Centro de Estudios y Acción Social Panameño.

McCain, William D. 1965. *The United States and the Republic of Panama.* New York: Russell and Russell.

McConnell, Malcolm. 1991. *Just Cause: The Real Story of America's High-Tech Invasion of Panama.* New York: St. Martin's Press.

McCullough, David. 1977. *The Path between the Seas: The Creation of the Panama Canal, 1870–1914.* New York: Simon and Schuster.

Meditz, Sandra W., and Dennis M. Hanratty, eds. 1989. *Panama: A Country Study.* Washington: Government Printing Office.

Mellander, G. A. 1971. *The United States in Panamanian Politics: The Intriguing Formative Years.* Danville, Ill.: Interstate Printers and Publishers.

Méndez, Roberto N. 1994. "Porqué NO deben permanecer las bases militares Norteamericanas en Panamá después del año 2000." Panama City: Publicaciones Nacionales, S.A.

Millett, Richard L. 1990. "The Aftermath of Intervention: Panama 1990." *Journal of Interamerican Studies and World Affairs* 32 (Spring): 1–15.

Mills, C. Wright. 1956. *The Power Elite.* New York: Oxford University Press.

Minor, Dwight C. 1966. *The Fight for the Panama Route: The Story of the Spooner Act and the Hay-Herrán Treaty.* New York: Octagon.

Miroff, Bruce. 1976. *Pragmatic Illusions: The Presidential Politics of John F. Kennedy.* New York: Longman.

Moffett, George D. 1985. *The Limits of Victory: The Ratification of the Panama Canal Treaties.* Ithaca, N.Y.: Cornell University Press.

Moore, Barrington. 1966. *Social Origins of Dictatorship and Democracy: Lord and Peasant in the Making of the Modern World.* Boston: Beacon.

Moreno, Miguel J. 1999. Former Panamanian diplomat. Interview by author. June 15. Panama City, Panama.

Morgan, Eduardo. 1998. *Memorias de una embajada.* Bogotá, Colombia: Editorial Grijalbo.

Morgenthau, Hans J. 1993. *Politics among Nations: The Struggle for Power and Peace.* Abridged ed. Revised by Kenneth W. Thompson. Boston: McGraw-Hill.

Morris, Charles. 1989. "The Panama Canal: 75 Years of Security History." *Security Management* 33, no. 9 (September): 68–74.

Morris, Edmund. 2001. *Theodore Rex.* New York: Random House.

Mosca, Gaetano. 1939. *The Ruling Class*. Translated by Hannah D. Kahn. New York: McGraw-Hill.

Moss, Ambler H. 1986. "The Panama Treaties: How an Era Ended." *Latin American Research Review* 21 (3): 171–78.

Mueller, John E. 1999. *Capitalism, Democracy, and Ralph's Pretty Good Grocery*. Princeton: Princeton University Press.

Muñoz, José Salvador. 1995a. "Panamá: Historia de sus partidos políticos." Panama City: Universidad Santa María la Antigua.

———. 1995b. *Panamá: Una nación*. Panama City: Universidad Santa María la Antigua.

Mussolini, Benito. 1975. *The Corporate State*. New York: H. Fertig.

Nanda, Ved P. 1990. "The Validity of United States Intervention in Panama under International Law." *American Journal of International Law* 84 (April): 494–503.

Niemeier, Jean. 1968. *The Panama Story*. Portland, Ore.: Metropolitan Press.

Noriega de Jurado, Jilma. 1999. "Verdad y miseria de nuestros partidos políticos." Panama City: Editorial Portobelo.

Noriega, Manuel, and Peter Eisner. 1997. *America's Prisoner: The Memoirs of Manuel Noriega*. New York: Random House.

Nye, Joseph. 2004. *Soft Power: The Means to Success in World Politics*. New York: Public Affairs.

O'Brien, Thomas F. 1999. *The Century of U.S. Capitalism in Latin America*. Albuquerque: University of New Mexico Press.

O'Donnell, Guillermo. 1994. "Delegative Democracy." *Journal of Democracy* 5 (January): 56–69.

O'Donnell, Guillermo, and Philippe C. Schmitter. 1987. *Transitions from Authoritarian Rule: Tentative Conclusions about Uncertain Democracies*. Baltimore: John Hopkins University Press.

O'Donnell, Guillermo, Philippe Schmitter, and Lawrence Whitehead, eds. 1986. *Transitions from Authoritarian Rule: Prospects for Democracy*. Baltimore: Johns Hopkins University Press.

Olson, Mancur. 1968. *The Logic of Collective Action: Public Goods and the Theory of Groups*. New York: Schocken.

———. 1995. "Discussion." In *New Dimensions in Regional Integration*, edited by Jaime De Melo and Arvind Panagariya, 122–27. New York: Cambridge University Press.

Ortega C., Joaquín A. 1965. *Gobernantes de la Republica de Panamá, 1903–1968*. 3rd ed. Mexico: Editora Exélcior.

Ortega Durán, Oydén. 1986. "The Panama Canal and Panama's National Interests." *Contemporary Review* 249 (August): 74–77.

Padelford, Norman J. 1942. *The Panama Canal in Peace and War*. New York: Macmillan.

Paige, Jeffery M. 1997. *Coffee and Power: Revolution and the Rise of Democracy in Central America*. Cambridge: Harvard University Press.

Palmer, Bruce, ed. 1977. *A New Treaty for Panama?* Washington, D.C.: American Institute for Public Policy Research.

Pareto, Vilfredo. 1935. *The Mind and Society*. Translated by Andrew Bongiorno and Arthur Livingston. New York: Harcourt, Brace.

Partido Revolucionario Democrático. 1986. "Propuesta para el desarrollo y aprovechamiento del área canalera." Second National Meeting of Professionals. Panama City: Litho-Impresora.

———. 1987. "Suplemento histórico—Revista." Panama City: Partido Revolucionario Democrático.

———. 1996. *Seminario-Taller: El canal y las bases militares*. Panama City: Partido Revolucionario Democrático.

Pastor, Robert. 1995. *El remolino*. Princeton, N.J.: Princeton University Press.

Pearcy, Thomas L. 1998. *We Answer Only to God: Politics and the Military in Panama, 1903–1947*. Albuquerque: University of New Mexico Press.

Peceny, Mark. 1999. *Democracy at the Point of Bayonets*. University Park: Pennsylvania State University Press.

Pedreschi, Carlos Bolívar, editor. 1974. "Las negociaciones sobre el Canal de Panamá y la Declaración de los Ocho Puntos." N.p.: Imprenta Barcenas, S.A.

———. 1987. "De la protección del canal a la militarización del país." Panama City: Litografía e Imprenta LIL, S.A.

———. 1993. *Panamá: Visión geopolítica y testimonial de su drama*. Cali, Colombia: Carvajal, S.A.

Peeler, John. 2004. *Building Democracy in Latin America*. 2nd ed. Boulder, Colo.: Lynne Rienner Publishers.

Pereira, Renato. 1979. *Panamá: Fuerzas armadas y política*. Panama City: Ediciones Nueva Universidad.

Pérez Balladares, Ernesto. 1999. Former president of Panama. Interview by author. June 10. Palacio de Las Garzas, Panama City, Panama.

Pérez, Orlando J. 2000a. "The Past as Prologue?: Political Parties in Post-Invasion Panama." In *Post-Invasion Panama: The Challenges of Democratization in the New World Order*, edited by Orlando J. Pérez, 125–46. Lanham, Md.: Lexington.

———, ed. 2000b. *Post-Invasion Panama: The Challenges of Democratization in the New World Order*. Lanham, Md.: Lexington.

Pérez-Venero, Alex. 1978. *Before the Five Frontiers: Panama from 1821–1903*. New York: AMS Press.

Perigault Sánchez, Bolívar. 1989. *¿Que sabe usted acerca de las intervenciones Norteamericanas en Panamá?* Panama City: Imprenta Franco.

Phillipps Collazos, Sharon. 1991. *Labor and Politics in Panama: The Torrijos Years*. Boulder, Colo.: Westview.

Pineda González, Pedro. 1996. "Democracia y vida cotidiana: El caso Panameño, una propuesta teórico-metodológica y consideraciones sobre la transición democrática." *Identidad Centroamericana* 3 (August): 153–66.

Pippin, Larry LaRae. 1964. *The Remón Era: An Analysis of a Decade of Events in Pan-*

ama, 1947–1957. Stanford, Calif.: Institute of Hispanic and Luso-Brazilian Studies, Stanford University.

Pizzurno Gelós, Patricia. 1990. *Antecedentes, hechos, y consecuencias de la Guerra de los Mil Días en el istmo de Panamá*. Panama City: Ediciones Fomento.

Pizzurno Gelós, Patricia, and Celestino Andrés Araúz. 1996. *Estudios sobre El Panamá Republicano (1903–1989)*. Panama City: Manfer, S.A.

Plan Estratégico de Seguridad Nacional. 1999. *El Panamá América: Informe especial*. November. Available at www.epasa.com/documentos/seguridad/.

Porter, Charles O., and Robert J. Alexander. 1961. *The Struggle for Democracy in Latin America*. New York: Macmillan.

Presidential Commission for Canal Affairs. 1994. "Transition Plan for the Transfer of the Panama Canal," Panama City. January.

Priestley, George. 1986. *Military Government and Popular Participation in Panama: The Torrijos Regime, 1968–1975*. Boulder, Colo.: Westview.

———. 1994. "Panama Elections: The Opposition Returns to Power." *NACLA: Report on the Americas* 28 (September/October): 11–14.

Pringle, Robert. 1975. "Panama: A Survey." *Banker* 125 (October): 191–210.

Przeworski, Adam. 1991. *Democracy and the Market: Political and Economic Reforms in Eastern Europe and Latin America*. Cambridge: Cambridge University Press.

Raven, Melba A., and Gloria Manfredo, eds. 1997. *Universal Congress of the Panama Canal: Proceedings*. Panama City: European Commission and Universal Congress of the Panama Canal.

Richardson, Neil R. 1978. *Foreign Policy and Economic Dependence*. Austin: University of Texas Press.

Ricord, Humberto E. 1989. *Panamá en la Guerra de los Mil Días*. Panama City: H. C. Ricord.

Riker, William H. 1982. *Liberalism against Populism: A Confrontation between the Theory of Democracy and the Theory of Social Choice*. San Francisco: W. H. Freeman.

Rippy, J. Fred. 1964. "The U.S. and Panama: The High Cost of Appeasement." *Inter-American Economic Affairs* 17 (Spring): 87–94.

Ritter, Jorge. 1999. Former Panamanian foreign minister and minister for canal affairs. Interview by author. June 23. Panama City, Panama.

Rivera, Pedro, and Fernando Martínez. 1998. *El libro de la invasión*. Mexico: Tierra Firme.

Robinson, Linda S. 1989–1990. "Dwindling Options in Panama." *Foreign Affairs* 68 (Winter): 187–205.

Robinson, William Francis. 1999. "Panama for the Panamanians: The Populism of Arnulfo Arias Madrid." In *Populism in Latin America*, edited by Michael L. Conniff, 157–171. Tuscaloosa: University of Alabama Press.

Rodrígues, José Carlos. 1885. *The Panama Canal: Its History, Its Political Aspects, and Its Financial Difficulties*. New York: Charles Scribner's Sons.

Rodríguez M., Alexis. 1996. "Derechos humanos, transición democrática y movimientos sociales en Panamá, 1990–1993." *Identidad Centroamericana* 3 (August): 132–52.

Román Lemaitre, Eduardo. 1972. *Panamá y su separación de Colombia.* Bogotá: Banco Popular.

Ronning, C. Neale, and Albert P. Vannucci, eds. 1987. *Ambassadors in Foreign Policy: The Influence of Individuals on U.S.–Latin American Policy.* New York: Praeger.

Ropp, Steve C. 1982. *Panamanian Politics: From Guarded Nation to National Guard.* New York: Praeger.

————. 1990. "Military Retrenchment and Decay in Panama." *Current History: A World Affairs Journal* 89 (January): 17–20, 37–40.

————. 1992. "Explaining the Long-Term Maintenance of a Military Regime: Panama before the U.S. Invasion." *World Politics* 44 (January): 210–34.

————. 1993. "What Have We Learned from the Noriega Crisis?" *Latin American Research Review* 28 (3): 189–96.

Rosenau, James N., and Mary Durfee, eds. 2000. *Thinking Theory Thoroughly: Coherent Approaches to an Incoherent World.* 2nd ed. Boulder, Colo.: Westview.

Rudolph, Gloria. 1999. *Panama's Poor: Victims, Agents, and Historymakers.* Gainesville: University Press of Florida.

Rueschemeyer, Dietrich, Evelyn Huber Stephens, and John D. Stephens. 1992. *Capitalist Development and Democracy.* Chicago: University of Chicago Press.

Rustow, Dankwart A. 1970. "Transitions to Democracy: Toward a Dynamic Model." *Comparative Politics* 2 (April): 337–63.

Ryan, Paul B. 1977. *The Panama Canal Controversy: U.S. Diplomacy and Defense Interests.* Stanford, Calif.: Hoover Institution Press.

Sabonge, Rodolfo R. 1997. "Long-Range Canal Traffic Scenario." Paper presented at the Universal Congress of the Panama Canal, ATLAPA Convention Center, Panama City, Panama, September 7–10.

Sahota, Gian Singh. 1990. *Poverty Theory and Policy: A Study of Panama.* Baltimore: Johns Hopkins University Press.

Sánchez G., Salvador. 1997. *El financiamiento de los partidos políticos en Panamá.* Panama City: Ediliber.

Sánchez, Peter M. 1997. "Race and Democratic Consolidation: The Dominican Republic, Guatemala and Peru." Paper presented at the Latin American Studies Association Meeting, Guadalajara, Mexico, April 17–19.

————. 2002. "The End of Hegemony? Panama and the United States." *International Journal on World Peace* 19 (September): 57–89.

————. 2003a. "Bringing the International Back In: US Hegemonic Maintenance and Latin America's Democratic Breakdown in the 1960s and 1970s." *International Politics* 40 (June): 223–47.

————. 2003b. "Panama: A 'Hegemonized' Foreign Policy." In *Small States in World Politics: Explaining Foreign Policy Behavior,* edited by Jeanne A. K. Hey, 53–74. Boulder, Colo.: Lynne Rienner Publishers.

————. 2003c. "Panama: The Limits of Sovereignty." In *Latin American and Carib-*

bean Foreign Policy, edited by Frank O. Mora and Jeanne A. K. Hey, 63–83. Lanham: Rowman and Littlefield.

———. 2003d. "Panamanian Democracy One Hundred Years after Independence: Prospects and Problems." *South Eastern Latin Americanist* 47 (Summer/Fall): 97–118.

Sands, William Franklin, in collaboration with Joseph M. Lalley. 1944. *Our Jungle Diplomacy.* Chapel Hill: University of North Carolina Press.

Sarti, Roland. 1971. *Fascism and the Industrial Leadership in Italy, 1919–1940: A Study in the Expansion of Private Power under Fascism.* Berkeley and Los Angeles: University of California Press.

Sartori, Giovanni. 1987. *The Theory of Democracy Revisited.* Chatham, New Jersey: Chatham House.

Schmidt, Brian C. 1998. *The Political Discourse of Anarchy: A Disciplinary History of International Relations.* Albany: State University of New York Press.

Schott, Joseph L. 1967. *Rails across Panama: The Story of the Building of the Panama Railroad, 1849–1855.* New York: Bobbs-Merrill.

Schoultz, Lars. 1998. *Beneath the United States: A History of U.S. Policy toward Latin America.* Cambridge: Harvard University Press.

Scranton, Margaret E. 1991. *The Noriega Years: U.S.-Panamanian Relations, 1981–1990.* Boulder, Colo.: Lynne Rienner Publishers.

———. 1993. "Consolidation after Imposition: Panama's 1992 Referendum." *Journal of Interamerican Studies and World Affairs* 35 (Fall): 65–102.

———. 1995. "Panama's First Post-Transition Election." *Journal of Interamerican Studies and World Affairs* 37 (Spring): 69–100.

———. 2000. "Electoral Reform and the Institutionalization of the Electoral Tribunal in Post-Invasion Panama." In *Post-Invasion Panama: The Challenges of Democratization in the New World Order*, edited by Orlando J. Pérez, 101–24. Lanham, Md.: Lexington.

Selser, Gregorio. 1988. *Panamá, autodeterminación versus intervención de Estados Unidos.* Mexico City: Programa de Estudios de Centroamérica del Centro de Investigaciones y Docencia Económicas.

Sheehan, Michael J. 1996. *The Balance of Power: History and Theory.* New York: Routledge.

Shue, Henry. 1980. *Basic Rights: Subsistence, Affluence, and U.S. Foreign Policy.* Princeton: Princeton University Press.

Sieder, Rachel, and James Dunkerley. 1994. "The Military in Central America: The Challenge of Transition." University of London, Institute of Latin American Studies, occasional papers, no. 5.

Simon, Maron J. 1971. *The Panama Affair.* New York: Charles Scribner's Sons.

Singer, Matthew M. 2005. "Presidential and Parliamentary elections in Panama, May 2004." *Electoral Studies* 24 (September): 531–37.

Sisnett, Octavio. 1972. *Belisario Porras o la vocación de la nacionalidad.* Panama City: Universidad de Panamá.

Skidmore, David. 1993. "Foreign Policy Interest Groups and Presidential Power: Jimmy Carter and the Battle over Ratification of the Panama Canal Treaties." *Presidential Studies Quarterly* 23 (Summer): 477–97.

Skinner, James M. 1989. *France and Panama: The Unknown Years, 1894–1898.* New York: P. Lang.

Skocpol, Theda. 1986. *States and Social Revolutions: A Comparative Analysis of France, Russia, and China.* London: Cambridge University Press.

Slater, David, and Peter J. Taylor, eds. 1999. *The American Century: Consensus and Coercion in the Projection of American Power.* Malden, Mass.: Blackwell.

Smith, Adam. 1976. *An Inquiry into the Nature and Causes of the Wealth of Nations.* Oxford: Clarendon Press.

Smith, Gaddis. 1994. *The Last Years of the Monroe Doctrine, 1945–1993.* New York: Hill and Wang.

Smith, Peter H. 2000. *Talons of the Eagle: Dynamics of U.S.–Latin American Relations.* 2nd ed. New York: Oxford University Press.

Soler, Ricaurte. 1989. *Panamá: Nación y oligarquía, 1925–1975.* 4th ed. Panama City: Ediciones de la Revista Tareas.

———. 1991. *La invasión de Estados Unidos a Panamá: Neocolonialismo en la posguerra fría.* Mexico City: Siglo XXI Editores, S.A.

Soler Torrijos, Giancarlo. 1993. *La invasión a Panamá: Estrategia y tácticas para el nuevo orden mundial.* Panama City: Centro de Estudios Latinoamericanos.

Solórzano Martínez, Mario. 1997. *Cuando los políticos cumplen: Experiencias del proceso de negociación Panamá 2000.* Panama City: Programa de las Naciones Unidas para el Desarrollo.

Sosa, Juan B. 1999. *In Defiance: The Battle against General Noriega Fought from Panama's Embassy in Washington.* Washington, D.C.: Francis Press.

Speller, Jon P. 1972. *The Panama Canal: Heart of America's Security.* New York: Robert Speller and Sons.

Spence, Edgar. 1989. "Panamá: Modelo para armar un enclave político-militar." *Pensamiento Propio* 17 (July): 9–56.

Spence Herrera, Edgar M. 1988. "El comando sur: El complejo militar Norteamericano en Panamá." Professional Thesis, Universidad Nacional Autónoma de México, Mexico City.

Steinsleger, José. 1986. *Bases militares en América Latina.* Quito: Editorial El Conejo.

Stepan, Alfred. 1986. "The New Professionalism of Internal Warfare and Military Role Expansion." In *Armies and Politics in Latin America,* rev. ed., edited by Abraham F. Lowenthal and J. Samuel Fitch, 134–50. New York: Holmes and Meier.

Stevens, Ricardo. 1987. "Metamorfosis de las fuerzas armadas en Panamá, 1968–1986." Copy at the Centro de Estudios y Acción Social Panameño, Panama City.

Stockholm International Peace Research Institute. 2002. "SIPRI Data on Military Expenditure." Stockholm: SIPRI. www.sipri.org.

Strong, Robert A. 1991. "Jimmy Carter and the Panama Canal Treaties." *Presidential Studies Quarterly* 21 (Spring): 269–86.

Summ, G. Harvey, and Tom Kelly, eds. 1988. *The Good Neighbors: America, Panama, and the 1977 Canal Treaties.* Athens: Ohio University Center for International Studies.

Sutley, Stewart. 1992. "The Revitalization of United States Aterritorial International Logic: The World before and after the 1989 Invasion of Panama." *Canadian Journal of Political Science* 25 (September): 435–62.

Szok, Peter A. 2001. *La última gaviota: Liberalism and Nostalgia in Early Twentieth-Century Panama.* Westport, Conn.: Greenwood Press.

Tack, Juan Antonio. 1995. *Ilusiones y realidades en las negociaciones con los Estados Unidos de América.* Panama City: Manfer, S.A.

———. 1998. "CMA: La soberanía si me alimenta." Panama City: La Prensa.

Tapia L., Octavio. 1994. *La idea de esperanza social en el Panameño urbano.* Panama City: Universidad de Panamá.

Tate, Mercer D. 1963. "The Panama Canal and Political Partnership." *Journal of Politics* 25 (February): 119–38.

Tate, Mercer D., and E. H. Allen. 1969. "Proposed New Treaties for the Panama Canal." *International Affairs* 45 (April): 269–78.

Tierney, John J., Jr. 1995. "The U.S. Still Needs Military Bases in Panama." *Heritage Foundation,* executive memorandum #426, August 21.

Tilly, Charles, ed. 1975. *The Formation of National States in Western Europe.* Princeton, N.J.: Princeton University Press.

Tondel, Lyman M., editor. 1964. *The Panama Canal: Background Papers and Proceedings of the Sixth Hammarskjöld Forum.* New York: Association of the Bar of the City of New York.

Torres A., José Eulogio. 1999. *Los grandes desafíos que plantea la reversión del canal y sus áreas adyacentes a Panamá y al comercio mundial.* Panama City: Imprenta de la Universidad de Panamá.

U.S. Department of Defense. 1976. "The Military Value of the Panama Canal." *Commanders Digest* 19, no. 7 (March 25).

U.S. General Accounting Office. 1995. "Panama: DOD's Drawdown Plan for the U.S. Military in Panama" (GAO/NSIAD-95–183). Washington, D.C.: U.S. Government Printing Office.

U.S. Information Service. 1998. "Press Bulletin." Panama City: U.S. embassy. April 14.

U.S. Southern Command. 1996a. "Southern Command Spent $333 Million on Panamanian Economy in 1996—Down 9% from 1995." News release. Headquarters, U.S. Southern Command, Quarry Heights, Panama. December 19.

———. 1996b. "U.S. Forces Good Stewardship of the Environment and Its Installations in Panama." Fact sheet. Headquarters, U.S. Southern Command, Quarry Heights, Panama. August 1.

———. 1997a. "Department of Defense/U.S. Southern Command Counterdrug Efforts in Central and South America." Fact sheet. Headquarters, U.S. Southern Command, Quarry Heights, Panama. February 12.

———. 1997b. "Nuevos Horizontes Engineering Exercises: Cornerstone of U.S. Southern Command's Nation Assistance Program in Latin America." Fact sheet. Headquarters, U.S. Southern Command, Quarry Heights, Panama. January.

———. 1997c. "Panama Canal Treaty Implementation Plan." Fact sheet. Headquarters, U.S. Southern Command, Quarry Heights, Panama. August 22.

———. 1997d. "Profile of the United States Southern Command." Fact sheet. Headquarters, U.S. Southern Command, Quarry Heights, Panama. August 19.

———. 1997e. "U.S. Military in Panama Now." Fact sheet. Headquarters, U.S. Southern Command, Quarry Heights, Panama. August 14.

Valdés, Manuel M. 1932. *Las intervenciones electorales en Panamá*. Panama City: Star and Herald.

Valdez, Eduardo. 1975. *The Roots of the Problem: A Positive Approach to the Panama Canal Issue*. New York: Vantage.

Vance, Cyrus. 1983. *Hard Choices*. New York: Simon and Schuster.

Vanhanen, Tatu. 1990. *The Process of Democratization: A Comparative Study of 147 States, 1980–1988*. New York: Taylor and Francis.

Velásquez, Osvaldo. 1993. *Historia de una dictadura: De Torrijos a Noriega*. Panama City: Litho Editorial Chen, S.A.

Veliz, Claudio. 1980. *The Centralist Tradition of Latin America*. Princeton: Princeton University Press.

Vergara G., David. 1995. *Acuerdos militares entre Panamá y Estadios Unidos, 1903–1977*. Panama City: Rios.

Von Mettenheim, Kurt, and James Malloy, eds. 1998. *Deepening Democracy in Latin America*. Pittsburgh: University of Pittsburgh Press.

Waltz, Kenneth N. 1959. *Man, the State, and War: A Theoretical Analysis*. New York: Columbia University Press, [1954].

Watson, Bruce W., and Peter G. Tsouras. 1991. *Operation Just Cause: The U.S. Intervention in Panama*. Boulder, Colo.: Westview.

Weeks, John, and Phil Gunson. 1991. *Panama: Made in the USA*. London: Latin American Bureau.

Wells, Henry, ed. 1968. "Panama Election Fact Book, May 12, 1968." Washington, D.C.: Institute for Comparative Study of Political Systems.

Wendt, Alexander. 1992. "Anarchy Is What States Make of It: The Social Construction of Power Politics." *International Organization* 46 (Spring): 391–426.

Westcott, Allan, ed. 1999. *Mahan on Naval Warfare*. Mineola, N.Y.: Dover.

Westerman, George. 1980. *Los inmigrantes antillanos en Panamá*. Panama City: Impresora de la Nación.

Wilkie, James W., and Carlos Alberto Contreras, eds. 1989. "Announced U.S. Assistance to Latin America, 1945–1988." In *Statistical Abstract for Latin America*, vol. 28. Los Angeles: UCLA Latin America Center Publications.

Williams, Mary W. 1916. *Anglo-American Isthmian Diplomacy, 1815–1915*. Washington, D.C.: American Historical Association.

World Bank. 1995. "Panama: A Dual Economy in Transition." Report no. 13977–PAN. July 20.

———. 2004. *World Development Indicators* [CD-ROM]. Washington D.C.: International Bank for Reconstruction and Development.

Yao, Julio. 1975a. "El anuncio conjunto Tack-Kissinger." *Tareas* 30 (January–April): 7–34.

———. 1975b. "La Política Exterior de Panamá." *Desarrollo Indoamericano* 27 (April): 49–58.

———. 1978. "Los Tratados Torrijos-Carter algunas lecciones." *Dialogo Social* 97: 18–21.

———. N.d. *El libre tránsito militar de EE.UU. en Panamá, 1846–1977*. Mexico City.: Ediciones Raíces.

Yerxa, Donald A. 1991. *Admirals and Empire: The United States Navy and the Caribbean, 1898–1945*. Columbia: University of South Carolina Press.

Zentner, Federico. 1984. *Nombres y apellidos de forjadores de la patria*. Cali, Colombia: Carvajal, S.A.

Zimbalist, Andrew, and John Weeks. 1991. *Panama at the Crossroads: Economic Development and Political Change in the Twentieth Century*. Berkeley and Los Angeles: University of California Press.

Zimmermann, Warren. 2002. *First Great Triumph: How Five Americans Made Their Country a World Power*. New York: Farrar, Straus, and Giroux.

Index

Peter M. Sánchez teaches political science, with a focus on Latin America and U.S.-Latin American relations, at Loyola University Chicago. He lived in Panama from 1984 to 1986 while stationed there as a U.S. Air Force officer, and from 1997 to 1998 as a Senior Fulbright Research and Teaching Fellow.